i'm

supposed

to protect you

from all this

RIVERHEAD BOOKS
NEW YORK
2016

i'm

supposed

to protect you

from all this

A MEMOIR

NADJA SPIEGELMAN

RIVERHEAD BOOKS
An imprint of Penguin Random House LLC
375 Hudson Street
New York, New York 10014

Copyright © 2016 by Nadja Spiegelman
Penguin supports copyright. Copyright fuels creativity, encourages
diverse voices, promotes free speech, and creates a vibrant culture. Thank you for buying
an authorized edition of this book and for complying with copyright laws by not reproducing,
scanning, or distributing any part of it in any form without permission. You are supporting
writers and allowing Penguin to continue to publish books for every reader.

ISBN 9781594631924

Printed in the United States of America
1   3   5   7   9   10   8   6   4   2

Book design by Gretchen Achilles

Most names in this memoir are changed. I have tried, to the best of my ability, to
accurately portray other people's memories as they were presented to me. But in the act
of turning their lives into narrative, the necessary editorial choices were my own. This work
reflects my personal understanding of a complex, shared, and subjective past.

Penguin is committed to publishing works of quality and integrity.
In that spirit, we are proud to offer this book to our readers;
however, the story, the experiences, and the words
are the author's alone.

For my grandmother
and
for my mother

La mémoire ne nous servirait à rien si elle fût rigoureusement fidèle.

—PAUL VALÉRY

i'm

supposed

to protect you

from all this

chapter one

W hen I was a child, I knew that my mother was a fairy. Not the kind of fairy with gauzy wings and a magic wand, but one with a thrift-store fur coat and ink-stained fingers. There was nothing she couldn't do. On weekends, she put on safety goggles, grabbed a jigsaw, and remade the cabinets in her bedroom. She ran a hose from her bathroom to the roof to fill my inflatable pool. She helped me build a diorama of the rain forest, carving perfect cardboard birds of paradise with her X-Acto blade.

"Maman," I asked her when I was four, "when will I be a fairy like you?"

"When you're sixteen," she replied. And so I waited, and I watched her.

ONCE, DURING A THUNDERSTORM in Brazil, my mother pulled the rental car over to the side of the highway by a dark, deserted beach. She beckoned to my brother and me. We uncurled from the backseat and leapt out into the electric rain. We followed her, leaving my father shouting her name from the road, his voice barely carrying over the storm. We stripped down to our underwear. My mother held out her hands, one for each of us, and we ran straight into the water. The ocean picked us up and slammed us down against the sand. We screamed with laughter. We ran back in. The sky fractured with lightning, opened, fell into the ocean. The waves reared twice as tall as my mother.

At the car, my father was pale, his voice quiet with awe and anger. "*Jesus,* Françoise," he said, shaking his head. We were late now, as usual, and my mother drove the car fast down the highway toward the pitch-black sky. Though we had been in two accidents, I did not know my mother was a reckless driver until I was in my twenties, when friends told me so. The things my mother did not see about herself, I did not see, either. We fell asleep in the backseat, my brother and I, mouths open, gritty with salt and sand, our hair drying in wild curls.

My mother disdained most dangers as American constructs, invented by timid women who washed their vegetables. She was always certain that nothing would go wrong. "No one ever *told* me it was dangerous to swim in a lightning storm," she would say when I laughingly mentioned the memory years later. Her voice pitched defensively; she did not like to be teased.

There were other vacations, too—the vacation when my mother, sick of the other moms who complained about the lack of apple juice at the breakfast buffet, absconded from the resort and let me drive the rented stick-shift jeep along the dirt roads, even though my feet barely reached the pedals. The vacation when my mother booked no hotels in advance, just took off driving down the coast of Costa Rica, buying us all the strange fruits that they sold by the roadside. My father rarely came with us. Once, in a forest, my mother scooped the earth into her hand and put some in her mouth and ours while she explained about building immunities. We were often sick as children, and then rarely. We knew, my brother and I, that it was only fear that led to danger. My mother cast around us her conviction that we would always be safe, and it held us like a force field.

"Do you know when I finally felt free of my mother?" my mother asked me. It was a story she told several times, more allegory than anecdote.

I was a baby, six months old, and she'd taken me to France to meet her family. This was during the golden years, the ones I'll never remember: the years when she never put me down. She wore a big coat and me strapped underneath it. We shared a body. In the night, she woke and came to feed me before I'd even opened my mouth to cry.

But on this evening, when she arrived at her friend's home for a dinner party, she was instructed to leave me in the host's bedroom. She did so reluctantly. As food was served and wineglasses refilled, I began to cry. My mother leapt up from the table.

"Leave her," the French friend said. "The noise doesn't bother us." My mother continued to move toward the door.

"She'll never learn to stop crying if you pick her up each time," the friend said with the tone of absolute authority the French often invoke when imparting wisdom. *You'll catch a cold if you go out with wet hair, bread is more caloric when it's underbaked, you'll never sleep if you drink ginger tea in the evening.*

My mother hesitated, then sat back down. My wails grew louder.

"She'll tire herself out," another friend declared. But my mother had already left the table again and gone to take me into her arms. As she soothed me, rocking me, pressing me to her body, she heard fragments of the chorus of disapproval from the other room. *Now, the baby . . . When my child . . . She's just got to . . . It will only encourage her . . .*

This is what it would be like, my mother thought as I quieted against her. *This is what it would be, if I raised her here. Everything would happen all over again.*

She thought of her loft in Manhattan, with its high industrial ceilings. She thought of the streets where we were invisible, she and I, in the jostling Chinatown crowds. And she knew she was free.

"I realized that I could reinvent motherhood," she told me now. "I was so far from all this in America. I had no blueprint, no rules. And so I invented it. Every piece. I had no idea what I was doing. But I knew that it was going to be different."

Now, now that I knew her past, I saw both. I saw all the ways in which she worked to be a very different mother from her own. And I also saw how much the past, so long kept secret, pulled us into formations like a deep ocean current, from so far below that we barely knew we were not moving on our own.

My mother ran away from Paris to New York City when she was eighteen. My family had always lived in the SoHo loft she moved into her first year in America, in 1974. I tried to recognize the space as it was in the old photos. It was a jumble then, crowded with furniture she'd hauled up from the street, the rooms partitioned by bookshelves and makeshift screens. Shortly after my birth, my mother created real walls and doors and staircases, leaning ladders to mezzanines and rope ladders to nowhere, trapezes carefully drilled into anchor beams—the floor plan inside which I stored my childhood.

We visited her family in France twice a year: her divorced parents, her two sisters, a cousin. They were all the family I had. Nine people in all, if I counted myself. There was no one left on my father's side.

My grandmother would not let herself be called *Grand-mère*, so we, like everyone else, called her Josée (she spelled it sometimes with a final *e*, sometimes without, and pronounced it *joe-ZAY*). Josée lived on a houseboat moored on the outskirts of Paris, where the Seine doubled back to touch the city's northwestern border. She had purchased it as a shipping barge and transformed it into a luxurious home in a style entirely her own. There were cream-colored carpets and sliding Japanese doors. There was a Jacuzzi in the center of the space beneath an octagonal skylight that opened like a flower, and a table that rose out of the floor at the touch of a remote control. You took off your shoes at the entrance, or, if you preferred, there were little plastic bags that you could slip on over your heels. This houseboat, and the several others she had renovated and sold before it, had been featured in magazines. She kept them in a stack beneath the hanging red lacquer fireplace. In the guest bathroom, the walls were covered in pictures of her travels: in a sari on an elephant, in blackface and leopard pelts, in leather chaps and nothing else (alongside a certificate stating that the "bearer bared her knockers at Mardi Gras 1998"). My grandmother was beautiful long after she was beautiful. She carried and dressed herself in a way that left no question. She had blue eyeliner tattooed around her eyes. She never asked me about myself.

There was always a moment of held breath as my grandmother seated us around her table, her choices as deliberate and pointed as a queen's. Those seated close to her were in her favor, those seated far away were not. Love was a zero-sum game. My mother, because her presence was rare, was often seated close. Her sisters, from the far end of the table, tried not to glare.

Even at a young age, I was aware that my aunts were trapped in their parents' orbits, like moths with singed wings around a flame, though how I knew this I am not sure. They were grown-ups, yet not grown-ups. They pitched their voices to the same resentful whine in response to their mother as I did to mine. Andrée, six years younger than my mother, felt closer to my own age. She broke her knees in motorcycle accidents, lived in Paris's roughest neighborhoods, and had wild love affairs. Sylvie, older than my mother by a year and a half, was constantly leaping up to serve and clear the plates, sighing loudly as she did so, the family martyr. But when she talked to the children—her son (our only cousin), my brother, and me—she was capable of great bursts of laughter, the glugging unself-conscious guffaw of a child.

During these visits, I followed my mother's lead. I knew in my bones that her family was dangerous, and she had taught us to be wary of them, like fast food or crossing Canal Street. She treated her sisters with the polite reserve she displayed toward women she didn't trust. With her parents, she was as effusively kind and respectful as she would have been with someone else's parents. I followed suit. My voice went up an octave in Paris. I said mostly *merci, oui, merci, s'il te plaît, c'est delicieux, merci.* I stood on tiptoe to kiss an endless number of cheeks.

When I was young, I watched my mother brace herself before each encounter with her family—the hard looks she gave herself in the bathroom mirror, the lipstick applied like armor. At the table, much of the conversation took place in language too encoded for me to decipher, but I sensed that the banter was laced with barbs, a poison center to every compliment. And I heard the comments that were directed at me—the grave pronouncements of disaster over my newly cut bangs, the way everybody agreed, with knowing nods, that I certainly didn't need a second slice of cake. I dreaded those dinners, but I adored the cab rides home. In the backseat, I felt awash in the safety of our family, finally shrunk back to its correct four-person size, a rare feeling of unity between us.

My mother was giddy with relief. "The best thing I ever did was move my life an ocean away from them," she often said in those moments.

"I'm so lucky I escaped," she said at other times. "It's the only way I survived. Can you imagine, can you imagine what it would have been like?"

But I couldn't imagine. The past was always there on her body, but I couldn't see it. It was in the scars that I traced with a fingertip as a child, in the strange things that set off her anger. It was even in my own body, a feeling of damage and danger that had no name and no explanation. It was underneath everything else: that deep foundation on which we were both built. But like her French accent, which forty years in America could not fade—and which her children, so used to her voice, could not hear—the past was too present for me to see.

How could my mother ever have been a girl? I knew what it meant to be a child, how emotions could knock you flat with their sheer strength, and how adults never seemed to understand. But of my mother's childhood, I knew almost nothing. Most of her scars were from accidents. A nose that broke four or five times. The place where the sharp metal spike of a fence had pierced all the way through her arm. A gash in her head from a sharp corner in a corridor of her family's apartment. ("I didn't know you had a red pillow," her grand-mother Mina said when she found my mother lying down in her room afterward.) Those were the funny stories. It was the scars on her wrists, the scars on the soft hidden places inside her body—those were the scars she didn't tell me about, and I didn't ask.

"After the divorce, my father used to come into my room and . . . ," my mother began once, then caught herself. "I'll tell you when you're older." When I told her that my high school girlfriend had cuts all over her arms, she said, "You know, when I was that age . . ." Then, with a quick sigh: "I'll tell you when you're older." There were moments when details slipped, when she seemed not to realize how strange certain things sounded, or forgot for a moment that I knew how to listen. Her father had wandered the hallways naked, terrifying the young maids. One Christmas, he had pre-emptively removed her appendix. But when I asked her directly about her life, she told me only the funny stories, the easy ones: the time she and her sister broke the bed and blamed it on their obese grandmother, the time she cut her sister's hair while she was sleeping. I saw only the edges of the holes, the aftershocks of the explosions. "I'll tell you when you're older," she said when I tried to reach for more. My mother understood: There was room for only one of us to be a girl. There was room for only one of us to be a woman.

AS A CHILD, I tried to cast spells of my own invention. I spun my dolls around three times, spat on teddy bears, put pieces of wire be-neath my pillow. I lived in awed fear of a faded pink fairy figurine that I believed controlled not only my fate but that of the other toys. The real world was overlaid with a shimmering second world of signs and symbols. I continued to believe in a magic realm long after my friends had stopped. I did not want to grow up. I did not care about my clothes. What stood on the other side of childhood—an uncomfortable awareness of my body, my mother's growing anger—held no appeal for me. I wanted only to fall out of this world, with its looming dangers, to that other, shimmering place.

I believed many things without question: that my mother could read my mind but chose not to; that the tiny red stinging bugs in the Astroturf on our roof were evil omens; that, while brushing my hair in the morning, I could tune in to the conversations of people I had never met, their banal statements—*I told you, it's all the way in the back*—drifting crystal clear through my mind. An upright plastic bottle in my path on the sidewalk would shimmer with importance, as if it were a message I could almost decode. I did not want to accept the random disorder of a world without narrative. That is what magic was for me: meaning superimposed on chaos.

On the morning of my sixteenth birthday, I stared into the mirror opposite our kitchen table in profound disappointment. I had not quite realized that I had still been waiting to become a fairy, but I had been. My mother walked in, wearing the faded pink nightgown that had belonged to her grandmother. I saw her for an instant the way you rarely see the people you've known your whole life. I saw the purple under her eyes, her olive skin growing thin and soft with wrinkles, the gray roots of her hair that had been going gray for years. And yet I knew, still knew, that she was a fairy. I knew it from the way she could make me feel invincible with just the right words. I knew it from the way she called my cell phone three seconds into each first kiss. I knew it from the way she took one look at my face that morning and asked me if I could fly.

WHEN I WAS SIX, and my brother a year and a half old, my mother accepted the position of art editor at *The New Yorker*. It was the first job she'd ever had for which she needed to wear nice clothes. She hired us a string of babysitters, ambitious French-speaking young women who were guaranteed to leave within a year or two and whose names I can now barely remember. She woke at six-twenty each morning to drive us to school, ripping up the FDR Drive to Twenty-Third Street before bringing the car back to SoHo and heading off to her office high above Times Square. She was home for dinner each night, even if the babysitter cooked, even if it meant that we ate long after the sun had set.

When I was sick or school was closed, my mother took me to work with her. I sat on the couch in her big office and watched as artists came with their sketches for magazine covers. She circled the pictures with her red pen, climbed on a chair, steady in her short leather skirt and heels, and tacked the sketches to the wall. She pulled proofs, ran down to the printing department, corrected colors, told the fact-checkers (who checked every image with shocking literalness) that rabbits could be pink when it was Easter. Sometimes she gave me scissors and I made crazed snowflakes from her scrap paper, trying to imitate her constant motion. I gave my creations to every person on the floor, running between the offices, never doubting their gratitude for a second. When I was with my mother, I felt invulnerable.

But when my mother drove us to school in the morning, the air was charged with a different energy. She slapped the steering wheel in frustration. Her French exhalations, her *argh*s and *pff*s, crowded the air like comic book sound effects that left no room for speech. And yet she insisted on driving us. She didn't want us to be made to go to school alone, as she had. It seemed strange, once I knew the full story, that this was the only part of her childhood that she allowed herself to resent.

I tried to picture her young, but I saw her exactly as I knew her. I'd seen not a single photograph of her between eight and eighteen. As far as I knew, none had been taken. She'd told me she drank coffee as a child. I tried to imagine her making it for herself in careful silence in the gray light of a Paris morning while the rest of her family slept. Seeking a road map to her, I petitioned for years to be allowed to drink coffee as well.

Outside our home, my mother's name was almost always appended to my father's. "An impressive woman in her own right," the articles said. My father's graphic novel *Maus* about his parents' experiences in the concentration camps, won a Pulitzer Prize when I was five. The spotlight of his fame projected a larger-than-life version of him to the world that even he often struggled with. But inside our home, it was my mother who loomed large.

"Françoise takes care of reality and I take care of everything else," my father often said, jokingly. And even though it was true that my mother handled the finances, the plumbing, the carpentry, our education and our vacations, while my father often disappeared for weeks at a time to his studio, I saw her wince when he said this, not taking it as the compliment he intended.

"My girlfriends and I talk about how much we hate you," a friend of my mother's once told her. "You're French, you've got the best job in New York, you've married a successful man, you're beautiful, you're thin, you've got two wonderful children. It's not fair. You're perfect."

My mother wasn't perfect. My mother was intense. Things didn't happen because they were possible, they happened because she decided they would. She once fit a couch through a door frame that was several inches too small simply by pushing with all her strength and saying, "Couch, go in!" But, as anyone who has read a fairy tale knows, all spells come with a cost. The magic pulled on hidden sources. My brother referred to her exertion of will as "the fireball technique." She could set the universe aflame, but she used herself as fuel. Somewhere inside, the earth was scorched.

ONE AFTERNOON, when I was eight years old, my mother caught me sharply by my wrist as I wandered back to my room from the kitchen. She was furious. I stared at her in surprise.

"You can't walk around naked when the plumbers are here!" she said. The bathroom door was still open and the plumbers working there could hear, though they didn't speak French. I spent a lot of time naked as a child. I had never been scolded for it before. But now I burned with a sudden and vivid shame. "It's indecent!" she said, and I could see in her eyes the real shock that I had not already understood this. I understood it then, all at once.

A woman's body was a private thing. My body was a private thing. My body was a woman's body. My mother was a woman. My mother was a private thing. There were dangers. There were secrets. There was something to guard.

I had thought that my shame had seared the memory deep only for me. But when I brought up this incident twenty years later, my mother nodded in recognition. I felt a small thrill. There were so few memories that we actually shared.

"Yes, there were these big men in the house that were strangers, and you . . . ," she said. "That was when I knew that something was really off. You never had . . . modesty." I burned with shame all over again.

My mother was a ferociously private person. She did not gossip and never betrayed secrets. She did not easily forgive these things in others, either. She did not go through my drawers or read my diaries. It never occurred to me that she would. She never asked questions of my friends or tried to remember their names. She talked disdainfully of American mothers who put themselves on the same level as their children. The boundaries between us were clear: the parents in the front seat, the children in the back. They were the source of her power. I tried to break them. I told her too much about myself. I told her about my crushes and my petty fights with friends. I told her all the things she would never ask.

I knew she expected me to respect her privacy in return. The older I got, the more difficult it became. When she wasn't home, I spent hours in her walk-in closet, touching her clothes and going through her boxes. I found her old diaphragm, her love letters from my father, her lingerie. I felt guilt only about how little guilt I felt. It wasn't until I read the papers in her desk, letters from long ago, that I stopped, sleepless with questions I could not ask.

As I HIT PUBERTY, and my body began to change, a dangerous new tension arose between us. My mother thrust Rollerblades at me in the morning and insisted I get myself to school, get some exercise, while she drove my brother and his friends. On weekday evenings, when the huge industrial skylights went dark and night fell in our living room, I knew better than to be on the couch when she came home. I gathered my books and comics and went to my room. I knew in the way one knows the things that can never quite be said that it made her furious to see me sitting still. I would listen for her "*Bonsoir!*" hurled from the door like a warning flare. It was only a matter of moments before my bedroom walls shook with the sound of my name. "*NAA DJAAA!*" Two guttural cries of frustration. I sat braced for this and yet I jumped each time. My heart raced. "Can you at least help set the table?" she would say, tears of exhaustion in her eyes, when I appeared in the kitchen doorway. And if the table was already set, if the dinner was already made, then it was a sock I had dropped in the bathroom, or shoes I had left in the hall, or something else I had done or not done that sparked her fury. Sometimes I roamed the house before her return, trying to guess the thing that would set her off and correct it. But the patterns were etched deep and felt inescapable. I felt it was not the sock or the shoes or the house but my body itself that refused to meet her expectations.

We were not allowed television (ours played only VHS tapes), so I escaped into books. I read in the bath, in the car, walking down the street, in the corner during adult dinner parties. Mostly I read books about ordinary girls in ordinary worlds who suddenly discovered their magical powers. But there was one book that I read often and kept hidden on my highest shelf. I had not wanted to return it to the library and so had paid the fine from my pocket money. *Don't Hurt Laurie!* It was a slim pink book with too-big type about a girl who was abused. Laurie's mother's anger was vicious and unpredictable. Laurie's mother told the nurses at the hospital that Laurie had fallen down the stairs. I knew my mother would never hurt me. She had left tiny pitchers of milk and bowls of cereal in the fridge when my friends slept over when we were five. My mother kissed me good night each evening and praised the stories I wrote. But I recognized something familiar, though grotesquely exaggerated, in Laurie's mother: the outbursts that made the house tremble and just as quickly disappeared. And I envied Laurie. I envied her black-and-blue marks and her bandaged wrists. I envied her clear-cut proof that something had actually happened.

THROUGHOUT MY ADOLESCENCE, my mother's reality threatened to overpower my own. One evening might pass without incident, then the next she would call me to the kitchen, shaking with fury, and accuse me of opening a second container of milk. It did not matter that the first had spoiled. It did not matter that I hadn't. When my mother was angry, the anger consumed her. Her gray-green eyes turned a lethal black. "Just apologize," she would say. And yet I was incapable of apologizing for things I had not done, no matter how small. I could not admit to throwing away all the spoons, to moving her papers, to hiding the mustard. I knew that to cede even this much ground was to lose all sense of myself. I would go to my room and scream at the top of my lungs, hoping that she would hear the intensity of my pain, how wronged and innocent I was, and come running with apologies. But my room, which had once been my father's office, was soundproofed, and my mother could not hear me from the other side of the loft.

Soon afterward, those fights had never happened. "You're

exaggerating, Nadja," she would say, a week later. "How could I have kicked you *up* the stairs?" I'd wonder, shakily, if she was right. I developed a code in my sporadically kept diaries—a big circled *R* on each page that detailed a fight with my mother, a reminder to myself that these events were "REAL." Often, it was easier to allow the past to become a blur.

Most families retell anecdotes, reinforcing their legends to draw closer: that time she overturned the game board, that time he gave the dog a haircut. We did not. Instead of anecdotes, we had narratives. My mother condensed whole swaths of our shared past into a sharp tool with which she explained and ordered our present. Reminiscing led to bitter arguments. Memories that contradicted my mother's narrative were picked apart in their details. That babysitter had not worked for us during the summers. We had stopped visiting that cabin in 1998. I felt myself clinging to my version of reality as if some essential part of my selfhood might get washed away. But when proof could be produced—a restaurant receipt, a map, a diary entry, a Google search—my mother simply shifted the subject. Like many couples, my mother and father could not tell a story about their shared past without arguing about which street corner they had been standing on. Once, during a particularly drunken dinner with the writers Siri Hustvedt and Paul Auster, Siri attempted to diffuse an argument between them with an anecdote of her own.

"One morning in the country, while Paul was still sleeping, our daughter and I saw a bird—it was a vision—through the window. A heron, majestic. I held her and we watched it in silence," Siri said. "Later, I overheard Paul tell the story at a party—but now he had seen the heron. He had held Sophie. I hadn't been there at all! Because of course we had told him all about it."

"I really thought I had seen it," Paul said with a gravelly laugh, an open sweep of the cigarillo in his hand.

"And I believe him," Siri said, leaning forward, her blue eyes wide and earnest. "And it doesn't matter. The point is: the heron was seen."

I served myself again from the Chinese takeout cooling on the table, even though I was no longer hungry. My mother was the only other one still eating. She never ate, then she ate like a wolf. I put the food in my mouth without tasting it. *The heron was seen.* How blissful to be able to find that kind of peace with the past.

"I have a terrible memory," my mother said then. She sounded tipsy, which surprised me. She drank wine every night, but she rarely got drunk. "All of my memories," she continued morosely, "all of my memories have my children in them. Even the ones from before they were born."

"So your life began twenty-three years ago," Paul said. That was my age at the time.

"I guess so," my mother said.

"But that's very sweet," Siri said.

"Is it?" my mother said. "It seems a bit sad to me."

But I do not think my mother meant that she remembered only her life after my birth. I think she meant what she said: that we were in all of her memories, even though we could not be. The narratives were part of my mother's power. The past shaped the present, but the present also reshaped the past.

OUR RELATIONSHIP CHANGED abruptly when I went away to college. It was as if my mother had been molding me my whole life, and now suddenly she stepped away, as if I were complete, as if she liked what she saw. The absence of her anger terrified me as much as the anger itself had. I still felt far from complete. The year I left, my mother added a second full-time job to her first. She began her own children's book publishing company in the ground floor of our building. She told me she knew my brother would be leaving a too-short four years later, and she refused to allow her life to feel empty without us. She made time for me whenever I called but very rarely called me first. Sometimes we went two months without speaking. I felt the free-floating horror of freedom. It took two years before I stopped jumping up from my seat in my too-quiet dorm room, hallucinating her screaming my name.

My junior year, I moved off campus at the last minute and found myself in an apartment with no furniture. The school year hadn't yet begun, and other people's parents were driving them to Ikea in their SUVs. I called my mother in a panic.

"What do I do? I don't even know where to start!" I said.

"You figure it out, Nadja," she said. She was busy, she had deadlines, she had an artist sitting in her office. "It's not that hard. You don't need much."

"But where will I sleep tonight? How does one even buy a mattress?" I said.

"I don't know," she said. "Borrow an air mattress. Sleep on the floor a few nights. I have to go." I wound up on a friend's doorstep in hysterical, self-serious tears. The next weekend, my mother stopped by on her way to the country. She had strapped a sofa bed to the top of the car. She furnished my apartment in two hours flat.

While other people joked bitterly about becoming their mothers, I longed to. I didn't even understand how she had become herself.

———

THE WINTER BEFORE my last semester of college, my mother and I were having dinner in a sushi restaurant in Paris. I was anxious about my upcoming graduation, unsure what I would do next or who I would become. My mother met every worry with an unshakable certainty that I would be fine. Right then, I wanted only her sympathy.

"Well, of course you don't get it," I said bitterly. "You've always known who you were."

My mother shook her head. And then she began to tell me about a time, a time before. I scrambled for my digital camera, hoping to use its movie function to record her voice. I didn't want to miss a word.

"I think," I told her a few weeks later, unsure how to broach the topic, "that I would like to write about you. About your coming of age."

"I'm flattered, but . . . are you sure?" There was a sadness in her eyes that I couldn't place. She wouldn't meet my gaze. I told her that I was ready. I wanted her to think so. I didn't want to be protected anymore.

My mother did not agree right away. She thought about it carefully. And then, having decided, she held nothing back. The boundaries between us fell, and fell suddenly. She let me in. There was nothing I couldn't ask. She answered me with a searching honesty rare even in the privacy of one's own thoughts. She made time for me in her overcrowded life. We talked at our kitchen table, in her downstairs office, on the couch. We talked until early-morning light streamed through the skylight and the cars started honking again on Canal Street. We went away together, just the two of us, to a country cabin and talked for days. I graduated from college, I moved into my parents' house, I moved out of my parents' house, I took my first job and then my second. We talked for years.

Early on, my mother prodded me carefully. "You know . . . what we're doing, it's a lot like *Maus*. Like what your father did when he interviewed his father."

"Of course," I replied, surprised that she thought I had not noticed. "That's part of it. I want to write, and I can't do it until I address what he did. I'm doing something parallel and yet it's completely different. And also, I suppose, I'm doing the one thing he could never do." My father's own mother had killed herself when he was twenty. His father had burned her diaries.

"That was the moment," my mother told me later, "when I knew I could trust you. I trusted you to know you were ready."

At first I used my laptop, the waveform spiking up and down on the screen as she spoke. Then technology changed and I used my iPhone. I didn't trust myself to remember. Many of the stories were so difficult to listen to that I would wake up disoriented the next day, a vague blackness in place of our conversation.

My mother and I spoke in French, the language so natural to me with her that I only noticed I'd shifted to it when I spoke to her on the phone in front of my friends. When I was three, she'd urged me to go join the children in a playground in the Jardin du Luxembourg. "*Mais Maman!*" I'd replied, wrapping myself in the wings of her long coat. "*Je ne parle pas français!*" It took me years to realize that the private language I spoke with my mother was a language other people could understand. But although I could speak French, I never learned to write it properly. So I transcribed our interviews in English, translating as I typed. My mother's words rolled through my head in her language and out through my fingers in mine. Her memories became my own. One evening, she told me that there was no one else she could talk to this way. Not my father. Not her friends. By that point, she could reference any moment in her life with barely a hand gesture. I sometimes felt I knew her past so intimately that I could read her thoughts.

"But with you," she said, "you're so close. Like when you were a baby. I don't . . . I can't worry about how you'll see me. You're a part of me."

For her, the stories dissolved us into one. I was the infant she'd never put down, whose cries she heard before my mouth had opened. But for me, the stories gave me the distance I needed to see her whole. "I'll tell you when you're older," she'd said, and now I was old enough. It would take a long time before I would understand the sadness in her eyes when I'd first asked.

chapter two

When she was a child, my mother was a boy. Her father brought her to his barbershop, where they cut her hair as short as his. Her mother dressed her all in blue, polo shirts and shorts. Most of the time, Françoise didn't mind. She was lithe and athletic. She scaled fences, jumped off jungle gyms.

My mother's older sister, Sylvie, was fourteen months old when Françoise was born, still nursing and barely walking. Josée had believed she couldn't get pregnant while her breasts were still full of milk. She hadn't wanted a second child so soon after the first. Unaware that she was pregnant, she'd gone on vacation, riding camels across the Egyptian desert. But she'd been stubborn, my mother, even then. She took root and held on.

A second daughter. Her father left the Paris hospital moments after her birth, his face such a mask of grief that nurses came to check that the child was still alive. He disappeared for a few days to a casino on the edge of Paris and came back just in time to legally declare the birth.

He insisted on naming her Françoise, his grandmother's name, common and down-to-earth, not Catherine, as Josée had wanted and expected. This child was his. The lines were drawn early.

"You were the ugliest baby," Josée liked to tell Françoise around the time of her birthdays. "Your nose was squashed flat against your face and your head was long and oval, like a suppository." But she'd grown into a beautiful child, one that strangers stopped to exclaim over in her stroller. She had her father's dark curls, her father's intelligent, combative gaze. "Brown eyes just like Paul's," Josée told me once, although my mother's eyes were a piercing gray-green. I supposed she meant that my mother's eyes weren't blue like hers.

Andrée had followed six years after Françoise's birth. Another man's child, Paul claimed. The product of a conjugal rape, insisted Josée. An attempt to save their failing marriage, I was once told. The final *e* was appended in the maternity ward, when it was discovered that this child had also refused to be a boy. Andrée's birth was often used to mark time in family stories. It coincided roughly with the beginning of Paul's major professional and financial success, with the moment when he and Josée were able to purchase the floor below their own for his medical practice. Before, they had been relatively happy. After, there was far too much money.

For the most part, the older girls learned to be invisible. On the many nights when their parents held dinner parties in the dining room, the children ate in the kitchen, handed out peanuts and olives in their pajamas (blue for Françoise, red for Sylvie), then went obediently to their room. In the bed they shared, Françoise whispered gruesome stories about martyrs. She had decided that she would grow up to be Joan of Arc. She couldn't see herself becoming a woman like her mother, with perfectly done nails. She would dress in men's clothes, die for a cause, change the history of France.

Sometimes the girls found moments of sisterly closeness. But most of the time, tensions between them ran high. They felt like the racehorses on which Josée and Paul placed bets each Sunday. Sylvie was her mother's horse and Françoise her father's. Françoise nearly always won—she couldn't help competing and couldn't help winning. She learned to swim the same year Sylvie did, her small arms straining to keep pace. She loved school and always came in first in her class. She skipped a year and shared classes with her sister. With each of Françoise's small victories, Josée's rage seemed to grow, and Françoise felt stinging regret.

Françoise admired her father. She liked the way people's eyes grew wide when she told them about the work he did—pulling the skin of her face back with her palms, explaining about smaller noses, smaller breasts. Paul was one of France's first cosmetic plastic surgeons, the profession's handsome spokesperson. She forgave him the embarrassment he caused by flirting with each shopkeeper or waitress. He was extraordinarily charismatic, and on the days he was in a good mood, his loud singing filled the house and no one, not even Josée, could keep from smiling. It went without question that Françoise was her father's daughter and would one day take over his practice. But it was her mother she truly worshipped.

In a photo from the early days of her marriage, Josée looks the part of the perfect 1950s housewife, a string of pearls on and a bouquet of flowers in hand, eyes tilted demurely upward at my grandfather behind the camera. But that was not the sort of woman she was cut out to be. When she threw dinner parties, as she was expected to do, they were lavish and extreme—oyster-eating contests, a rack hung with dried sausages in the center of the buffet, whoopee cushions on the seats, forks that bent in half when you tried to use them, trick glasses that spilled wine down starched, monogrammed shirts to her guests' raucous delight. When she made herself beautiful, as she was expected to be, she was one of the most beautiful women in Paris, with her wasp waist and legs for miles and her gaze that could lure a man from across a room. When she dressed well, as she was expected to do, she set the fashions. When her husband cheated on her, as he was more or less expected to do, she had wild affairs of her own. But when it came to being a mother, she did not have the time.

Josée came home in the evenings laden with shopping bags that she dropped by the door as she ran to the bathroom.

"I haven't even had time to piss!" she'd exclaim. Young Françoise watched her dash by with wide eyes, deeply impressed by the busy schedule this implied. In retrospect, it was not exactly clear what took Josée's time. She got her hair done nearly daily. She bought antique furniture and restored it herself in the building's courtyard, frequently enough that the concierge thought she was an antiques dealer. She helped organize the international plastic and reconstructive surgeons' conferences. She planned the dinner parties, recording in a notebook what was served and which of the stuffy surgeons was seated next to which of their wives. She made annotations such as "P arrived late" or "JM prefers rosé to white." She noted her own outfits, careful never to repeat them.

Neither Josée nor Paul had been born into money. Paul had been raised in a small town in Corrèze, an insular region in the center of France, the only child of a veterinarian. When Josée first visited her in-laws, their bathtub was filled with potatoes. Josée's own upbringing was darker and more complicated, and the details of it were murky to her daughters. It was never discussed in public. Still, the two of them had seduced and charmed their way into the staid circle of the upper class. They had retained their pasts only as the weapon they used to cut each other deepest.

Their fights were constant, intense, violent. More than once, the police were called.

"I have always been able to cry on command," Josée commented one Sunday afternoon, as her husband and children were gathered around a towering pile of seafood. They turned to watch as tears began to roll down her face. Then she stopped as abruptly as she had begun, fixing her husband with her impenetrable blue eyes. His face turned red and he shook with rage. "Don't smirk at me, with your dirty little bastard's smile," he said. His dinner plate whizzed past her ear, shattering against the wall. Josée barely blinked.

They were most at peace when they were getting ready to go out in the evenings. They knew what a glamorous couple they cut. They were as proud of each other's looks as they were of their own. Paul sang to himself as he arranged his thick black curls, sprayed his cologne. Françoise hovered silently as Josée added false eyelashes, pinned to her head the extra ponytail of blond hair. Françoise felt she would explode with love. Her admiration for her mother burned so bright that she was sure it must be visible, a strobing light that pulsed from her chest. But Josée never seemed to see her small, boyish daughter glowing behind her in the mirror. As Josée put on her shoes, as Paul extended his elbow to her, Françoise edged closer, hoping for a kiss good night. But then they were gone, the sound of their laughter on the stairs, a faint trace of Shalimar in the air. After they left, Françoise snuck into Josée's closet and pulled the dresses around herself.

"If I go to bed now, will you come and tuck me in and kiss me good night?" Françoise begged Andrée's nurse. "Just this one time?"

"I can't," the woman said. "I have children of my own."

Françoise wanted only to be allowed to love her mother. She brought her offering after offering—drawings covered in hearts, an ashtray, a clay vase she had made in school. If only the gift was good enough, beautiful enough, it would capture all the love she could not communicate, and Josée would be forced to notice that her daughter was madly in love with her. But Josée was used to people being madly in love with her. She tossed each object aside with some vague criticism. The clay vase remained on the mantel of the formal living room for a few days, and Josée laughed as she demonstrated to guests how water poured into it dripped right back out through a hole in the bottom.

Françoise kept trying, crawling into her mother's bed in the mornings when Josée was still sleepy and soft, kissing her cheek. "Go away," Josée would say, tossing onto her side. "I don't like to be touched." One Mother's Day morning, Josée's face was swollen by a particularly agonizing toothache. Françoise overheard her complaining. Josée refused to leave the bed, unwilling to show her face to the world. But Françoise still found her mother heart-wrenchingly beautiful. She went into Josée's room with a song she had prepared: *"Maman, Maman, c'est toi la plus belle du monde,"* Luis Mariano's popular hit at the time. She had memorized all of the lyrics. She sang it with such passion that she felt her lungs might burst. "Beautiful mother," Josée scoffed as she pushed Françoise out of the room. "Now there's an oxymoron." She locked the door.

It was two in the morning when my mother finished telling me this story. We were curled together on the couch, her legs across my lap. The skylight overhead had long since gone dark. There were no windows in this part of our loft but it took visitors a minute to notice, because the ceilings were high and the walls were covered in framed pictures, original comic book pages and lithographs given to my parents by friends. There was a large stop sign my mother had found in the street. There was a mural painted straight on the wall, dating back to the days when my parents had used this space to self-publish their underground comics magazine. And hanging directly in front of us were four paintings I'd made one weekend when I was twelve, unremarkable portraits of four female faces, each with a different color hair. The blue-haired girl wore a T-shirt that said HELL. People noticed them immediately when they walked in. I used to blush when my parents' friends felt compelled to bestow some faint praise on them. In the kitchen, large-scale kindergarten paintings of a witch and a devil hung above the table. In my mother's bathroom, a beautiful glass curio cabinet contained my brother's clay sculptures. The entire wall by her desk was covered with doodles, poems we had written about her, letters we had left for her. On her mirror, a note I'd written in glow-in-the-dark pen, a misspelled "*je ta dore maman*" surrounded by hearts, had never been erased.

I nestled my head into my mother's shoulder, trying to get comfortable. She laid her hand on my head.

"Remember when you were little and we cuddled in the mornings?" my mother asked. "'It's all hard!' you'd say, jabbing my shoulder."

"It's still hard," I said, laughing.

"I can't help it!" she said with genuine hurt.

I grabbed a throw pillow and placed it on her chest.

"It's okay," I said. "I can fix it." We lay there a moment in silence, her hand in my hair. I listened to her muffled heartbeat through the pillow and smelled her faint, familiar scent of Shalimar.

———

LATE INTO THE NIGHT Françoise read in the bathtub, where no one would scold her for keeping the light on. She often became so absorbed that she forgot the running tap and flooded the downstairs neighbors. Much of her education depended on rote memorization and she could recite whole plays after one or two readings. Her father ran a tab at the *papeterie* across the street, and she read through the entire bookstore alphabetically. Her collection of paperbacks overflowed her bookshelf and began to creep across the radiator. But when the time came in eighth grade for her to choose a track in school, her parents decided Françoise would opt for science. They even came to her school, rare and vivid visions, to speak with the principal. It went without saying that Françoise would be a doctor like her father. That there were extraordinarily few female surgeons worried no one. Françoise felt a slow-growing discomfort. It was not so much that she did not want to be a doctor—plastic surgery held little appeal but other branches of medicine might have interested her. It was the creeping realization that there were choices, big choices, being made about her future without her.

Sylvie, on the other hand, was encouraged to paint. She would make a good wife, her parents agreed. Or perhaps she would be a masseuse. Her mother liked to point out her big strong hands. "*Brave* Sylvie," her parents said, shaking their heads sadly. Sylvie was a good cook, she was creative and artistic, she was kind and *serviable*, she was what women were. Françoise, it was agreed, was intelligent, ruthless, sullen, and mean.

"Look," Josée said laughingly to Françoise, "even baby Andrée starts to cry when you walk into the room!" Françoise scowled and walked back out. At least their older daughters had one thing in common, Josée and Paul agreed: neither had any sense of humor.

The roles were cast and there was no escaping them. It didn't matter that Andrée always smiled when she saw Françoise—that she was, in fact, the only family member who ever seemed happy to see her. Some things were said so often that they became true. Françoise practiced smiling in the mirror, her father's wide open grin, her mother's come-hither smile, but she couldn't shake the dark cloud that seemed to follow her from room to room.

For the first decade of their lives, Françoise and Sylvie were each other's constant companions, if only by necessity, and fractiously. Françoise put chewing gum in her sister's hair, and Sylvie left huge scratches down her sister's arms. One evening while their parents were out, they were roughhousing in the medical office below. Sylvie, fooling around in a wheelchair, backed into a glass-front cabinet and broke a figurine. The girls thought it might be an Egyptian artifact. Certainly it was expensive and rare, as all of Paul's belongings were.

"Just leave it there," Sylvie said. "They'll think it was the maid."

"But she'll lose her job," Françoise said.

"Better her than us," Sylvie replied.

"Where will she go?" Françoise said with genuine horror.

"Not our problem," Sylvie said.

"If you don't tell them, I will," Françoise said, and she did. Both girls were punished. *I am Joan of Arc*, Françoise told herself. But Sylvie was becoming less and less interested in her stories of martyrs.

In the space of a summer, a chasm had opened between the two sisters. At ten years old, Sylvie was formed—that was what the French said when a girl first had her period, *"Elle a été formée."*

In Sylvie's case, the expression was literally true: she had breasts, she had curves. She looked like a woman.

That summer, Sylvie was sent away to summer camp. It was the first time the two older girls had been separated. The following fall, Josée sent Sylvie to Paul's mother, Mamie, in Ussel, a year's exile.

"She has jaundice," Josée declared. "She needs to be in the country." But it was clear to Françoise that that was not the reason.

Françoise slept alone now. Josée had made a new bedroom down the hall for Sylvie when she came home. "Sylvie is a young woman now," Josée said. "She needs her own room."

Françoise stared at her unchanging child's body in the mirror. She didn't envy Sylvie her year with Mamie. Mamie's breath smelled bad, she rarely bathed, she was very fat, and her voice quaked like a bleating goat's when she spoke. In Françoise's opinion, Mamie was a small-minded provincial woman whose company was to be avoided at all costs. She was nothing like Mina, Josée's mother, who lived in Paris in a grand apartment, who read, who worked over the weekends on the typewriter in her living room.

But in Ussel, Sylvie found something she had been longing for. Mamie, lonely Mamie, smothered her granddaughter with unconditional love. She loved *big*, like this, Sylvie would say, her arms stretched wide. Mamie gave Sylvie a pot of Nutella every afternoon at four. She used a stick of butter in each meal. Sylvie took it all in, the love and the food, insatiable. She returned to Paris on weekends and school vacations, her face growing steadily rounder. After a year away, she had gained twenty pounds.

Josée's anger trained itself on Sylvie in full force. There was no space for an unbeautiful daughter in the world she and Paul had made for themselves. "My parents *invented* superficiality," my mother told me once. The girls were made to feel that physical appearance was the only measure of worth. Josée had meticulously decorated their apartment for receiving guests, and it was irreproachable, if oppressively somber. Heavy curtains, heavy furniture, heavy carpeting—everything was calculated to give the appearance that they had been rooted in this life for centuries. But now it was as if, in Sylvie's body, the ghost of their pasts had refused to stay buried. Paul's provincial roots were showing. His mother's body had reemerged, uninvited, in his daughter's.

Josée claimed for herself the new bedroom Sylvie had barely had a chance to inhabit. She needed her own space, she declared, installing a rigid blue settee barely large enough for one. Sylvie was relocated to the medical floor below, in a small, dark room whose window gave onto a grim interior courtyard. She could hear the floorboards creaking overhead as her family moved around and she knew that she was no longer part of them. During the day, she sidled past her father's patients in the waiting room, designer heels and bandaged noses, and up the dark servants' stairs to reach the bathroom. At night, she was the only person on the whole floor. This banishment is what, years later, she would resent most.

"Why didn't you take the room below for yourself?" Sylvie asked Josée at dinner one night, nearly fifty years later, not for the first time. Now it was Josée who scooped crème fraîche onto her carrots and Sylvie who scolded her for it, but the helpless little girl was still there in her voice. "It would have given you a very private access."

"I wasn't about to go sleep somewhere else in my own home," Josée replied, indignant.

"So you thought it was *normal* to send an eleven-year-old—"

"Well, who else was going to go down there? I suppose your father could have . . . but otherwise, yes. You sent the kids."

"And you thought it was—"

"Now that you say it, yes. We could have sent Paul."

"Because you figured that for a child—"

"His whole medical office was down there. It would have been convenient," Josée acknowledged with a beatific smile and a shrug. "And I could have taken his room then! Well, I've only thought of that just now. No luck for you."

"I HAVE ALWAYS LOVED both my children equally," my mother said to me when I was an adult, with unwavering conviction. That my mother favored my brother was for me one of the most basic facts of our shared past. She tended carefully to his minor scrapes and bruises. When he bit me on the back and drew blood, she scolded me for provoking him. My brother was a cherubic child with a halo of soft curls and long-lashed brown eyes. But when he was angry and we were alone, he curled his fingers and let loose a long, breathless wail so intense his face went red and his head shook. Then he lunged, clawing and punching and biting. He looked just like her, my mother used to say. When I'd asked who I looked like, she'd said, "your paternal grandfather."

One summer, at a city pool with a particularly inattentive babysitter, my brother held me underwater so long the world went black. He held me by my growing breasts. He had learned that this caused me so much pain I could not fight back, and so he used the tactic often. I came up gasping, terrified, convinced I had almost died. When I reported on this later to my mother, certain that this time I would find sympathy, she looked at me stonily. She sent me away and called my brother into her room. When they emerged, she told me that she wouldn't punish either of us. I must learn to stop trying to drag her into our arguments. "But you should be ashamed of yourself for what you did," she said to me. "You know exactly. Now, end of discussion."

I clung to the moment one of her friends pulled me aside and told me that the imbalance in our treatment wasn't normal. It was the only proof I had. Neither my mother, my father, nor my brother remembered things the way I did. I tried to remind myself we could each have our own versions. My mother's was not more real than my own. But I never quite believed this was true.

WHILE HER FAMILY SLEPT, Sylvie crept up the servants' stairs to the kitchen to raid the refrigerator. She ate fruit in syrup straight from the can. She stole money from the grocery wallet. She bought herself bags of candy at the *boulangerie*. She bought roses by the dozen and gave them away to strangers in the street. At the girls' communion, a fancy affair where they had been instructed to say hello and politely stay out of the way, Sylvie drank so heavily she wound up flat on her back under the table.

Françoise watched her sister with horrified awe. Sylvie's year in Ussel had left her unprepared for her return to Paris, and her grades failed. Rather than repeat the year and thereby fall behind her little sister, Sylvie was sent to a series of boarding schools and local private schools, a rarity at that time even for well-to-do Parisians. Sylvie was friends with boys. She went to parties; she drank and smoked. Françoise was never invited along. She spent most of her time alone in her room, with her unchanging body and her perfect grades.

Sylvie had sanitary napkins. Sylvie had a bra. When Sylvie had cramps, Josée would lie in bed with her *"pour lui donner ses fesses,"* curling herself into her daughter's abdomen so that the warmth of her buttocks would ease the pain. Françoise's stomach clenched with jealousy. She was tired of being a boy. The jealousy was the same in the more difficult moments. Françoise stood outside Josée's locked bedroom door, listening to the thwacking sounds intercut by Sylvie's cries of pain. At first Josée used her hand, then a hairbrush. *When my turn comes, I won't give her the satisfaction of crying out,* Françoise resolved. Now when she snuck into her mother's bedroom, she hit herself with the hairbrush. She tried hard to make it hurt and to stay silent. She watched herself in her mother's mirror, practicing a stoic mask. But her turn never did come, and that hurt most of all.

"A BRA?" Josée said when Françoise finally mumbled her request. "A bra for what?" She shouted to Paul and Sylvie. "Did you hear that? Françoise wants a bra!" Sylvie laughed loudest.

Josée had slipped into the 1960s with ease—miniskirts and Brigitte Bardot bangs. Her body was made for the era—the breasts she spent a lifetime complaining were too large, the waist so small two hands could nearly fit around it. Françoise grew fixated on the maxi-coat her mother wore over her shortest skirts. If only she had a coat like that, she thought, she might be seen as a woman. But she was still dressed by her mother, in school uniforms and utilitarian clothing designed not to fade or tear. Occasionally Paul might take Françoise shopping, flashing rolls of cash in Paris's most expensive stores. But she was only his prop then, trying on a parade of preppy outfits as her father boldly flirted with the saleswomen. He would never buy her a fashionable coat like her mother's.

Instead, Françoise gathered her carefully saved pocket money. She bought a cheap department store raincoat. She cut it and sewed it, then put it on and twirled in front of the mirror. It wasn't the coat she'd envisioned, but, Françoise thought, if she moved like this, swayed like that, one might mistake it for elegant, one might forget its uneven hem and plastic sheen. She swooshed through the house in it, imagining the admiring looks.

"What is that supposed to be?" Josée said. "You can't seriously want to leave the house in that!" Françoise looked down and watched the spell transform her Cinderella gown back into plastic. She never wore it again.

Every Sunday, on her way to the racetrack with Paul, Josée dropped Françoise off at her mother's house. Often, she pulled over only long enough for Françoise to climb out of the car. Sometimes she stopped in quickly to give Mina her hand-me-downs, designer dresses past their season, in a stiff exchange that was more payment than present. Mina's house was filled with faded luxuries from a different time. She loved fine things but she sewed her own clothes or repaired Josée's old ones, preserving her threadbare elegance as best she could. Françoise never thought to wonder why Josée never sat down in her mother's house. The two women existed in separate worlds. Despite the tinted photograph of a young Josée on Mina's wall, it never occurred to Françoise that Josée might once have lived there. Josée didn't exist in Mina's world, and Mina didn't exist outside of it. Mina was never invited over to Josée and Paul's house, not even at Christmas, when Paul's mother and Josée's father, the mismatched grandparents who seemed to get along beautifully, sat in the living room, eating the chocolates the patients had left as presents.

Françoise loved being with Mina. Here she wasn't a sister or a daughter, a child or a woman. Here she was finally at ease. After she'd had her bath, Mina would perfume her, tickling her all over— *une friction d'eau de cologne*—while she squirmed with pleasure, delighted to be touched. As she grew older, she and Mina talked for hours, though very rarely about the family. Instead, Mina taught Françoise to sew a button or clean a kitchen, things that at home were done by the help. Mina often brought her secretarial work home over the weekends. Françoise was very impressed by her grandmother's job. She could not imagine becoming a wife, like her mother, or a plastic surgeon, like her father. She convinced Josée to buy her a practice book and an old typewriter, and she taught herself how to type like Mina.

One afternoon Mina said, "What a nice chest you're developing!"

Françoise puffed with pride. "Oh really?" she said. "Do you think so?" She arched her back, showing her fuller left profile.

"Yes," Mina said, "absolutely."

Françoise caught a glimpse of herself in the mirror and her face fell.

"You're going to need a bra soon," Mina said, and when she caught the spark her words set off, "in fact, you must have one right away."

It was not possible simply to go into a store and try on clothes. Everything had to be asked for and fetched from beautiful shop clerks who looked down their noses at little girls. Françoise was terrified of the ordeal buying a bra would entail. Surely the saleswoman would laugh. Surely she'd throw them out. But Mina strode into the store with her back very straight.

"My granddaughter needs a bra," Mina announced. The woman glanced at Françoise, her eyes flicking down to her chest.

"Something with a lot of *support*," Mina said in a tone that left no room for questions. The woman pressed her lips together and nodded. She pulled several padded bras off the wall.

"Yes," Mina said. "Precisely what we were looking for."

Françoise wore the bra home. She held her back straight, her chest pushed out. Josée never noticed.

IN 1966, JOSÉE AND PAUL purchased a slope-side triplex apartment in Avoriaz, a ski resort in the French Alps. Both Françoise and Sylvie loved to ski, and the girls were enrolled in regional races. Françoise passed the gold-level tests before Sylvie had even passed the bronze. Sylvie soon lost her taste for skiing. Françoise went on to train with the junior Olympic team.

One afternoon, Françoise announced that, as a treat for the family, she was going to make a lemon pie. The announcement was met with skepticism. It was a known fact that Sylvie could cook and Françoise could not, though Françoise had never tried.

It took some effort—the new home was high up the mountain, and the lemons had to be brought up by ski lift from the town below. Françoise worked in the kitchen all afternoon. She had no cookbook, so she invented a recipe. She mixed flour with water until it formed a dough, rolled it out, covered it in sliced lemons and sugar. "What is this ungodly thing?" Josée teased as she passed by. "I've never heard of a pie that takes all afternoon to prepare."

The family gathered for dinner. Françoise leapt up several times to check on her pie. When it was time for dessert, the family sat waiting.

"Françoise has decided to poison us all and yet we're going to die of hunger before it even arrives," Josée said.

Françoise emerged from the kitchen and placed the pie in the center of the table. Paul took a knife and tried to cut it.

"It's too hard," he declared. He exaggerated his difficulty, grimacing, pantomiming, until Josée, Sylvie, even baby Andrée collapsed in giggles.

"We need a hammer," Paul declared.

"We need a saw!" Josée chimed. Sylvie laughed hardest of all.

Paul rose to fetch a saw. Everyone collapsed in merriment—everyone except Françoise. No one ate the lemon pie, though to this day they still talk about how awful it tasted.

My mother's mouth became very small as she told me this story. She cast her eyes downward, her voice hollow with hurt. I could see on her face the same expression she must have had that evening, the little girl appearing under the thick eyeliner.

Although we knew how much my mother hated to be teased, my father, brother, and I regarded as entertainment our periodic missions to empty the fridge of bright green cheese and sour cream long past its expiration date. "Filet of celery, anyone?" my father would say, holding a stalk so limp it flopped toward the floor. My mother tried to laugh with us, but as soon as our laughter exceeded hers, her mood darkened. She would grab a knife and stomp to the counter, roughly chopping the mold off the cheese in order to make us sandwiches.

"It's perfectly edible," she'd say. "It's you kids that are spoiled."

And so we learned to clear the fridge in secret. We rarely teased my mother and she never teased us.

Some weekends, my brother and I baked cake. It was a game I thought I had invented. Under my direction, we concocted recipes with whatever we found—unsweetened cocoa powder, oatmeal, dried apricots, entire jars of ground cinnamon. I knew we needed flour and eggs, but I guessed wildly at the quantities. We baked our creation at any temperature we pleased, until it became solid. The cake would emerge as a dense brick, somehow having shrunk in volume rather than rising. I would turn it out on one of my mother's fancy cake plates and adorn the wet lump with strawberries. It almost always tasted like pencil erasers and sawdust, barely sweet. We would call my mother from her room and proudly serve her a slice.

My brother and I ate happily. We were starved for sugar and eager to eat it in any vehicle possible. My mother would slather her piece in fat-free vanilla yogurt and eat with us at the dining table. "Mmm," she would say every time. "Truly delicious. The best one yet."

FOR A SHORT TIME, there had been happy summers in Deauville, on the Normandy coast. It was only two hours north of Paris, and Josée and Paul's social circle flowed easily between the two cities. They entertained in lavish rental homes and danced in the ballroom of the grand casino. Haute couture designers gave Josée samples of their dresses to wear. Paul drove up to join his family most weekends. The best restaurants produced their best tables at the mention of *le grand docteur* Mouly. Josée bought an abandoned *pressoir*, where apples were crushed for cider, just outside the city limits, with the intention of renovating it into their summer home. Françoise pored over the architectural plans, marveling at Josée's ability to create glamour from ruins. It seemed to her an incredible magic trick. But then something happened. The plans for the *pressoir* were abandoned midstream. The building was resold. The family was no longer to summer there. Françoise suspected her father's increasingly out-of-control gambling, but the reasons were not explained to the children, nor would it have occurred to the girls to demand answers.

Now, Paul decided, the family would summer near Ussel. His parents had left him a farm four miles from his hometown, where his mother still lived, and Josée would renovate it. It was an appealing image—his beautiful wife and fancy cars, the luxurious vacation home they would create. What better measure of his own success than the envy of his former schoolmates?

Les Bezièges, the home was called, and Josée, with far less enthusiasm, drew up a new set of plans. In Ussel the sun didn't shine with the gold heat of the Mediterranean or the cool blue light of the north. It was gray, always gray, over the small and unbeautiful homes in the town. Josée drove in at the start of each summer, daylong drives of listening to the girls squabbling in the back of the hot car, while Paul stayed behind to work. The longest stretches of time Josée spent alone with all three children were likely those car trips that bookended each vacation, and years later she would complain about them often.

The arrival of the Parisians raised the local eyebrows. Ussel was a tight-knit community, and the disdain was immediate and mutual. The renovations on the farmhouse proceeded. It had a double-height ceiling, a mezzanine, a grand formal living room. Josée had a patch of land by the barn flattened for a tennis court, the only true tennis court in the region. Jacques Chirac, not yet president but already on the National Assembly, came over to play doubles. But often the house echoed emptily unless friends from Paris made the long drive. Josée would walk straight to the front of the line at the butcher's shop and order thirty of the finest lamb chops for her visiting guests. When she had a stand of trees razed for their new driveway, the town gossiped that she was building a helipad.

In mid-August, Paul drove down from Paris in his Porsche. He stayed only a few days, soaking in the praise that the butcher and baker bestowed on his lovely wife and his three healthy girls. Then he was off again. His patients awaited him in Paris, he told his family lightly, though there seemed little doubt that he was headed for yet another casino, yet another woman's arms.

Josée had created two bedrooms for her three daughters—a young lady's room for Sylvie and a children's room for Françoise and Andrée to share. Françoise did not mind sharing a room with Andrée. Her love had settled easily on her inexplicably cheerful little sister, who sang to herself each night even after Paul, unable to sleep, stormed into her room and broke her bed. When Andrée had walked her first stumbling steps into Françoise's outstretched arms, Françoise nearly cried out with pride. It was only decades later, when she had children of her own, that she realized children learn to walk without ever being taught.

Andrée, Josée had declared, was anorexic. It was true: she often refused to eat. Josée had insisted that someone (rarely herself) sit and coax Andrée bite by bite, late into the night, until a reasonable amount of food had been consumed. The popular parenting advice of the time held that to be potty trained, children must understand the relationship of food to their bowels. Baby Andrée was seated on a plastic potty at the dinner table and encouraged to eat and eliminate in tandem. Françoise suspected that this arrangement was the major cause of her refusal to eat, but still, she was happy to take on the task.

The two of them stayed at the table long after the end of each meal, Françoise pressing forkfuls of food against her sister's smiling, firmly closed lips. Andrée delighted in the attention. She became Françoise's toy. They spent hours playing school, and Françoise tried, with great patience, to teach her too-young sister to read.

Françoise enjoyed her first quiet summer with Andrée. She did not have to compete with the nanny for her time, as she did in Paris. Besides, in Ussel, Sylvie ran wild with the friends she'd made in her year at Mamie's, while Françoise had no friends there of her own.

But the following summer, Josée announced casually, "You're not to play with Andrée anymore." Françoise stared at her, speechless with shock.

"I've asked Renée's little girl to come stay with us so that Andrée will have a friend her own age," Josée continued.

"But *why?*" Françoise asked as the news sank in.

"Your attachment to her is unhealthy," Josée said. "She calls you *maman.*"

The two girls continued to share a room, but now Josée monitored them closely during the day to make sure they remained separate. For Françoise, it was the beginning of a permanent sense of isolation from her family. The days stretched out, impossibly long. Sylvie pointedly did not invite her to join her friends in their mysterious teenage mischief. Françoise was alone, with only her books and her increasingly unhappy mother, who insisted Françoise strip and sand antique furniture until her knuckles ached. Andrée barely seemed to notice the shift. She was delighted to have a playmate her own age. It did not take long for her to stop calling Françoise *maman.* Françoise, on the other hand, felt the loss acutely. Long after I myself stopped being a child, my mother would often accidentally call me Andrée.

IN THE FALL OF 1968, Françoise turned thirteen and began to lose control of her body. It was not in the way she had hoped, not in the way that Sylvie's body had performed its quiet overnight transformation—the curves, the cramps, the spots of blood. Instead, it was around that time that the fits began.

"Make your bed," Josée said, angrily flinging open the door to Françoise's room. It was an arduous process, to transform the bed back into a couch.

"But why?" Françoise said. "This is my room now. No one else comes in here."

"Don't talk back to me," Josée replied. She was capable of saying things so terrible they blacked out the sun. "No one will ever love a girl like you," she might say. "How could you expect them to? A disagreeable, insolent, unpleasant girl like you?" The words shot darkness over Françoise's future and blotted out all hope. She was miserable. She would always be miserable. There was no escape.

When Françoise fought with Sylvie, she wasn't afraid of her own anger. She hit her sister as hard as she could, she pulled her long hair. But when she fought with her mother it was different. The pain was unbearable. It grew inside her, like an object with a physical shape. It expanded her chest and jabbed into her rib cage. Her hands trembled.

Françoise began to hit her head against the wall, rhythmically, so hard that her ears rang and the room spun. She clawed at her face until it opened and bled and there was skin beneath her nails.

She wanted her mother to see how much she was hurting. She wanted the pain to stop.

"You're out of your mind," Josée said. "You are crazy. On top

45

of everything else." She dragged Françoise roughly to the bathroom and put her under a cold shower. She pinned her wrists and slapped her across the face. Françoise, shivering and gulping water between huge, heaving sobs, calmed down.

But the fits continued.

Crises de nerfs, Josée called it. *Hystérie.* Françoise knew her Greek. She put her hand to her uterus. The fits only happened around her mother.

"She's crazy," Josée told her husband. "Something's wrong with her."

They brought Françoise to a neurologist. He performed an encephalogram. Cold white electrodes were placed on her scalp until her whole head was covered. All around her, a halo of wires. It looked like something out of a bad horror movie, but it was advanced technology then, and the doctor was proud of it.

"With this machine," he told her, "we can read your brain." Françoise was terrified. What terrible things would he find in her thoughts? She tried to make her mind as blank as possible. She watched the needle jerk up and down over the scrolling paper, drawing a shaky chart. The doctor frowned at the results.

The machine read only electrical energy. If it had any use at all, it was to detect epilepsy. The doctor called Josée into the room and gravely told her that he couldn't figure out what was wrong.

"You should send her to a psychiatrist," he suggested.

The psychiatrist was an unpleasant man. He made Françoise feel very small in his dim office.

"Tell me about your parents," he said.

"My parents?" she said.

"Yes," he said.

"Is this confidential?" Françoise asked.

"Strictly," he said. "Absolutely."

Two days later, Josée walked into Françoise's bedroom and slapped her.

"How dare you tell that man those things about me," she said. Françoise barely remembered what she had said. She began to skip her appointments with the psychiatrist, using the time to read in the park. The psychiatrist didn't mind. He said nothing to her parents and continued to bill them. By the time her absences came to light, it no longer mattered. A second kind of fit had begun.

In math class one day, Françoise's breathing began to come quick and shallow. Her pinky and her ring finger slowly but resolutely curled in on themselves. She stared at her traitorous hands. Between gasps, she asked to go to the infirmary. The heavyset school nurse sat on her chest facing her. She folded Françoise's arms up at the elbows and attempted to pry open her cramped hands, as if by simply forcing her fingers to relax, the rest of her body might follow. Françoise panicked and hyperventilated, her chest fluttering like a hummingbird's.

Once, this happened at home. She lay down on the couch in the formal living room, unable to slow her breath. Her father was out and so her mother summoned the neighborhood doctor. She rarely saw doctors who were not her father's friends. This doctor was calm and kind. He gave her a shot. He spoke to her softly. *Just breathe*, he said, *just relax*. She did, and her fingers uncurled. The fit was caused by a lack of calcium, he said, common in adolescents. He gave the fit a name: it was a *crise de tétanie*. It'll pass, he said, though it didn't. The problem would persist for a decade. But the hysteria stopped. It faded from memory. Now, when Françoise fought with her mother, her breathing went shallow, her fingers curled.

THE PHYSICAL PAIN was not enough to stop her dark thoughts. Her father kept a large array of medicines in the bathroom, but she'd read enough to know how easy it was to take too many or too few. Françoise stepped up onto the ledge of the big bay window in her bedroom. The wrought-iron rail came up to her shins. She leaned out over it, her arms braced against the window frame, and looked down the façade to the street below. This was before the city was scrubbed to a postcard-perfect pearl beige. The buildings of Paris were all gray with soot back then.

Françoise's vision blurred, then cleared. Someone had told her—her mother, maybe—that those who jumped off the Eiffel Tower sometimes landed on the people below. But this was a sleepy residential neighborhood, and the street was mostly deserted. The real problem was her own body, the resistance it put up. She swayed unpleasantly, the sidewalk swimming closer.

This was when the events that would unfold after her death still mattered to her. She pictured Josée running down to the street. Perhaps Josée, even the whole neighborhood, would come to life with a siren call of grief. The pain would explode beyond the apartment's walls, beyond the confines of her mind, and become public. Her body would be proof.

Her arms tensed, her knees bounced, but whether to grip the stone or to push off it, even she didn't know. She removed her hand from the window frame, barely aware of how hard it was shaking, and ran it through her short hair. The world around her dulled until there was only throbbing. Her skull was a shrinking cage. Her thoughts sounded as if they were being screamed. Her mother's words: *No one will ever love you. No one will ever love you.*

When she could think again, her thoughts were the lyrics of a song. Mina had given her a few old 78s, and there were two records Françoise listened to over and over. One of them was "Un Jour, Mon Prince Viendra." *One day my prince will come.* She could not understand. Which prince? Which day? Where had he been until now? And then what? How could you hope something so vague would save you? She played it repeatedly, trying to parse the emotion it contained.

But it was the second song that played through her head now. "Non, Je Ne Regrette Rien." *Not the good things they did to me / Nor the bad—it's all the same to me,* Edith Piaf sang. *JUMP*, she was telling Françoise. The meaning seemed crystal clear.

She stood in the window for a long time. She wasn't afraid of death. She longed for it. Death was blissful oblivion. But even as she saw herself jumping, again and again, her body would not move. It reminded her of the dreams she had early on school mornings, where she woke and brushed her hair, only to find, as she was leaving the house, that her body had stayed behind in bed. Now she felt the sped-up rush of air around her, the shock of adrenaline flooding her veins, the impact of the concrete. But each time, she found she was still there, standing in the window.

No one looked up. Night fell, and she went back inside. Four stories up might not be far enough to die. Her mother might not cry.

AT THIRTEEN, I was still a child, much more a child than any of my peers, with their lip glosses, their first kisses, their boyfriends. When all the other girls began wearing tight jeans with brand names emblazoned on the back pockets, I still wore the stretchy floral leggings my mother picked for me. When my mother, brother, and I went for walks in the forest surrounding the cabin we rented in Connecticut, I looked for archways formed by falling trees. I knew they were doorways to the fairy world, which looked suspiciously like ours and yet wasn't. I counted each arch I walked under, entering and leaving, so that I could be sure which world I was in. On the crumbling stone walls that crisscrossed the landscape, the remnants of boundaries between cornfields long since overgrown, I built pyramids of twigs and pinecones as offerings.

I was still a child then, but my body kept a schedule of its own. Each morning I awoke to new betrayals. Now, as I rode home from school on the public bus, men sat next to me and asked where I was going. Now, when I stayed after class to ask questions, male teachers stared at my chest.

"That one there in the orange," one balding man said loudly to his friend as I walked by, "I'd like to fuck her brains out." I could imagine only the violence of this, my brains spilling out on the floor.

"Breastfeed me sometime *mamacita*!" another man said as I walked past, and again the image was disturbingly literal.

When I tried to talk to my mother about these incidents, she told me to act as if such comments were compliments.

"I always say thank you and smile," she said. But then she saw my face, and understood that perhaps I could not do as she did. "Or ignore them," she said then. "Don't give them the satisfaction of a response."

My father's friends, men who drank heavily, men who spent their days exploring and drawing their sexual depravity, men who had come of age in the free love of the sixties and had laughed at the new wave of feminists, began to treat me very differently. My parents, overhearing them, laughed as if their comments were only the jokes

they appeared to be on the surface. But I felt the menace underneath. My body was whispering to the adults around me in a language I did not understand. It was promising unkeepable promises.

I felt as if I had awoken on a remote island and found myself
wearing the body of a native. They recognized me as their own, yet
I had none of their culture. It would soon be discovered that I was
an intruder. There would be anger at my deception. There would
be consequences. I did not want to be there, but I could not leave.

My body was dangerous not only to me but to others. I saw this
in the wariness with which my mother had begun to treat me. More
and more now, she became enraged at my closeness with my father.
If I walked arm in arm with him, if I tried to sit between them at the
movies, if he and I laughed at a joke that she had not heard, she
became angry and frustrated, sometimes to the point that tears
sprang to her eyes. Between my father and me, the innocent closeness that had always been there remained unchanged. But my mother's anger provoked in me the deep confusion of an answering guilt.

As fully as I knew that among adults my body was dangerous,
I knew that among those my own age I was neither feminine nor
desirable. I had always been a heavy child, not fat but solid, with
rounded limbs and too much strength. I'd envied my girlfriends
whose mothers insisted that they eat. Now my body changed further and faster than theirs, and the gulf between us grew infinite.
In one strange middle school health class, we sat in a circle on the
floor and were made to list the qualities we found attractive in the
opposite sex. The boys invariably listed petiteness and fragility,
blond straight hair. I longed to be one of those girls, with bones
like glass and legs still perfectly smooth, who could be picked up
and spun around, who was still small enough to make a twelve-
year-old boy feel like a man. I could have picked up and spun all

of the other girls in my class, and many of the boys as well. In schoolyard jokes, in the pop culture I absorbed through my skin even though I wasn't allowed television, I learned that there was nothing more shameful for a man than to be associated with a woman who wasn't thin. At school dances in the cafeteria, where girls and boys solemnly placed their hands on each other's shoulders and swayed, an arm's-length apart, I knew that if I asked a boy to dance I would humiliate him. I found no power or pleasure in my changing body, only the deep unease of being found desirable when I didn't want to be and undesirable when I did.

It was in those years that I began, secretly, to buy Halloween-sized bulk bags of candy. I stole money from the grocery wallet or fudged the count on the change my mother gave me to get home. I was amazed to discover that candy cost very little. I shoplifted as well, for a brief time. Other girls shoplifted with friends, giddy with giggles and adrenaline, but I stole alone, slipping lip glosses from chain pharmacies into the pockets of my backpack. I gave out the lip glosses in the cafeteria, explaining that my mother had bought me too many. My mother did not buy me any makeup, or even deodorant (which she considered too American), although I did not ask very often. I chewed the candy methodically, late into the night, reading young adult novels about ordinary girls who could freeze time, until my teeth ached and wrappers spilled out from beneath my mattress.

I gained fifteen pounds in a year. I had always been in the ninety-fifth percentile for my height and weight, but now my pediatrician worriedly charted my weight up into the ninety-sixth, ninety-seventh, ninety-eighth. I dreaded stepping on scales. It seemed to me that magic was involved here, too, that the right thoughts and shapeless prayers before a weighing might bring the needle back down. But it always rose, and that too felt controlled by magic, a punishment for some far broader badness than eating. I suppose it's clear with hindsight that I ate to bury my curves, to slow this precipitous womanhood, to become invisible. But back then nothing was clear. My weight gain felt to me as unstoppable as the blood that began to flow, as the hairs that began to appear. Even while I ate compulsively, I dreamed at night of unzipping my body and stepping out of it, svelte and smooth and flawless.

It seemed to me that in those years my mother only became more and more beautiful. My heart swelled with pride on the rare occasions when she came to school. Short skirts and black turtle-necks, tailored red skirt suits with padded shoulders—everything hung perfectly on her frame. And yet despite her long thin legs and her high cheekbones, she never embarrassed me with her beauty. She wasn't the kind of mother the boys in my class might whisper about. She was the kind the other girls envied. Men stammered around my mother, but they knew she owed them nothing. She carried herself with elegance, intelligence, self-possession. Adults treated me with new respect after they had met her.

Our bodies were different in every way possible, her broad shoulders and my broad hips. She went braless in the summertime and I wore thick one-piece bathing suits (not because I was deemed too young to wear a bikini but because, as my mother said, how could I want to?). She was photographed for spreads in *Vogue* and inter-viewed for a book titled *French Women Don't Get Fat*. I was asked to model for *Teen People* only to find out they wanted me to model the "curvy" body type in "Real Jeans for Real Bodies."

I felt that my mother was ashamed of my weight. Throughout high school, it seemed to me that my body was the main battle-ground between us.

One of those summers in the South of France, my mother and I drove into town to buy baguettes for dinner. They were still warm from the oven as I held them in the passenger seat, and I ripped off the end of one and took a bite. My mother told me not to ruin my appetite, but I took a second bite. She grabbed the baguette from my hands and beat me with it as hard as she could while still driving.

My body didn't look like my mother's, and it was clear even then that it never would. But still I believed that she, not I, was what a woman was meant to be. It seemed to me that either I would become like her, spare and androgynous, or never truly become a woman at all.

One weekend around that time, we were in the cabin in Connecticut. My brother was out front playing in the weeds that grew wild there, and my mother and I were sitting in the wood-paneled living room, with its cathedral ceiling and the smell of mice in the yellowing foam cushions. She was sitting by the fireplace on the dusty wooden floor, working a puzzle my brother and I had abandoned. I watched her back as I gathered my courage. I was going to tell her. My mother was a woman of solutions. For any problem, large or small, concrete or existential, she provided step-by-step advice with the efficiency of a doctor scrawling a prescription.

"Maman," I said at last, my voice shaking, and she turned. I felt that it pained her to look at me and thought that this was both because of my femininity and my lack of it.

"*Oui, mon chat?*" she said, beckoning me to come sit by her.

"I have to tell you something," I said.

"What is it?" she asked, concern in her voice, her hand on my knee.

I wasn't sure I could find the words. "I've been . . . I've been . . . I've been ripping out all of my hair. You know, all of the hair that grows . . . down there," I said. For months, for nearly a year, I had been tearing out my pubic hair by the handful, furious with my body. The skin was raw and scabbed.

I felt her stiffen, saw the discomfort in her posture. I had crossed a line with her, for neither the first time nor the last. I could not seem to learn where she stopped and I began, what I should and should not share.

"Is this also while you're touching yourself?" she said, her voice held even.

"No!" I said, horrified at the idea that my mother would think I masturbated, although I did.

Perhaps this was the wrong answer, or perhaps my mother felt uncomfortable with herself for having asked. Either way, she shut down, withdrew her hand, went cold.

"Then don't worry about it," she said.

"But—" I said.

"I said don't worry about it. Why is it a problem?" she said.

"I feel . . . I'm . . . I feel . . . horrible," I said.

"Then stop doing it," she said.

"I tried. I can't," I said.

"You'll stop eventually, when you're ready to," she said dismissively. I could hear in her tone the disgust I had so feared. My face flushed pink, and I flooded with shame. Tears spilled down my cheeks.

"It's really nothing to cry about, Nadja," she said absently. "It's not very serious." She got up from the floor and went to the kitchen, calling my brother in from outside to help her make dinner.

PARIS WAS ONLY AS BIG as home and school and back again. Françoise knew the butcher and the women at the bakery. She knew the Parc Monceau, with its bright off-limits grass. She knew the sleepy streets where doctors and lawyers lived with their wives and well-dressed children and small dogs. She did not know how to get to the foot of the Eiffel Tower, though she could see it, toy-sized, through the low buildings of the seventeenth arrondissement. She rode the Métro to school, and yet it never occurred to her that the line stretched on past her stop, snaking into uncharted parts of the city.

But that May of 1968, in the center of the city, a wild fever was spreading. The news came through the radio and the papers. The students, it was said, had laid siege to the universities. The factory workers were on strike. The radio was on constantly, the latest events an increasing buzz at the dinner table. The students were ripping up the pavement. The students were throwing Molotov cocktails. And then the news broke that De Gaulle had threatened a siege of his own. Josée had been about Françoise's age when the Germans took Paris, and Paul a few years older. They knew what it meant, a city surrounded by an army.

"Go to the store," Josée said. Françoise hesitated. Her mother always gave her a list when she sent her shopping.

"What should I buy?"

"Everything you can find," Josée said. "Nothing that might spoil."

At the store, the line already stretched down the block. All the neighborhood grandparents were there. They had their baskets; they looked straight ahead. They appeared prepared to wait hours without complaint. It was as if everyone around her had fallen into the steps of a dance that she had never known existed.

The trains went on strike, the schools shut down. Fresh provisions were becoming scarce. Tanks had rolled up to the city's perimeter and no trucks were entering. On the radio, the government urged people to leave so that it would be easier to isolate the students. They warned citizens not to stockpile gasoline in their bathtubs, as some had done during World War II.

It was as if the past three decades had folded up and disappeared.

All through the neighborhood, the fear was palpable. Josée began to pack. But Paul was not scared. The uncertainty excited him. He announced that he would stay. As a doctor, he got an ample ration of gasoline. If he chose to leave later, he would still be able to.

Françoise pleaded to be allowed to remain in Paris, "so that I can be useful to Papa." It was as if she felt the city pulsing, ready to open itself to her.

Josée warned her that she might find herself all alone. But all alone meant no domestic help, and that's just as it was on weekends and holidays. All alone sounded wonderful. Besides, Françoise argued, someone would need to help Paul with his medical work.

And so in the end, the rest of the family left Paris, and Françoise and her father stayed.

In the middle of that first afternoon, she went for a walk by herself. The shops were closed. The streets were completely deserted. There were no cars, no people. It was spooky, this ghost city.

But Paul was in extraordinarily high spirits. That evening, he led her to the kitchen. "So!" he said, clapping his hands. "We have to make food!"

"What do you know how to make?" Françoise asked dubiously.

"Mayonnaise," Paul said. Françoise was impressed. She had never seen her father in the kitchen before.

"We'll make deviled eggs then," she suggested, as this she had been shown how to do. She put a pot of water on to boil.

"You know, before I met your mother, I often cooked for myself," Paul said. Françoise couldn't quite imagine this. Paul was upset by her incredulity. "It is very important to know how to make a good mayonnaise," he told her. He gave her a seminar on the emulsification of oil and egg yolks and the proper quantities of mustard, until somehow, through his bluster, a mayonnaise mounted.

The following night they ate hard-boiled eggs, and after that he drove them to one of his favorite expensive restaurants, which had managed to stay open through the turmoil. It was the first time they had ever been to a restaurant together, just the two of them, and Françoise felt herself exist in his eyes.

Many evenings, when he had returned from the half-closed clinic, he suggested they go see what was happening in the Latin Quarter. They had the city to themselves and Paul sped through red lights, the wind riffling Françoise's short hair. She was not scared. Her heart was full. She was so grateful to her mother for leaving her behind.

In the Latin Quarter, the lights were on and the streets were crowded. The students had occupied the universities, but the doors were wide open and anyone could walk in. The halls were filled with sleeping bags and mattresses. The walls were covered with posters. BENEATH THE PAVING STONES, THE BEACH! Françoise read each one carefully, inspired by their design. There were no policemen in sight. The whole quarter was *en liesse*—in a state of communal, collective jubilation.

The students weren't hippies, like their counterparts in the United States. The boys didn't have long hair and the girls didn't wear flowers. They seemed more passionate about their ideas than about any particular style of dress. In nearly every room she and Paul walked into, an assembly or a heated debate was taking place. The word *"solidarité"* bounced through the buildings. Each time a new factory went on strike, the news was shouted victoriously from person to person.

Paul wandered freely through this landscape without pretending to listen to any of the speechifying. He was neither against the students' uprising nor for it. He was simply the usual jovial self he was with strangers, the kind of man who always tried to make cashiers laugh. For Françoise, though, these students—only six or seven years older than she—were adults. They had brought the entire city to a standstill, and she was awed by their power.

Back in the apartment, she played secretary to her father. She took dictation at the typewriter, grateful she had learned to type. She worked the duplicating machine. The mysterious language of medical reports arranged itself into clear, satisfying meaning. She distinguished benign moles from melanomas, surprised at how simple it all was to learn. Paul showered her with compliments. For those few weeks, the two lived in easy harmony. Françoise cooked them rudimentary meals in the kitchen. She sat at the desk his secretary usually occupied. "You do this so much better," Paul said, his hand on Françoise's shoulder.

Françoise was happy, so happy, so happy. As my mother told me this story years later, she choked on "happy," and it came out as a strangled shout—*heu-reuse*—as if the word, unable to contain the great many things she felt, had broken in two. Her father finally saw her as an adult. They worked so well together, in perfect synchrony, and this is what her future could one day hold.

"This is my favorite daughter," Paul had always said when he presented her to his friends. "She's going to be a doctor one day, just like me."

"It seemed . . . ," my mother said, then hesitated. "It seemed too beautiful to be true."

The electricity cut out more and more often. The portable radio, their only source of news, ran on batteries, and there was no way to replace them. They no longer kept it switched on all the time. In the Latin Quarter, the inherent paradox of students on strike showed through the ragged places where fervor wore thin. Who but their own parents cared if the students refused to attend classes? And yet the siege continued. Each day became a victory for its own sake. They could not stop now. They had already gone this far.

One evening toward the end, when the electricity had been off for longer than usual, the atmosphere in the Latin Quarter was festive and tinged with wildness. The restaurants, the contents of their freezers in danger of spoiling, were serving free meals on the street. Paul and Françoise seated themselves at a table. The waiters came with course after course, unasked for. Wine flowed. Spirits soared. It could not hold but they did not care. It was the feast at the end of the world.

ON MY SECOND or third full day of high school, I was making use of my morning free period to complete my math homework in the library. Stuyvesant was a beautiful high school, the jewel of New York City's public education system. I was eager to leave behind the person I had been in my small private school and re-invent myself in this incoming freshman class of eight hundred students. The building's ten stories were linked by escalators. A million-dollar pedestrian bridge arched from the school over the busy West Side Highway. The library was lined with windows that looked over the Hudson River and the downtown skyline.

A crowd was gathering by the library's windows. One by one students left the round tables where they were working and pressed their noses to the glass. I kept my back to them, focusing on the neat row of numbers that unspooled before me. A thud reverberated through the walls like a sonic boom. I remember the unruly diagonal line my pen made on the graph paper.

"Someone must have dropped a weight in the gym upstairs," said the librarian. She laughed too loudly at her own joke.

The bell rang to signal the change of classes.

"Nadja," someone said as I was leaving, "did you look out the window?" I said I didn't want to be late and kept walking.

"Go look," the person said, catching my arm. "Really, just go look."

I went, elbowing my way through the crowd. It was the most elaborate movie set I had ever seen. A painted version of the skyline had been hung over the skyline itself, obscuring it entirely. A hole had been cut in the World Trade Center. A flap of fabric hung down. Billowing smoke, from a hidden dry-ice machine, came through the tear. That is really what I saw.

"There was a second plane," said one boy to another, his voice giddy and cracking. "It's a terrorist attack."

Boys, I thought to myself, with a huff through my nose. They watched far too many movies.

Over the loudspeaker, the principal announced that we would not, then that we would, then that we would not be allowed out for lunch that day. The next time I looked out a window, I looked only down. I saw men and women in business suits, talking on cell phones, swarming the streets. I had never seen so many people in the park by the river, though I'd played there often as a child. I noted to myself that the area was busy at lunchtime and did not allow myself to wonder further.

Our English teacher, a pretty young woman with a soft, lilting voice, abandoned the lesson plan she had prepared for the day. Instead, she asked us to talk about our mornings.

Then the building shook again. The lights flickered off, then back on again. I stared at my hands. They were gripping the edge of my desk. My knuckles had turned white. Why were my hands doing that? I felt on the brink of a realization.

"It's just interference from a plane passing overhead," the teacher said, tucking a wisp of hair behind her ear, "like cell phone static when you walk under a bridge." My fingers loosened. On the loudspeaker, the principal announced that we would not be following our regular schedules. We were to report to our home-rooms to be counted. I felt a flicker of annoyance—my math homework, now complete, would not be collected.

I do not remember running into my best friend in the hallway, but she told me later that I had. She was a friend from childhood, one of the few people I knew in this huge, unfamiliar school. She told me I had been delighted to see her. She told me I had not noticed that she was sobbing.

My homeroom was several flights up. A new friend of mine had her leg in a full cast. The administration had shut down the escalators and the elevators. As my friend negotiated each step, I held her crutches. My emotions focused into fury that they had shut down the elevators. We pushed open the door of the stairwell on the tenth floor. A girl stopped and stared.

"Nadja!" she said. "Your dad has been looking everywhere for you."

"My dad?" I said. And there he was, coming down the hallway toward me. His face flashed like a kaleidoscope: relief, anger, terror.

"*There* you are," he said and wrapped me so tightly in his arms I could not breathe. I had never seen my father look scared. He grabbed me by the hand and we ran back down the stairs.

My mother was in the lobby, her face streaked with tears. We squeezed awkwardly out through the doors, my mother unwilling to let go of me.

"Should I take my bike?" I asked my father.

"If you don't, you'll never see it again," he said. My hands trembled as I undid the lock. My mind felt leaden and would not function. Even then, I did not let myself wonder what was going on. We joined a thick stream of people walking uptown along the pedestrian path by the river. In my memory everyone was eerily quiet, talking in whispers if at all. And then we all stopped and turned.

I do not know how to describe what I saw. There was the World Trade Center, half a mile away. There was only one tower. And then the gray of it peeled off, infinitely slowly, gathering on itself as it rolled down. As the gray descended it revealed a skeleton of red beams. They hung in the air, shimmering. And then they too became powder, became particles, became the air and fell, and everything fell, everything fell.

My mother screamed the name of her friend who lived beneath the towers. A huge white cloud was moving toward us. I watched as my school disappeared. All around us, people turned and began to run uptown. I had grown up in a city of skyscrapers. They weren't supposed to fall down.

"*Run!*" someone shouted at us as he passed. "The smoke will kill you!" And then I was very high up in the air. Somewhere on the walkway below, a girl turned and began walking. From where I floated, I could just make out the words she was saying: "*My friends, my school, my friends, my school!*" Over and over, like an incantation. A stranger offered her water. She didn't respond.

She should take that water, I thought. *She needs to calm down.*

My father took the water and pressed it into my hands. And then I was back in my body. The words were coming out of my own mouth. I forced a sip down my throat.

We turned away from the river, onto Canal Street, and became just the three of us once more. The street was achingly familiar. We had walked this way many times, my family and I. But it was different now, in a way I could not name.

Ahead of us, a man had set up an easel on the sidewalk. He was absorbed in his painting. *Look,* I said, tugging on my father's arm. On the canvas, the towers burned. But past him, in the real skyline above, the towers were gone.

I TOLD THIS STORY so many times over the years that it ceased being a memory. On rare occasions, when speaking to a close friend, I could still feel the aftershocks of emotion. But most times I simply felt myself stepping through a series of empty images that I had stepped through many times before. I could not turn my head left or right. I could not see the details I hadn't already told. Once, at a party, a girl said with delight, "*Ooh,* you're giving me shivers!" and I felt the twisted pleasure of doing myself violence.

For the most part, I stopped talking about it. When I did, I never included the man painting on the street. That's my father's story now, immortalized in the comic he wrote about the day. I wonder, at times, if I can still see that red skeleton of beams hanging in the air or if I only see the drawing he made of them. We'd talked about it, he and I, before he drew the image: how you didn't see that in the newsreel. So you saw it, too, he said, and I had. I had seen it, too. But my memories were so easily overwritten by his. They squared themselves away into comic book panels that contained pictures of me I had not even posed for.

They sent us back to school while the ruins were still red embers. We showed our high school ID cards to the federal guard stationed at Canal Street, downtown still off-limits to most. Our return was televised: the brave students of Stuyvesant High School. Journalists found and called our home phone numbers. Our teachers spoke over clanging metal as cranes lifted pieces of the skyscrapers onto the barges outside our windows. A man in a full yellow hazmat suit stepped into our classroom and told us to ignore him. The small device in his hand went *beep beep beep BEEP-BEEPBEEP*. He made a few notes and left silently. A social worker handed out a worksheet: *If Lucy feels alienated from the adults around her, if Lucy has trouble sleeping at night, if Lucy becomes anxious when watching the news, then Lucy has post-traumatic stress disorder.*

My hand shot straight up in the air. "Lucy sounds like a normal teenager," I said with righteous fury. "Have you *seen* the news these days?"

The social workers begged us to talk to them. We didn't even talk to one another. The hallway walls filled with messages sent from schools nationwide. "Our prayers are with you," surrounded by multicolored handprints of paint. Why would anyone pray for *us*, we wanted to know. We did not want pity. The smell of death was all around us but I knew no one who knew anyone who had died. We were fine. We were not damaged. This seemed very important to prove. When tourists began to ask the way to Ground Zero, we told them to walk to the river and jump in. When tour buses passed and pointed at our school, we threw our empty soda cans at them. When the subway stopped in a tunnel without warning, we gripped the poles in silence but did not acknowledge why. It would take me years to realize that not everyone had nightmares about bombs and planes.

In those nightmares, I was not afraid. I was in the cool lucid place beyond fear. In all of them, I had a small child with me. In one, I drove us through a road filled with land mines. In another, I hid us in a basement while men with guns shot anyone who moved. When the shooting stopped, I crept out and found us water. My dreams were not about death. They were about survival. They diminished in frequency, but they never stopped. One morning in my late twenties, I awoke with the realization that I was also the child. The building had fallen and split me in two. The world moved on too quickly for me, looking back before the moment had even passed. Part of me had stayed frozen, floating above the West Side Highway. The self that had kept walking, had found water, was a different me, profoundly altered.

I avoided all media related to the event, until avoidance became a deeply ingrained habit. Footage of the towers falling never ceased to feel like an assault. It felt obscene to watch.

On the one-year anniversary, I came across a magazine on our kitchen table. On the cover was a glossy photo of people standing in the windows of one of the towers, poised to jump.

"Maman?" I said.

"You didn't know?" she said, surprised.

Even a decade and a half later, I would find it intolerable that a memorial had been built, and a new tower. How dare they reconcile that event into an ordered past. It was still happening. It was still incomprehensible.

The morning it happened, my parents had gone out to vote in the mayoral primary. They had just left our house; they were on our street. My mother saw a plane fly low overhead. She followed it with her eyes. She watched it leave a hole in the tower.

My mother counted the stories. The tower had been breached. The top might fall. She saw it in her mind's eye, falling. She saw the radius around it, saw my school. My father had gone upstairs to check the news. My mother screamed his name in the street, wild with fear. Onlookers stared. She called his cell phone frantically until he came downstairs. She dragged him into the heart of the chaos that others were already fleeing. For nearly an hour, my parents searched the school building for me.

It is posed as a theoretical question, whether a mother would run into a burning building to save her child. It is not one that many people know the answer to.

chapter three

Recently, an old schoolmate of my mother's sent her two class photos. Blown up to well beyond their original size, they were grainy and unfocused.

"If I hadn't seen these," my mother said, "I would have told you that I was always like this." She pointed to the first photograph. "That I was always shy, invisible, a little girl. Miserable." In that photo, she sat with her legs crossed at the knee, hands in her lap, looking up at the camera sweetly. But in the second photo, her eyes locked confidently with the camera. Her shoulders were thrown back and her spine was straight.

"Your father found me right away on the second one. He said, 'Oh, you were already yourself!'"

"What happened?" I asked.

"I don't know," my mother said, and paused, her finger lingering on the paper. "I suppose I became myself."

IN THE SUMMER OF 1970, in Ussel, Sylvie began a small romance. Jean-Michel Guérin was a local boy. He was not particularly handsome. He was not very tall and his strong features fought for room on his face. But his unflappable self-confidence lent him an air of mystery. It was as if he knew he possessed a special destiny that no onlooker could divine. His parents deferred to him with a mixture of pride and fear. As often as possible, he broke free of them and hung out with the other local teenagers. They drank and danced and drove too fast down the curving country roads. Sylvie, during her year in Ussel with Mamie, had been accepted as an honorary member of their gang. Françoise was still regarded as a summer visitor, a haughty *parisienne*. She watched Sylvie come and go from afar.

The romance began as an innocent flirtation in the August heat, barely sullied by kissing. Jean-Michel delivered grand compliments—*your eyes, the stars*—that sounded new and adult to sixteen-year-old ears. Sylvie, freed for brief moments from being the family's ugly duckling, warmed to him with a radiant new beauty. It was a small, sweet romance, a romance that even in the present tense of that summer the two of them did not take entirely seriously. But the terrible calculus of the family was such that any love given was love elsewhere taken away. That small romance would have a heavy cost.

That fall, back in Paris, letters began to arrive for Sylvie, instantly recognizable by the pictures Jean-Michel had doodled all over the envelopes. Josée snatched them from the mail and called to her eldest daughter. The two of them disappeared into Josée's room, where they collapsed in girlish giggles over Jean-Michel's amorous declarations, rendered in the highest literary French. It was jarring to Françoise, this sudden complicity, and she felt even more adrift. She had a boyfriend of her own that year, a sweet, dull young man she had met skiing. In fact, her quiet, intense self-sufficiency regularly drew admirers. But unless they had the courage to step right in front of her and ask her to dance, as this boy had, she rarely noticed them. Josée approved of this boyfriend, mildly—his mother was a famous journalist—but she did not take Françoise into her room to read his letters. In fact, she paid very little attention to what passed between him and Françoise at all, and it was only thanks to his mother's early return home one afternoon that Françoise was still a virgin. Now Françoise listened to the laughter drifting from behind Josée's closed bedroom door and her stomach twisted with a familiar jealousy.

In October, Sylvie began campaigning to be sent to the girls' boarding school in Clermont-Ferrand, an industrial town an hour from Ussel. Ussel had no adequate high school, and so many of its students were sent to Clermont-Ferrand to continue their education. The girls' school was across the street from the boys' school Jean-Michel attended. Françoise was surprised by Sylvie's request. For Parisians, boarding school was a punishment reserved for those too unruly to keep at home.

Paul immediately opposed the plan. He had spent his own boyhood in boarding schools and he hadn't come this far only to send his daughter back there. Besides, the semester was already under way in Paris. But Josée was tickled by the idea of Sylvie continuing her *petite aventure* with Jean-Michel. She quickly set about convincing her husband to change his mind. She and Paul had a monthlong trip to Australia planned for that winter. It would be convenient if the girls were already situated elsewhere. Soon, Françoise, too, began to see the virtues of the scheme. Home was becoming intolerable, and she had no desire to be left there to bear the full brunt of her parents' rages. She joined Sylvie's cause.

She pleaded with her father. Strings were pulled. The girls entered the boarding school in November.

The Lycée Jeanne-d'Arc faced the Lycée Blaise-Pascal, each of them occupying a city block of Clermont-Ferrand. Of the thousand or so students at Jeanne-d'Arc, only about two hundred boarded. Most of the boarders came from small farms and villages in the region, too far to commute. Sylvie and Françoise shared their dormitory with fifty other girls, in row after row of bed-nightstand-bed-nightstand configurations. They were given beds far away from each other, Sylvie near the door and Françoise against the back wall.

Only a few of the other girls had heard of the Beatles. None of them had ever been on an airplane. Françoise had flown alone to Morocco when she was eight years old. She knew about the Beatles *and* the Rolling Stones, though she preferred Boris Vian and Georges Brassens. She felt her sophistication rolling off her, a new sense of cool that she had never conceived of having. That the Mouly girls had been sent here from Paris, in the middle of the school year, meant that they must be very bad and very dangerous. That their parents were going to Australia, a place so far away as to be spoken only in a whisper, only added to their aura.

Françoise began to fit herself to her newfound reputation. In Paris she had always been a model student, sitting quiet and attentive in the first row. At boarding school, she became the kind of student teachers warned one another about. She asked questions constantly. She demanded to know the reasoning behind the school's strict and arbitrary rules. She shot spitballs at a substitute until the woman left the room in tears. She snuck a banana peel out of the dining hall and dried it on the bathroom windowsill for weeks, then scraped off the pith and rolled it in a strip of waxy brown toilet paper and lit it, showing the other girls how to inhale deep into their lungs and hold down the smoke.

When Françoise and Sylvie were allowed off the school grounds on Thursday afternoons, they did not linger with their classmates. They followed Jean-Michel and the other Ussel boys from Blaise-Pascal to a café near the university where the college students gathered, and the coolest of the lycée students spent their free hours. Occasionally they ran into two brothers from Ussel whose parents knew theirs. Éric and Christian were a year and a half apart, just like Sylvie and Françoise, and their parents had often joked that their daughters would marry the two boys. By this logic, Françoise knew that she was destined for Christian, but she harbored a secret crush on the older Éric. He was handsome and reckless, and his disregard for women made them flock to him. But although Françoise hung on his every word, he treated her with the same dismissive kindness as he had when she was a child.

Françoise watched Jean-Michel and Sylvie carefully in the café. They rarely touched, beyond cheeks pressed together in hello and good-bye. But there was little time in which to observe. A few weeks after they arrived, Sylvie's privileges were revoked. She had smuggled a bottle of liquor into the school and invited another student to drink with her in the bathroom, one of the few places in the institution with a door that locked. The girl, not as adept at drinking, drank so much that she had to be sent to the hospital. Sylvie, the clear instigator, was no longer allowed to leave the grounds.

Now Sylvie watched from the window as her little sister came and went on Thursday afternoons. Françoise walked out the big main gates of the campus and headed to the café alone. She packed a book in her bag and sat reading in the back room until people she knew arrived. The café was a place that would come to mark a time in her life. She loved the pinball machines and the *demi panachés*. She loved the casual hours spent around others almost as painlessly as if she were alone. But most of all, she loved the fervor of the political debates. The college students crowded around the small tables, plotting the uprising of the working class. They slammed their fists so hard their drinks spilled. They leapt up so swiftly their chairs fell over. They reinvented the world. Here, finally, was her very own May 1968. Here were the student demigods who brought cities to a halt. And here, finally, far from Paris, she was in the heart of it all.

She listened. She grew bold enough to challenge others' ideas and form her own. She returned to the lycée, her head buzzing with revolution. But when she opened her mouth to share her excitement with her sister, Sylvie's glare froze the words in midair. The resentment was so strong that it nearly had a smell. The exact nature of the reproach remained unspoken, but it was clear. Françoise had usurped her world. "If you had invited me drinking that day," Françoise told her through tight lips, "I gladly would have come."

Françoise tried to tell herself that she had done nothing wrong, but guilt bubbled uneasily in her stomach. She spent her study hall periods devising her sister's escape. In the library's broom closet, unseen by the monitor, she scraped at the mortar in the brick wall with a spoon. The bricks came loose one by one. On the other side of the wall was the street. After Françoise had removed a few, she brought her sister to the broom closet and showed her what she'd done. She offered her a second spoon so that they could work side by side.

"And what will I do when the hole is big enough?" Sylvie asked angrily. "Just pop out into the street in broad daylight? Hope no one notices? What if I lose my weekend privileges as well?"

Françoise kept scraping. But she also kept going to the café alone.

It didn't take long for her to fall in love with Jean-Michel. He filled the small bar with his voice. He noticed how Françoise quietly followed his movements with her deep, intense eyes as he spoke. They spent hours chain-smoking and talking. Françoise smoked Gitanes with filters, like her doctor father, because she knew about the latest advances in health. Jean-Michel smoked Boyards, so strong they made nearly everyone nauseous but were worth it, because the thin corn-paper stuck to your lip and the cigarette hung there as you talked, the very epitome of cool.

"What are you doing this weekend?" Jean-Michel asked Françoise one Thursday as he walked her back toward the boarding school. The next Thursday, he leaned across the table in the café and kissed her.

It seemed to Françoise thrilling, unbelievable, that anyone so charismatic should find her interesting. But she pictured Sylvie, bitterly pacing the confines of her dorm room. Perhaps this was a one-time thing, she thought. Perhaps she didn't have to tell. But the following week, Jean-Michel kissed her again.

"What about my sister?" she asked him, pulling back.

"What about your sister?" he said. He assured Françoise that it was over between him and Sylvie. It had never even begun. He had simply wanted a recipient for his poetry. Sylvie had sent him far more letters than he had sent her. They had just been friends.

"I have to tell you something," Françoise told Sylvie soon after, her voice shaking. "Jean-Michel seduced me."

"How dare you!" Sylvie replied. She was angry, but then again, my mother commented as she told me this story, Sylvie was always angry. She preferred to be angry. And, she pointed out, Sylvie hadn't said, "How dare *he*!"

"Maman is going to be furious with you," Sylvie said. And they both knew that this was true, and that this was the real problem, though neither of them could explain why.

On the rare afternoons when the girls called home, Françoise hung anxiously by while Sylvie murmured into the receiver. "She was late for a dinner," Sylvie would say, hanging up. Or, "Her voice was tired, she didn't feel like talking anymore." Even at a distance, Françoise felt the force of Josée's anger like a physical thing. It hunched her back and made her hands shake. She had to keep moving. She carried the fervor of the café back within the high walls of the school. There was a new wild look in her eyes. She was ready to sacrifice herself to the first cause that presented itself, like a woman compelled by a spell.

The students were allowed to smoke in the dorms and toilets and study hall but not outside in the courtyard. Françoise declared this a staggering injustice. She had begun smoking two years earlier, at thirteen years old. In Paris, she kept ashtrays in her bedroom. She was scolded only when the concierge tattled that she had seen her smoking in the street. "Only loose women smoke in the street," Josée told Françoise angrily. Now, for the right to smoke in the school's courtyard, Françoise staged a hunger strike that lasted twelve days, sucking on sugar cubes and her pride.

The headmistress was at a loss. Françoise was impossible to punish. Most girls fell into line as soon as the school threatened to contact their parents. But letters and phone calls to Josée were met only with sighs. Françoise was an *enfant terrible*. She took after her father. Josée had never been able to keep her in line.

"*Libérez Guyot!*" Françoise cried one spring day to the girls gathered for recess in the courtyard, cupping her hands around her mouth. "If we all leave, they can't punish us all! Unite! Take back the power!" Local activists, college students she'd met in the café, stood just outside the boarding school gates, cheering the girls on. They'd rerouted a protest march past the high school at Françoise's suggestion.

"Together we cannot be defeated!" she cried. "Who's with me? *Libérez Guyot!*"

"Any girl who leaves will be suspended immediately," the headmistress shouted back from the steps of the school.

"She can't suspend us all!" Françoise cried. "*Libérez Guyot!*"

The headmistress took hold of a megaphone. "If Mouly leaves, she'll be suspended."

"I'm leaving!" Françoise screamed, transported by revolutionary fervor. "Follow me!" She walked out without looking back. Eight other girls broke away from the group and followed with shaky steps. The others simply stared after them, then filed quietly back into the school.

Joined with the other activists, Françoise marched through the streets of the sleepy city. "*LIB-ÉR-EZ GUYOT! LIB-ÉR-EZ GUYOT!*" At the university, they stood in a huge amphitheater and listened to impassioned speeches. A young woman grabbed the microphone.

"I've just come from the Lycée Jeanne-d'Arc," she said. "And I want to let you all know that one brave activist among us, Françoise

Mouly, was expelled for joining our cause." The crowd erupted in cheers and whistles.

"Mouly! Are you here? Come up onstage!" the girl said. The crowd parted around Françoise as she made her way forward.

"I'm going to call the school," the girl announced. The crowd quieted as the phone rang.

The school secretary answered.

"Put me through to the headmistress," the student said. She identified herself as secretary-general of their organization, which had quite an official-sounding name. The phone clicked, and the headmistress picked up, exasperated.

"I'm calling to verify that you indeed expelled your student Françoise Mouly this afternoon."

"Yes, *bien sûr*," the headmistress said. "I warned her not to leave and she left."

"Is that so?" the girl said. "Because, madame, I am calling to inform you that we will be voting to form a direct action support committee devoted entirely to this cause." She rattled on in this fashion, sounding threatening. "She used such impressive words!" my mother told me, remembering not the exact words but the hushed awe they had inspired in her.

"Of course, um, the decision has not yet been finalized," the headmistress said. "There are many factors to take into consideration, and rules, and exceptions, of course."

"Can you confirm that the expulsion will not go through? Your voice is currently being broadcast to an assembly of six hundred people, and we all stand ready to vote," the girl said.

"Well, yes, certainly, I have nothing against Mouly," the headmistress said. A wild cheer ripped through the crowd as Françoise's savior hung up the phone.

Françoise returned to school giddy with power. For the rest of that spring, whenever the headmistress reprimanded her, Françoise responded with veiled references to her "friends at the organization." She felt invincible.

But when Josée came to pick up her daughters for Easter vacation, she breezed past Françoise without a glance.

"*Viens, ma chérie,*" she said to Sylvie. "Oh, how I've missed you, you poor dear." The two of them walked out of the school lobby arm in arm. Françoise stood clutching her suitcase, unsure whether to follow.

"WHO WAS GUYOT?" I asked my mother. Three years had passed since she had first begun telling me her story.

I was sitting at the kitchen table while she stood at the counter, chopping a head of romaine with manic speed. Guests were arriving in an hour. She had come home from work later than planned, as usual, and the roast she'd left to start cooking on an automatic timer was burnt to a crisp.

"What are we going to do about the dinner?" she asked me. "There's almost nothing left of this." Her voice shook.

I got up to pour her a glass of wine. "We can order Chinese," I said, handing it to her.

"We ordered Chinese last time," she said. "It's embarrassing."

My childhood memories were dotted with dinner parties in this windowless space with its huge mirror on one wall and skylight above, the wine flowing for hours and the lazy ceiling fan swirling the cigarette smoke. We ate with our elbows on the table and stuck our forks straight into the serving dishes. My mother moved easily between stove and table, nudging me to help her clear plates or pass out dessert spoons. As I grew older, I often thought fondly of that "dinner party feeling," surrounded by adults and allowed to just listen, coming and going from the table unnoticed, my attention drifting around the room. But gradually I became aware, too, of the bright energy-efficient lightbulb that hung too close to the table, of how cramped it was when we sat eight, of my mother's underlying insecurity about how these dinners compared to those her friends hosted in return, in formal dining rooms with unchipped plates.

In my new separate life, I'd filled my Brooklyn apartment with plants and thrifted furniture and read articles about how best to create atmospheric lighting. I threw elaborate dinner parties, first using the four recipes—ratatouille, pot-au-feu, choucroute garnie, couscous—that my mother had always made for company, but soon learning how to cook Indian and Vietnamese and how to invent my own recipes as well. For a long time I thought that because these things were feminine, I had learned them from my mother. Now I saw our SoHo loft through a stranger's eyes, and I realized that I had not. More and more now, my mother turned to me on questions of hostessing, as if I were the authority.

"We can eat on the roof," I said. "That'll be special."

"Yes!" she said, taking a long sip of her wine.

"Will you sit with me for just a few minutes?" I asked softly.

She slid down into a chair with a loud sigh, letting her head fall back so that it rested against the seat. Her eyes closed. "What were you asking?" she said, lifting her head.

"Who was Guyot?"

"Oh, I don't remember," she said, laughing. "I didn't know even back then. But oh, how I wanted him to be free!"

"Is it possible that that's why Josée was angry with you?"

"That what was?" she asked, tensing.

"That you had been expelled."

"Of course not! The headmistress tried to expel me twenty-three times! I kept count," she said with a hint of pride.

"But . . . all the more reason, no?"

"No." She was adamant. "I don't think the headmistress even told my mother about Guyot. She understood . . . she knew things weren't okay between my mother and me."

"How would the headmistress know that?"

"I had . . . incidents at the school. Related to my mother. I don't remember the details."

"Related to your mother? How?"

My mother's eyes drifted shut as she tried to remember. "There were letters from her maybe, I don't know. Maybe we talked on the phone," she said. She slipped off her clip-on earrings and tugged gently at her earlobes. "She hated me. Hated me," my mother continued. *Elle me haïssait,* the verb a cry of pain in her mouth. I wanted to reach out to touch her, but she had folded in on herself, hands tucked into her armpits. "I sat in the backseat of that car in silence while she fawned over Sylvie. *Oh, ma pauvre petite chérie.*" She clipped the earrings together and unclipped them, looking down at her hands as they moved. "I knew I was supposed to be ashamed. And it made no sense. At the time, it made no sense at all." She sat up slowly, as if each part of her body had to be moved separately.

"I'm getting old," she said. "My whole body aches now."

"Don't say that," I said.

"No but it's . . . it's sort of wonderful, actually," she said. She looked at me as though she knew that I could not understand and yet wished I would.

"I'm old," she said. "Finally."

"No," I said. "Maman." As though I could prevent this.

"No," she agreed gently, and put her hand on mine. *"Jamais. T'inquiète pas."*

The doorbell rang.

"Americans!" my mother said angrily, looking at the wall clock. She had never stopped finding it rude when people arrived on time to dinner. But by the time they'd made it up our four flights of stairs, she was beaming as she kissed their cheeks. I stood behind her, wondering if they could sense the faint disturbance our conversation had left in the air. I turned to grab the tin plates we always used for Chinese food and she turned with me, reaching for the wineglasses, so that we moved with one movement, as if unfurling a tablecloth over all that was scratched.

"So you were in the school's courtyard, urging the other girls to join you, and the college students were waiting outside?" I was asking. Two more years had passed. I had called her on her cell phone at work and she had turned on the video function, as she often did, even when we were both walking down the street.

"Look at that! Can you see that?" she asked, swinging her phone toward the window.

"I can't see anything. I see a corner of your window frame."

"Oh," she said, disappointed like a child. "The clouds just descended on the skyline. It was so fast. Everything turned white."

"I see the white," I said.

"It's incredible, isn't it?" she said. A few months before, *The New Yorker* had moved into 1 World Trade Center, the building we had watched rise, bit by bit, from the ashes of 2001. While her coworkers spent months carefully packing their offices, my mother had piled on so many new projects that she staggered from the stress. She did not say she was afraid. She only moved faster and faster, until she became a blur. She barely slept. Sometimes she sank to the floor in public, leaning against a wall until she found the energy to keep working. She packed her Times Square office in two sleepless nights. But when I asked, now, about the new building, she would only tell me cheerfully about how nice it was to bike to work along the river.

She sat back down at her computer, the camera trained up at her face under the fluorescent lights, and I wondered when she had become so completely unself-conscious. The thick streaks of black eyeliner had blurred below her eyes, as they often did by afternoon. She looked tired—more than tired, exhausted—but I knew she heard this often enough and trusted me not to say so.

"So you were in the courtyard," I prompted once more, and the story unspooled from her easily yet again.

"What did the school look like?" I asked. At her suggestion, we both called up street-view images of her boarding school onto our computers.

"The entrance is so majestic!" I said. I had not pictured it like this: Gothic arched cathedral windows, mini-turrets, white and tan tiles decorating the exterior.

"Majestic?" my mother said. "It was hideous! It was so sordid. But look how white the buildings are now." She held her phone up to her computer as she spoke, to show me the buildings. I saw the psychedelic radial lines that appear on a screen within a screen, as if they are revealing images invisible to the naked eye. The grand entrance was used only by the parents as they picked up and dropped off their daughters in the cool calm of the high-ceilinged lobby. The students themselves used a small gate on the other side of the complex to access the oppressive, Soviet-style buildings where classes were held and boarders were housed. My mother showed me the dorms that had been hers. She clicked through the streets. I watched her face and I could see new memories begin to rise.

The hall supervisor wasn't like the other teachers, who were all small-minded women who had lost their enthusiasm decades before. She was young and pretty, and she was posted at the Lycée Jeanne-d'Arc for just that year, while she completed her training. Her name was exotic, though it escaped my mother now— Alexandra, perhaps. A gentle name that rang of faraway places.

"She was very kind to me," my mother said, "even when she didn't have to be. Especially . . . during those difficult incidents." She said this last in a mumble, with a wave of her hand, as if to brush aside the words she had just spoken.

"What incidents?" I said.

"I told you," my mother said, looking straight at me through her phone. Her look was clear: a pleading.

"You didn't," I said.

"I thought . . . ," my mother said, and looked up and away. The silence buzzed between us, a thick digital static.

"I told you this," she repeated. "I thought . . . I can't . . ." I let the silence grow, filling the rooms we were in like slowly rising water. My mother sighed and looked toward her closed office door. She blinked and wiped at her eye with the back of her palm.

My chest clenched, but I said again, more softly, "You didn't tell me." She had told me every story two or three times by then. I hadn't known that there was more to tell.

"I don't remember what set it off," she began, her voice hesitant at first. As she spoke, she forgot the phone she was holding and the image drifted toward her lap until the screen went black, so that I heard only her voice, muffled, from above.

Françoise was in the hallway, hitting her head against the wall. Her hands were at her face as if she might be able to open her body and step free of it. She was screaming. And then she was lifted, still flailing, and transported by strong arms to the infirmary. Hands struggled to tie her down.

The headmistress came in. She was a tight-lipped blond woman about Josée's age. Some part of Françoise watched everything with clear eyes even as her body fought and flailed. The headmistress had good intentions. She just wanted Françoise to quiet down. Françoise was rooting for the headmistress. She willed her to find the right words. If only the right words could be spoken, the spell would break. Until then, her own mouth could do nothing but scream.

"You're acting crazy," the headmistress said.

She said, "Calm down, or I'll have to tell your mother."

The headmistress was her mother. The three or four women around the bed were her mother. The unpleasant nurse was her mother. Françoise howled. A door inside her opened and gave way to pure force. She nearly succeeded in throwing the women off. She wanted to say, *The more you try to tie me down, the more I have to fight.* She wanted to say, *Just leave me alone, please, just leave me alone and I'll calm down.* But the quiet part of her knew that they were all trapped. They could not leave her alone until she calmed down, and she could not calm down until they left her alone. She wanted to stop screaming with such desperation that she screamed louder. The headmistress shook her head and left the room. A needle slipped under her skin. Blackness fell.

Later, the headmistress asked to see her in her office. She gestured to Françoise to take a seat in the chair that faced her desk.

"You're unhappy," the headmistress said. "What's wrong? Please, tell me what's going on."

From her tone, Françoise understood that the headmistress was trying. But the desk loomed between them, creating an interrogation chamber. If only the headmistress would sit beside her. If only she would take her hand. Françoise shook her head and looked at her feet.

"I can't help you if you won't talk to me," the headmistress said gently. Maybe if they stood, maybe if they both stood and the desk was no longer between them. But the woman remained behind her desk, her hands clasped in front of her. It was impossible.

"You're leaving me with little choice but to expel you," the headmistress said. "Maybe that's what you want? Do you want to be back with your parents? Do you miss them?"

Françoise's eyes snapped up to meet hers in mute terror.

"No," she said. "Don't send me home."

The headmistress sighed. Françoise was not expelled. Not then, and not on the many other times her expulsion was threatened. On the national exams for literature, administered at the end of the year, she received one of the highest scores in all of central France.

"I bet she was glad she didn't expel me then, *la connasse*," my mother said. She had picked up her phone and I could see her once more. Her anger swelled and strained her voice. The headmistress had not known how to save her. How dare this woman, who was an adult, who was supposed to know all things, have failed her. It was an impossibly young anger, the anger of the helpless.

Françoise was terrified that she was going insane. There was no one she could talk to. Not Sylvie, not her friends. Certainly not the headmistress, who loomed in her mind like a diabolical version of her mother. The more she worried about her sanity, the more she felt it slip away. She sensed that the adults were afraid of her, and that made her still more afraid of herself.

But the young hall supervisor was not afraid. She saw the pain underneath the violence. She knew to come find Françoise in private. She spoke to her softly. If Françoise could not confide in her either, it was only because she herself didn't know what was wrong. And the young woman did not say, "Everything will be okay." She did not say, "This will pass." Instead, she held Françoise when no one else dared to. She caressed her forehead.

The image wavered as my mother pushed the heel of her palm roughly against her eyes. I felt our distance acutely, and it lanced my heart. I wished I could throw my arms around her, though it was unclear to me if I wanted to comfort her or to be comforted.

According to neuroscientists, when we stir up a long-term memory, it floats in our consciousness, unstable, for a window of approximately three hours. During this time, the memory is malleable. The present infiltrates the past. We add details to fill in the gaps. Then the brain re-encodes the memory as if it were new, writing over the old one. As it sinks back down into the depths of our minds, we are not even aware of what we have gained or lost, or why.

Pure memories are like dinosaur bones, one neuroscientist

wrote, discrete fragments from which we compose the image of the dinosaur. They are only flashes: the examining room table in the nurse's office, the soft hand against the forehead. But memories we tell as stories come alive. Tendons join the bones, muscles and fat and skin fill them out. And when we look again, our memories are whole, breathing creatures that roam our past.

The stories we use to create our sense of self—the stories we tell new lovers at five a.m. so that they can understand who we are—are also the ones over which we have most heavily embroidered. They have been altered by the moods and settings in which we have told them. They have been altered by what we needed them to mean each time. The story involving poor forgotten Guyot, for example, had been pressed and shaped, through entering and leaving my mother's conscious mind, into a smooth block that lay at her foundation. It was one of the first she ever told me about her adolescence, and she had told it to me many times since. Even so, when I questioned her, certain details came loose. How was the phone call to the headmistress broadcast to an auditorium, I wanted to know. By pulling a rotary phone on a long cord onto the stage and holding the receiver to the microphone, she told me with certainty, though this did not strike me as fully plausible. Somewhere along the way, the episode had passed from memory to story to myth.

Even in retelling it now she said, "But you see, I have never understood how to follow the rules." She told me about showing a new colleague around the building that afternoon. She had gone through a door, then turned and noticed that he hadn't followed. He stood in the hallway, hesitating. The door was covered in signs that said DO NOT ENTER. It led through the building's technical core. It was a shortcut to her office. "It had never occurred to me to actually not enter," she said. "But I suppose to some people it would."

This new story that had emerged, however, the story of the fits at school, had not been smoothed. It did not fit neatly inside her. It did not build into the narrative of who she had become. She had told me stories that seemed far more difficult with dry eyes and a steady voice. Perhaps she had not omitted this story from her life because it was painful to recall. Perhaps it was painful to recall because it had been omitted.

She was glancing worriedly at her watch. She was late for a gala she had to attend with my father. She pushed back the curls from her face and looked at me through the phone. Her gray-green eyes crinkled with love.

"Let's talk soon," she said. She hung up the phone.

The eerie silence of my apartment rose up around me. I felt, as I often felt, the violence of my project. What right did I have to reach so deep into her past? I had asked my friends, women between twenty and thirty, if they had asked their mothers to tell them their lives in this way. Most said no. Most said they weren't sure they'd want to know.

Ten minutes later, my phone rang. It was my mother.

"Rebecca," she said, instead of hello. "I was just walking to the elevators and it came back to me: her name wasn't Alexandra, it was Rebecca. It would have sounded exotic to me then. Now that I think about it, she was probably Jewish. The way she looked . . . it would make sense." The elevator arrived, and she hung up again.

I thought of a story my parents often told with amusement. In my mother's first years in America, when she had been dating my father for several months, she had been surprised to learn that a good friend of theirs was Jewish. The man was so obviously so that my father laughed at her surprise.

"And him, too? And him? And him?" she'd asked, rattling off the very Jewish names of their friends, men with prominent noses and bushy eyebrows.

"Yes," my father assured her. Most everyone they knew was Jewish. It had never occurred to her. I pictured my mother now, as she rode the elevator down through the reinforced core of that gleaming new building. I pictured Rebecca's face morphing in her mind to fit the many she'd seen since, before settling again, changed, in the deep drifts. I remembered that long-ago dinner party, when my mother said my brother and I were in all of her memories, even those from long before we were born. It was true. I stirred the memories to the surface, and they changed as she told them to me. Bright threads of myself, embroidered upon her past.

THAT SUMMER, the summer of 1971, my mother discovered sex. All spring, she and Jean-Michel had rubbed against each other in doorways and on park benches, in the back room of the café, but he hadn't been allowed past the boarding school gate. That summer in Ussel, however, they found their way into the groundskeeper's cottage at Les Bezièges. It had been abandoned for years. There was no electricity or water, no furniture. They spent entire days on the dusty wooden floor, experimenting. "Like rabbits," my mother told me more than once. I let myself picture two white bunnies in a toolshed, noses twitching. Afterward, she and Jean-Michel lay on their backs, smoking and dreamily planning their *maison du paradis.* They would have a real home, theirs alone, filled with children and animals and a real bed, their bed, soft and bathed in sunlight. Curtains. A fireplace. A drafting table where Jean-Michel could work on his architectural plans. He was a year older than Françoise and would begin his studies at the Beaux-Arts in Paris in the fall. He talked of his grand plans, of how architecture could change society. Françoise listened, her head on the rise and fall of his chest. She knew by then that she did not want to be a plastic surgeon. She wanted to find her own path, but she didn't know what it would be. As Jean-Michel spoke, a new possible future opened before her. She had always loved to work with her hands. She traded her father's surgical tools for Jean-Michel's X-Acto knives, carving new noses for building architectural models.

In the evenings, when the long summer sun stretched pink rays across the cobwebs and rusty handsaws, they ran back to the main house just in time to sit down at the table, flushed and sweaty and smelling of sex, wood chips in Françoise's hair. Josée's perfect eyebrows rose, but she said nothing.

At the very end of August, when Paul came down from Paris, Josée called Françoise into the formal living room.

"Your father and I have something to discuss with you," Josée told her, her voice echoing off the double-height ceilings. "Are you and Jean-Michel having sex?"

"Of course not," my mother said with genuine indignation. How could she voice something so private across the expanse of this room? And with her father present! She wasn't even aware of lying.

"In front of my father!" she told me, the indignation still fresh years later. "If Josée had talked to me alone, maybe that would have been different."

As a teenager, I knew Prospect Park best by night, when we sat in the dugouts of the baseball field drinking forties of malt liquor. But during the day, amid families enjoying their first spring picnics, the vast lawns covered in colorful blankets, I blinked against the sun and did not know how to orient myself. This was Zane's park, though, his neighborhood, and I did not worry about getting lost. We paced the looping paths aimlessly, holding hands. I could hear in his voice that he was nervous, and I felt a small flicker of pleasure in my chest. I rarely seemed to make him nervous.

Zane had too-short hair and a crooked grin, a long thin nose and long lashes. He wore T-shirts with political slogans, and his pants were so torn from climbing trees that they seemed about to fall off his body. He carried around a beat-up copy of *On the Road*. I had a crush on him so big it flew out of me and above me like a helium balloon. Everyone knew. I'd memorized all of *Howl*, hoping to impress him. *I saw the best minds of my generation destroyed by madness, starving hysterical naked*, I mouthed to myself, as if each word were its own love song.

He asked me to hang out with him after school one day. We wandered to SoHo and sat on a public bench, watching the giraffe-legged models walk by to their photo shoots. In a roundabout way, he answered the question I hadn't asked. I was too young. Too sweet. Too nice. He didn't want to hurt me. I nodded, lips firmly pressed. I swallowed the hard knot that rose in my throat. "Peace love and anarchist applesauce," he said with a goofy grin as we hugged good-bye. It was his thing, that phrase, how he always said good-bye.

That evening, I sucked the insides of my forearms till they were covered with purple bruises. I did not want to be nice. *N* always stood for "nice" when friends made acrostics of my name. "Banish 'nice' from your vocabularies," my English teacher said that year. "It is the most meaningless adjective." It would take me years to unlearn that. To realize that nice was rare.

My mother arched an eyebrow in the morning, taking in my arms. "I wouldn't do that if I were you," she said. "It looks very unappetizing." I glared at her. What did she know of pain? But I tugged down my sleeves.

We were the same age, Zane and I, but I was young for a New York City fifteen-year-old. I had gaped when my new friends passed around a joint on our lunch hour, and I worried my naïveté would not be easily forgotten. Only two years earlier, in middle school, I had somberly cut and pasted a collage of blackened lungs and placed it on my mother's bed. SMOKING AGES YOU PREMATURELY, it read. Now I slid a cigarette out of the pack of Gauloises in her nightstand. My best friend and I sat on my fire escape and learned how not to cough. We plotted our path to the poets and stoners with military precision.

We were a high school of the uncool, and our standards were strange. Entry to Stuyvesant required a score in the top 3 percent on an SAT-like exam and nothing else. There were autistic students who wandered the hallways whistling to themselves, Russian kids who sold stolen graphing calculators from the inside pockets of their trench coats. We organized ourselves into separate constellations, based largely on ethnicity—Asian or white—with social hierarchies that did not overlap. The football team was called the Peglegs and lost nearly every game. It was cool to get good grades, though cooler still to get them without working hard. It was not uncommon for a student to cry in the halls over a bad test score.

And yet in my world, it was all about the beat poets and Audre Lorde. It was about protesting the Afghanistan war and wearing T-shirts to school that read FUCK BUSH. It was about the Great Books course with the charismatic teacher where we wrote our own versions of *The Sound and the Fury* and *Pale Fire*. Even the girls from the Upper West Side dyed hidden locks of their hair purple.

It seemed important, in those high school years, to knock off firsts as quickly as possible. First kiss, first hangover, first cigarette, first class cut, first joint rolled, first blowjob, first ride in a dealer's car. But at fifteen, I had never kissed anyone. Not even at summer camp.

My best friend and I went to CBGB. It was long past the punk rock luster of the 1980s, but it was one of the few places with live music that did not card us at the door. In the bathroom, we tried to open the bottle of wine I had stolen from my parents with the backs of our earrings, with a pen, with a safety pin, while heavy metal shook the walls. In bodegas, I bought us beer by speaking in fractured Franglais. "Twenty-one?!" I would exclaim. "In my country, it's sixteen!" It worked about half the time.

In the basement of the Brooklyn townhouse where the permissive parents filled the upstairs bathroom with marijuana plants, I spent long stoned evenings grabbing for my cell phone, sure my mother was calling and sure that I had forgotten how to speak French. My friend and I bought a glass pipe on Canal Street, but we had nothing to put in it, so we unrolled cigarettes and shoved the tobacco in the bowl. The first time I bought pot,

I said "twenty dollars' worth" to the dealer on the phone, and my friend went gray with embarrassment. We cut school one day to practice rolling joints until they were perfect cylinders. I learned to ask for "a dub" or "a dime." I learned to say "trees" and "bud" instead of "pot." I learned to say "word, he's mad chill" as I watched Zane disappear around corners to kiss other girls. I learned to make it all roll off my tongue, like so many exhalations of smoke. All of this happened very fast, though it felt long then. A few months, maybe. I shed childhood with a vicious shake.

Then, once or twice, he waited for me outside my math class, pulling faces through the window in the door. My exhilaration could have ripped the world in two. In college, a girl told me that she already knew she would never in her life be as happy again as the first time she tried cocaine. Sometimes I wonder if it's the same with love.

And then, miraculously, we had a date. He asked me out to the Film Forum, to see a documentary about the music of apartheid. I floated to the movie theater. When I arrived, his mother, father, little brother, and grandmother were there. I tried to hide my sur prise. We all went out to a diner for greasy burgers afterward. Under the fluorescent lights, I memorized a particularly unflattering angle of his nose, just in case. His family was kind. I hugged them all good-bye. I was a few blocks away and halfway home when I heard footsteps running behind me. I turned and he kissed me. My cell phone rang, my mother calling.

That night, I jumped up and down on my bed like I had when I was a child. I did not care that my head nearly hit the ceiling.

He held my hand in the hallways and rested his head on my stomach when we lay in large groups by the lockers. He kissed me between my classes, and though kissing was not like I had imagined—more invasive, less sensual—I liked it anyway. We went to protests and he fought with the cops. During the morning Pledge of Allegiance, a new post-9/11 policy in New York's public schools, he stood and said a "pledge of resistance" instead. He was reprimanded for it and continued. I traced his name with my finger in the article in the school paper, flushed with pride. I filled notebooks with the intense peaks and valleys of emotion I felt each time he smiled at me or didn't and tried not to let him see. It did not seem to occur to either of us to actually get to know each other. He told me about his childhood once or twice, only happy things. Mostly he told me the plots of movies I had not seen, acting out the parts.

He dropped acid after school even though I'd asked him not to. I was worried that it might change him and did not want anything to change. My father had told me a story about a man who dropped acid only once and now spent his days in front of a supermarket, slowly swallowing and then disgorging the same long length of rope. But then again, my father had also told me that hallucinogenics were the only drugs worth trying, back when he thought I would never grow up. Zane took acid anyway, which did not surprise me, then apologized, which did. He did not become a man who swallowed rope. He continued to be my boyfriend, a miracle so monumental it never ceased to leave me dizzy. I was newly uncertain about all my deeply held convictions. Two years before, I had been making antismoking collages. Now I smoked on my way to school. Were all the things I had once thought taboo supposed to be swept away, one by one?

We had been dating for five or six months when we took that walk in Prospect Park. Our intimate conversation felt perfectly private in the anonymity of the city. He named the two other couples who already had. He asked me gently if I felt ready. Somehow, I was surprised. It hadn't quite occurred to me yet that this was a thing that we might do. Blowjobs seemed complicated enough. A friend who was very proud of having already given one tried to show me in the school hallway. "One finger or two?" she asked, grabbing my hand for demonstration. None of my close friends had had sex yet. There was some competition about which of us would be first. But no one, including me, had thought it would be me.

I wanted to forge myself into a girl who was fast, rebellious, fearless, but I was not she and never would be. I liked the fumbling times Zane and I fooled around. I liked the terrible poem he wrote for me comparing my orgasm to a tsunami, liked it so much I did not tell him I had never had one. And yet, virginity was something one lost, and I was not sure I wanted to lose anything just yet. I sensed that he expected me to hesitate, and so, gratefully, I did.

Shortly after, my mother asked me if I would like to invite Zane to join us in the South of France that August.

"Really?" I asked, once again in awe of her gift for thinking of wonderful, impossible things. I had brought friends on family vacations to France before, their presence balancing the volatility of our nuclear four. But to bring Zane! To be with him, just him and me, far away from school, for days on end!

"Yes," she said, bemused. "Really."

But Zane did not seem eager. He told me that he planned to go to Cuba with a group of American activists that summer, as an act of resistance.

"You could come after," I said. And I also said, though it makes me cringe to remember it, "If you came, you could bring condoms."

His parents wanted to meet my parents first, which my parents found amusing. They planned a Fourth of July picnic in Brooklyn Bridge Park. The air was filled with fireflies. Zane and I played with our little brothers while our parents talked. I looked across the river at that strange, changed skyline. I realized, as I looked at that still jarring gap in the air, that there was no going backward. Some of the things I had put down so hurriedly could never be picked up again.

On the day Zane arrived in France, we walked together to the small medieval village on a hillside. He pointed out the graffiti on the abandoned cement structures by the path. FUCK YOGURT, one said in a scrawl, and we laughed. Then he told me that in Cuba he had kissed a girl.

"It was mad whack of me," he said. "If it makes you feel any better, my friend punched me in the face after."

"Oh no," I said, glancing to make sure he was not bruised. "Okay. That's okay, I guess." I was not going to let this small thing derail my joy.

My mother set up the pullout couch in the small cabin we had rented. My brother and I slept in twin beds in the same room down the hall.

Could my brother sleep on the couch? I asked. And Zane in our room?

Absolutely not, my mother said.

But my brother had said he wouldn't mind.

"Isn't it already enough that you have your boyfriend here,

without making your poor little brother sleep on the couch?" she said. *Why should my brother mind the couch?* I thought. It was bigger than our small beds.

"I'm sorry my parents are so lame," I told Zane.

"Now?" he asked, when we were kissing in the lit-up pool that night. But the pool was open to all the cabins, and people could appear at any time.

"Now?" he asked, in the middle of the afternoon, when my family was out. But they were coming back any minute.

"Now?" he asked, the night he and I babysat for family friends who were staying in a hotel. I could hear the children tossing in their sleep in the room next door. I looked at the bed, at those white hotel sheets.

"No," I said. I could sense his growing agitation. I worried that I had made a promise I'd be unable to keep. But I wanted a moment with magic. I wanted a moment worth remembering.

On our last day, we again walked together to the village. It was a small road, with few cars, that wound through vineyards and a shady forest. I spotted a field lit up gold in the early-evening light. Bushes shaded it from the road.

"Now," I said, and grabbed his wrist and pulled him toward it.

The itchy grass raised small welts on my sensitive skin. A grasshopper landed on my calf, sticky legs springing off again. Gnats aimed for my eyes. Zane was nervous, and it took a very long time and then a very short time. And yet, in that moment, I was thinking, *This is a story. A field at sunset in the South of France.* He looked into my eyes and seemed to realize for the first time that they were not brown but flecked with gold and green. *This,* I thought, as he curled his head against my shoulder like a small boy, *is a story I will tell my daughter someday.* Only later, when my best friend laughed at me, did I realize what a strange thought that was to have.

That evening, as I got ready for dinner, I looked at myself in the bathroom mirror to see if I had changed. I was too young then even to know how clichéd that impulse was. My face was flushed, and grass stuck in my hair. My parents did not seem to notice. Their friend did, however. He was a decade older than my father. He stared hungrily across the table. He put his hands on my shoulders to massage them. He told my boyfriend, several times, what a very lucky young man he was. My parents laughed. I pulled Zane away from the table when their backs were turned and we went and sat quietly under a tree.

That fall, my parents' friend sent a glossy photograph of me taken that summer, with a love letter attached. It was a surprisingly unflattering photo. My eyes were as dull and vacant as a cow's. My mother sat on my bed to read the letter to me.

"*Ew,*" I said.

"It's sweet," she said. "You should keep it." She left it next to the plastic pink fairy figurine I had not had the heart to place in the box with my other toys.

A few months later, I stood in the doorway of my mother's bathroom.

"*Maman,*" I said, "*s'il te plaît!* Just let me spend the night at Zane's house."

"The answer is no," she said, leaning into the mirror to adjust a curl.

"But why? His parents already said it was okay. Please?"

"I already said no, Nadja. Stop arguing with me."

"But give me a reason!"

"I don't need to explain myself to you. You . . . you don't want to go getting yourself into situations where you . . . where you will feel pressured to do things that you don't want to do," she said.

"*Mais, Maman*," I said, exasperated, "you don't have to worry about that. That's already happened, and I wanted it to." I thought this might convince her. It seemed impossible to me that she didn't already know.

She finally turned to look at me.

"The answer is definitely no," she said. "And you really shouldn't tell me these things."

FRANÇOISE DIDN'T REALIZE what had happened until that autumn. The knowledge came to her all at once, a sure and physical thing, like a ball she had caught without knowing it was being thrown. Her breasts were swollen. She slept all the time. She'd missed her period, though that had been easy to ignore, as it had begun only a few months earlier.

She wasn't nervous about telling Jean-Michel. Wasn't this what they had daydreamed together all summer long—children, a house of their own? He seemed at least hesitantly happy at her news. But she was terrified of telling her mother.

"I knew it!" Josée spat angrily. "Of course you are. Well. Will he marry you?"

Jean-Michel and his father, Louis, sat stiffly in the living room of the Paris apartment. Françoise had imagined her parents rendered silent by Jean-Michel's declarations of love—he was a big talker and proud of his eloquence. But now he sat quietly by his father, meek in his too-tight tie and shiny shoes. He kept his eyes on the ground as Louis and Josée worked out the details. Françoise fought a heavy wave of disappointment. It was just another sign, she told herself,

just another sign that they needed to escape these parents, these formal rooms, this deadening, stifling atmosphere, and build a home of
their own where their voices could carry as loud as they wished.

After Jean-Michel and his father left, Paul pulled Françoise
into the dining room and shut the door.

"You're not marrying him," he said. He wasn't going to stand
by and watch her throw her future away. She was only fifteen. She
hadn't even passed her baccalaureate.

On the contrary, it was perfect timing, Françoise said. She'd
have the baby in May, which would leave her a whole month to
study for her exams.

No, Paul said. She'd have an abortion, not a baby.

Françoise was adamant—she could already feel the baby kicking inside her, she told him—but Paul stood his ground. She was
still a minor. Her parents got to decide. There were clinics in
England that would take care of it.

"You'll have to force me," Françoise said. "I won't go willingly."

Françoise was not ashamed of being pregnant, nor did she
particularly care whether she got married or not. She was proud
of herself for calculating the months of her term and saw no
flaw in her plan. She argued firmly and rationally. This child
was her ticket out. It was the only way she saw to escape her
family.

Finally, her father gave in. "Fine," he said. "Fine. You can have
the baby. But you'll live at home and raise it here."

Françoise agreed to the abortion.

DECADES LATER, when I kicked inside her, my mother realized
she couldn't have felt anything so early on in her pregnancy. But

she had been telling the truth then—the baby was real to her, and she was certain she had felt it kicking.

I tried to imagine the older sister I'd never had. I reached back through the years for her barely formed foot but it slipped my grasp. This ghost child was conceived in August, to be born in May, just like me. Her birth would have prevented my own. I felt the strings that connected me to my mother's past pull tight.

They flew to London on a Thursday, Josée, Françoise, and Jean-Michel. Later Josée would tell me, laughing, how Françoise turned on her heel in front of the hospital and ran down the street. How Josée and Jean-Michel had to catch her. How Jean-Michel came as far as the hospital entrance, then turned around to begin the journey back to Paris. He couldn't afford to miss a quiz he had in school. "A quiz!" she hooted, the childish insignificance of it hilarious to her.

My mother didn't remember any of this, didn't remember that Jean-Michel was there at all. She remembered only the waiting room, only her mother.

"Maman, will you tell the nurse?" Françoise asked. "Will you tell her now?" The hospital rumbled around her, unintelligible and menacing.

Josée went to speak quietly in English with one of the doctors, gesturing over at her daughter. Françoise watched them carefully. She'd had only one request, which she was desperate to communicate. If she was going to kill her baby, she wanted to be there. She wanted to feel the pain, and she wanted it to be excruciating. She wanted to know the moment when the baby left her. She didn't want to be sedated.

The nurse came over.

"Follow me, please," she said to Françoise. She told Josée to wait in the reception area. She led Françoise to a room painted in soft tones with suffused lighting and told her to relax. Françoise lay on the hospital bed. The light was not strong enough to read by, but for once she did not mind. She wanted to be alone with her thoughts. The nurse prepared a needle.

"*Qu'est-ce que c'est?*" Françoise asked. She recoiled with her whole body, her hands waving in front of her. No.

"Yes, yes," the nurse said. Françoise recognized the word "mother," the word "yes." The nurse took her arm and slipped in the needle. Then she left, and Françoise was alone, alone with the strange silence of the hospital, the hum of machinery and the muffled voices out in the hall, alone with the gentle kicking of the child she felt inside her.

Two nurses entered the room, with Josée just behind them. The nurses had her lie down on a gurney. The hospital floors were roughly tiled. The rattling metal wheels shook deep in her bones, echoed off the walls. Her vision began to swim. The noise fell away and the walls of the hospital receded. She was falling and floating, all at once.

"What's happening?" she said. "What's going on?" The words fought their way out from deep inside her. Her lips were rubbery and her mouth felt filled with cotton.

"Shhh," her mother said. "It will be easier for everyone this way."

The nurse said something in English, and she could not understand. But she understood.

"*NON!*" Françoise shouted. She gripped the sides of the gurney until her knuckles turned white, trying to pull herself back into the world. She fixated with wild concentration on the ceiling, on her mother's hand. She tried to force her eyes to stay open. She screamed at the top of her lungs, though she couldn't hear if she was making a sound.

"*Espèce de salope!*" You whore! she tried to shout at her mother. But the words were lost deep inside her. She tried to grab the nurse's sleeve but her arm was already gone, asleep. The blackness slid up over the rest of her body, steady and unrelenting.

And then she was awake. Her lower body felt numb. She was alone, alone in an unfamiliar hospital room, and alone in her body. She felt an emptiness so deep she hadn't known it could exist. It was as if a new sense had been granted to her, only to be lost again. And then she began to shake, and she felt her body fill again as she flooded with impotent rage.

chapter four

"W ithout me, you would be nothing," Paul spat at Josée in anger one spring evening. This was the mythology of why she'd left him. This was the line she always quoted.

Divorce was still uncommon at the time, and it was especially unusual for a mother of three children, with a wealthy husband and no career, to initiate it. Yet only twelve-year-old Andrée was truly surprised. Josée and Paul hated each other with a passion. Josée and Paul each hired lawyers. They planned the details rather calmly. At first it seemed as if the divorce would be amicable. Paul's gambling addiction had barely dented their finances, and the money still flowed like water.

Josée was gone by July. She took Andrée and a suitcase. She first rented a houseboat just outside of Paris, far from the doctors and lawyers she had lived among for the past two decades. In a city with a finite amount of space, where laws against noise where often enforced and neighbors tiptoed around one another, the boats presented a rare kind of Wild West lawlessness. Some were hooked illegally to the city's power grid. Some were little more than planks of driftwood and garbage bags nailed together into makeshift squats. Josée's first boat was more like a country cabin, wooden and cozy, with bay windows in the living room that opened onto a floating terrace.

Sylvie had more or less run away from home by then. She was living on the street, in the maid's room above a friend's house, in a commune down in the South of France. Françoise remained at home, but she had made herself as invisible as possible. She came home late and shut herself in her room to study. She spent what little free time she had with Jean-Michel, who was enrolled in his first year of architecture school in Paris. She planned to enroll in the same school in the fall. Her father was profoundly disappointed that she would not go to medical school, and his disappointment emerged masked as anger.

"You would have made a good assistant," he told her angrily. "But you never would have been more than that." Maybe she would have been okay in a laboratory, but she lacked the human touch that made a great doctor. Still, at least she might have married one. She might have given Paul a son-in-law to take over his practice, he told her. He never warmed to Jean-Michel.

That August, Jean-Michel and Françoise traveled to Afghanistan for two and a half months. When they returned, everything had changed.

While they were away, Paul had gone to the houseboat with flowers.

"This is great," he told Josée. "It's peaceful here! It's different! I'll move in with you."

She'd shut the door in his face.

On his lawyer's advice, Paul hired a private investigator. Josée had been given a job by the real estate agent who had helped her buy her various homes. Now she managed construction sites, beating the workers there in the morning and not returning home until late in the evening. The private investigator tailed Andrée as she walked herself to school and back, the key to the boat hanging around her neck. She made her own meals, rowed the rowboat up and down the Seine by herself.

The private investigator followed Josée as well. He threw open the door of a hotel room. He snapped photos. He had caught her *in flagrant delicto.*

It was no longer to be a no-fault divorce. With a charge of adultery against her, Josée had no claim to her husband's fortune. But it was not the fact of the affair that made Paul go mad with rage. Josée had had affairs before. What drove Paul to madness was the man in the photos. Paul recognized him instantly. It was Louis Guérin, Jean-Michel's father.

Josée, with deadly accuracy, had managed to wound Paul as deeply as anyone could have ever done. She struck him in his pride. The two men looked alike, with a bearlike sturdiness and curly hair, but Paul was handsome and Louis was not. Louis was one of the local businessmen in Ussel. Paul was a surgeon, he'd "gone up" to Paris. Paul was tormented by memories of the summers in Ussel, how he'd driven down the main streets in his convertible, basking in his success. The grand doctor Mouly, returned for August with his beautiful wife and his three daughters. They praised him to his face, complimented his perfect family. But behind closed doors, the whispers must have been jumping from ear to ear. His wife had been sleeping with a local businessman. Everyone in town must have known. Everyone except him and Louis Guérin's wife. When she heard about the affair, they said, she grabbed a shotgun, went into the backyard, and killed the ducks and chickens. And with each echoing shot she'd screamed: *"Josée! Françoise! Josée! Françoise!"*

"It was *known*," Josée told me once with great pride. Oh, how the news of her affair spread. It was known all over France.

Paul had expected that Françoise would break up with Jean-Michel immediately out of filial duty. The boy had never been good enough for her anyway. When she didn't do so of her own accord, he ordered her to. She refused. He slammed his fist down on the table. The only explanation he could find for his daughter's stubbornness was that Françoise must have known about Josée's affair all along. He was wounded to his core, lonely, losing his mind with hurt and anger. Every night he came into her room and sat down on her bed.

"Your mother's a whore," he would tell her, jumping up to pace the floor. "Nothing but a dirty whore. When I married her, I thought she would be eternally grateful." Who else would have married a bastard girl? He should have listened to his parents. Look what she'd done to him! Look how she'd repaid him, the *pétasse*!

I recognized this as the continuation of the story my mother had begun all those years before. "My father used to come into my room and . . . I'll tell you when you're older." I let out a sigh of relief, and my mother glanced at me curiously before continuing.

"That's my mother you're talking about," she would remind her father, but he would not listen.

Françoise shook from the fallout of her father's hurt. It was more than she could bear. She packed her suitcases. Paul tore through her room, trying to unpack them.

"You can't leave me," he said. "You can't leave me here all alone."

He followed her down the stairs, screaming at her, while Françoise tried to float outside of her body. Out on the street, Jean-Michel was behind the wheel of an idling car. Louis Guérin had offered to rent a studio apartment for his son, as was standard at the time. It embarrassed Françoise to have Louis pay the bill, but she could no longer live with her father and she had nowhere else to go.

"You're just like her," he was saying now as he tried to wrest the suitcase from her hands. "Please. Don't you leave me too." Jean-Michel twisted in his seat and looked worriedly over his shoulder. He had never stood up to her father. She threw her suitcase in back and slammed the trunk. Paul was so close beside her that it clipped him on the forehead. He reeled back and punched her.

Then she was lying in the street, looking up at parts of faces at unfamiliar angles. A metallic taste filled her mouth. Her hand came away bright with blood. Her father kneeled and helped her up. She leaned on him. He brought her back upstairs to the medical office. He reset her broken nose. When she was able to think again, there was only one relentless, pounding fear: *What if this means I can't leave?* But her father was meek now, ashamed. He let her go, his eyes on the floor.

"Were you angry with your mother?" I asked my mother when she told me this. "For sleeping with your boyfriend's father?"

"I don't know how to answer that," she said, and there was a long silence. "Angry? I don't know what it would mean to be angry with my mother. That wasn't possible for me then. I still can't imagine what it would be, to feel anger toward her. I was angry with my father, for talking to me about her that way. That was easy. But my mother? She made me suffer. But being angry would have meant believing she could change."

IT WAS SOMETIME during my junior year of high school that my mother discovered the cookies were missing. One day some months before, she'd announced, "I've bought some snacks for your brother and I've hidden them." It sounded like a speech she had rehearsed in her head. "They're not for you. You don't need them. Okay?"

"Okay," I'd mumbled, grateful that she seemed willing to let the conversation end there. I hated talking about my weight. My body felt undefined. It seemed to shape-shift by the second. As long as no one mentioned it, I held on to a hope that perhaps I wasn't fat. But when my mother talked about my body, I immediately felt myself expand, the increased pull of gravity. Each second was excruciating. So I was willing to pretend with her that I didn't already know that in the low cabinet by the fridge was a stash of beef jerky, fruit roll-ups, cookies, and chips.

But when the snacks started disappearing, empty wrappers left behind, I was the obvious suspect.

"I didn't," I said.

"Admit it!" she said.

The fight lasted nearly a month. I was permanently grounded. I told my friends that my father had caught me smoking, embarrassed by the real reason. My mother could barely look at me.

"If I'd eaten them, I would tell you," I'd say. "All I want is to get out of this house. Why wouldn't I tell you the truth?"

"I don't know!" she'd say. "Why won't you?"

There was no way out. If I shouted at her, she shouted back louder. If I reasoned with her, she reasoned better. I punched pillows in my room but felt silly; screamed at the top of my lungs but ended up squeaking. I couldn't understand why she wouldn't believe me. I wanted, more than anything, for the fight to end. But it never occurred to me to admit to eating the snacks. I knew that I hadn't.

"*Menteuse, menteuse, menteuse!*" she screamed at me one day. Liar, liar, liar! Her trembling red face, too close to mine, was all that I could see. Her spittle hit my cheek. I lost control of myself. I slapped her, very hard. My palm stung. She reeled back, her eyes wide with shock.

"That's it," she said, her voice quiet and threatening. She turned her back to me and shuffled some papers on her desk. "I'm putting you in therapy."

My shrink was calm and kind, with sensible shoes. Sometimes she met with my parents as well. Together they explained to me that I was sleep-eating Chips Ahoy! in my pink cat pajamas, brushing the crumbs away with the sleep from my eyes in the mornings. There was no trace of those midnight raids inside me—I searched myself hard but found not even the lack of a memory, not even a hole. Yet eventually I began to believe it. I believed my mother more than I believed myself. I wondered how many other things I was doing without knowing. The possibilities seemed infinite. I was crazy. I was terrified. I withdrew from my friends, unsure who I was. I stopped holding on to my memories. They were too dangerous. I let them fall away.

Finally, I was allowed to sleep at a friend's house. We smoked pot and drank forties in the dugouts in Prospect Park, got the munchies and bought our own cookies. When I came back, there was an empty bag of potato chips on the floor of my room. I picked it up and brought it to my mother's room.

"I didn't do this," I said, holding it out to her, afraid that somehow I had.

"Oh," she said numbly. "Okay. Just put it there on the washing machine."

She turned back to what she was doing. I went back to my room. We didn't talk about it. I stopped thinking about it. I spent the summer in East Africa, breathing in the oceans between us. The following fall, my parents sat my brother and me down at the kitchen table. My brother was closed, too furious to speak. My mother made him apologize for framing me with candy wrappers. His apology stung, made it real.

It wasn't until three years later that I realized my mother had never apologized to me, and that I needed her to. I called her from my off-campus apartment, pacing the kitchen and eating Triscuits while we spoke. In this relationship, which had miraculously transformed when I left for college, I finally felt I could hold my own.

"I couldn't have known," she said. "It was inconceivable."

"I understand," I said. "I understand why you didn't believe me. But that doesn't change the fact that you hurt me. You made me think I was going crazy. And when you hurt someone, you apologize."

"Nobody could have known," she said. "Even you didn't know."

"But you're my *mother*," I said.

The conversation lasted two hours. We went in circles. We said the same things over and over. And then, finally, abruptly, she understood.

"You're right," she said. "Of course, you're right. I'm your mother. Oh my baby, I'm so sorry."

———

THE *BOULANGERIES* had delicate icicles of glass in their windows, sprigs of mistletoe and wreaths of pine. On the street corners, men in shabby coats with blistered fingers hunched over grills, scooping chestnuts into paper cones. Children pushed off the brown shells with their mittens, shoved the soft nuts deep into their cheeks. Chickens rotated lazily on their endless merry-go-round, thick drops of grease hitting the pan below. Paris was well suited to winter; it was a city that looked best in gray. It seemed the streets were filled with families, happy families, well-fed children, the glow of their warm homes still on them as they took a post-prandial stroll. The holiday cheer was like the muffled sounds of music in an apartment next door. It hung close around the passing mothers and fathers, stayed behind the glass of the shop windows.

Françoise drew her coat close around her neck. She fingered the coin in her pocket. Jean-Michel had gone home to be with his mother. Françoise had asked him to stay in Paris instead, but he'd said no without hesitation. He needed to be with his mother to console her, Jean-Michel said. She'd be spending Christmas without Louis this year.

When the door closed behind him, she'd scoured the empty apartment for loose change, her fingers plunging through the holes in coat pockets and underneath the mattress. She'd scavenged enough for one baguette a day. One baguette, and no more. She learned all the different feelings bread could have in her mouth, the many different ways there were to chew.

Ten days. She moved her tongue in her mouth to recover the

memory of speech. Their friends at architecture school called her Guérinette—Jean-Michel Guérin and his Guérinette. They were gone as well, and with them, her name. She hadn't seen her mother in months, and she had yet to be invited to the houseboat. She was too proud to see her father. The city was empty, chilly, strange.

When summer vacation came around, Jean-Michel took her with him to Ussel. Jean-Michel's mother didn't want them on her property, but his father gave them use of a small cabin outside the town. They were three now: Jean-Michel, Françoise, and their dog, Chivas. Françoise's fingers roamed through Chivas's fur, untangling knots and removing burrs. He was a stray they'd brought back from Afghanistan, part wolf she thought, and he grew bigger by the day. She loved the solid mass of him, his gravity. In the evenings, she rested her head on his stomach as it rose and fell, breathing in his familiar smell, and underneath it something wild.

She and Jean-Michel were together, but it was no better than when they had been apart. Jean-Michel had a car, places to go, friends to see, family to visit. Françoise did not know how to drive and would, anyway, have had nowhere to drive to. She had no friends there of her own. She felt trapped by the same loneliness she had felt the summer her mother had separated her and Andrée.

She began to worry that her depression had a smell. Her unhappiness seemed to cling to her, to drip from her, staining the air where she had been. She worried Jean-Michel would sense it and recoil. She went for long walks while he was gone, trying to lose herself in the open air. Chivas trailed after her. Jean-Michel grew still more distant. The further he went, the more desperately she grabbed for him.

At night they went out dancing. Jean-Michel liked to drink. His voice rose loud over a crowd. He pulled his childhood friends around him in a tight circle that left Françoise outside, watching. She envied the ease with which he made people laugh, the energy he took from the loud music and bright lights that battered her into a corner. She tried to loosen up, but she hated the swimming feeling of being drunk. She hated the loss of control. When she tried to dance her limbs moved awkwardly, resisting the music.

On the way back to the cabin, she gripped her seat as Jean-Michel tore around the curves of the country roads. It wasn't that she was afraid of dying. A day didn't go by that summer when she didn't fantasize about death—the blankness, the quiet, a state of being nei-ther empty nor full. But she wanted to die by her own hand. Jean-Michel insisted that the danger of driving drunk was part of the fun.

One morning, Françoise opened the front door to find Chi-vas's corpse there, his fur matted with blood.

The neighboring farmers told her they'd had to shoot the dog because he'd killed a goat. "Beast like that, once they get the taste of blood . . . ," they'd said, shrugging.

She called the police, the words fighting their way out of her, fury under the wave of tears.

"But what a *parisienne!*" The police officers laughed. "Crying over an animal!"

"Don't take it so hard!" Jean-Michel said. "It's the country. They do things differently here."

She felt the gulf between them grow infinite. Jean-Michel was so far away that she could no longer see him. Or rather, he could no longer see her.

He urged her to come dancing. She refused. They argued. He left, the door slamming behind him.

She was a weight on the world. She was a black stain. She was poison. Her unhappiness choked the air from the room and pushed itself up against the closed windows. She opened the door and found that her feet led her to the toolshed, to the paint thinner. If she was poison, then let her be poison utterly. She drank as much as she could, then she lay on the grass outside and waited to die. She imagined a blackness spreading inside until it reached her skin, turned her lips and fingernails black. If only she could kill a goat, be shot for her wildness. But she didn't even know how to dance.

And then she was on all fours, heaving. The poison came out in a flood. Her stomach contracted over and over, long after the poison had left it. Her traitorous body, all animal and no sense, chose life at all costs. She pulled herself upright and went back to the dark cottage. She fell into the sucking hole of her bed. She was asleep when Jean-Michel came home, got into bed beside her, slipped into his own heavy oblivion. In the morning when they woke, he kissed her gently. Alcohol on his breath, poison on hers, so heavy they could not taste each other. She said nothing.

In Connecticut one weekend, my mother and I were discussing fact and fiction. We'd recently found a diary she'd briefly kept, a diary that contradicted the chronology of the story she was telling me. She'd put it aside and continued to tell me the story as she remembered it.

"I'm saying that there is no objective reality, no true nonfiction," she was saying now. Nonfiction was a construction, albeit a construction that followed different rules from fiction.

"But what about newspapers?" I asked. "Wouldn't a newspaper story be true nonfiction?"

"Facts are transformed by being recounted," she said. "They're turned into stories."

"But still," I said, "in a newspaper article there's only one story to tell. One true story."

"No," she said, "there's always the question of what makes it in. Last week there was an accident around the corner, in Chinatown. The next day the story was in *The New York Times*. A van had been double-parked on East Broadway, but the driver had accidentally left it in reverse. The van backed up slowly onto the sidewalk and killed a four-year-old girl and a three-year-old boy. They'd been walking with their teacher, holding hands. It was a tragedy. But if the van had crashed into a storefront, it wouldn't have been a story. No, it was a story because there happened to be no car blocking the van's path to the sidewalk, because no one realized until too late that there was no driver, because the van happened to hit small children, because they were holding hands. Because you can see it all unfolding before you, a tragedy in the Greek sense, destiny carved out in advance."

"But still," I said, "it's nonfiction. All the events are real events."

"No," she said. "We construct reality. When I tell you I don't remember if something actually happened or not, it's because for me it's the same thing. There's no way to know if my memories are *solid*." She slapped the book she was holding to emphasize the word.

"They did a study," she said. My mother was the master of referencing psychology research to support her arguments. "They did a study where they measured a participant's brain waves while they watched someone dance. Then they asked them to imagine someone dancing. The patterns were the same. There's no physiological difference between what you experience and what you imagine. That's the reason we're always telling stories, why in every culture there are myths. We don't see things as they are, we see them as we interpret them. Take the ducklings who imprinted

Konrad Lorenz as their mother. They followed him everywhere because he really was their mother. They weren't thinking, *Oh, that's not my real mother, that's just my* fictional *mother.* The separations between fact and fiction are ones we create, and the better we control our fictions, the better we can control our reality."

"Oh," I said, a little lost.

As I wrote, I reminded myself: This is my mother's story, as she told it to me. This is my mother's story as I imagine her dancing.

SECOND YEAR OF *architecture school,* my mother had written next to a big bracket that swept up a whole year on the timeline I asked her to make in my notebook. In December: *Visit Mina in Cannes. Trip to Algeria* in March. It was not until the following June, June 1974, that the stories resumed.

"I think we should see other people," Jean-Michel said casually.

Françoise looked at him, uncomprehending.

They'd met when they were very young, he said. They should look around, explore, see the world a bit.

"Okay," she said, because there was no other answer. It had not occurred to her that this would happen. She felt blank, frozen. It wasn't that she was in love with him. How can you be in love with yourself? She didn't know where she stopped and he began. When he left, what of her would remain? Which thoughts, which likes and dislikes, which turns of phrase belonged to her? Guérin and Guérinette.

She would need a new name. Her mind began to turn again. She would need a new place to live. She had spent the past two years in the studio apartment paid for by Louis Guérin. Once a month, she visited her father in the cold empty apartment where he now lived alone. He had kept only the lower floor, for his medical practice. She sat with him at a table in the cramped room that had once been Sylvie's, the green and orange wallpaper still on the wall, the bed still in the corner, as his maid served lunch. He made her ask for the money every single time. He made her fight her pride and find the right polite words. He gave her barely enough to survive on. She couldn't afford to rent her own room.

She felt no anger or hurt. Only confusion, worry, and underneath that, a spark of excitement. She wasn't particularly eager to see other people, but she was eager to see herself. This body of hers, this mind of hers, what might they look like when they were hers alone?

But Paris was littered with ghosts of her past selves. She wanted a place so new it blinded her. A place that would pick her up and bleach her clean, a blank page on which a new story could begin. She wanted to go someplace no one she knew had been.

This was how she chose New York—it was the city that didn't exist. She'd seen it only in movies, dangerous and surreal. America to her was flashing lights on the Champs-Élysées advertising USA COOL JEANS! It was tacky, brash, and bright. But it was big, and it was far. She wouldn't run into Jean-Michel walking arm and arm with some new girlfriend on the streets of New York City. She decided she would take a year off from school. She'd see the whole thing, first New York, and then perhaps Chicago, because that sounded good in her mouth, very sophisticated—*Shee-cah-goh*—and then San Francisco. And then Texas. She would earn money in each place, travel cheaply. She would come back to Paris an adult, all of America inside her.

First, she needed money for a ticket. She needed a place to live. She searched desperately for work in Paris and found none.

"Come down south," her mother suggested. "Everybody's building summer homes by the Côte d'Azur; there must be work for an architect here."

Josée, Louis, and Andrée were spending the summer in a home Louis had bought under Josée's direction. Once the detective's flashbulb had gone off in that hotel room, the divorce had devolved into an interminable battle. Paul had sued for custody of Andrée and won. He took her off the houseboat and placed her in boarding school. Josée went wild. She phoned Andrée at the boarding school as often as she could, sobbing. She turned her bedroom on the houseboat into a shrine of sorts. Suddenly this daughter, who'd just hit puberty and was the spitting image of her own younger self, meant the world to her. Now that she had her for the summer, she barely let her out of her sight.

When Andrée saw Françoise, she ran toward the pool screaming, "MY favorite sister is—" and then, right as she leapt into the air, just before she crashed into the water "—*Sylvie!*" At twelve, she no longer remembered the puppet shows she and Françoise had put on together, the hours spent playing school. The girl who had once called Françoise *maman* was at last the center of her actual mother's intense and undivided attention.

Françoise circled ads in the local paper and took the first job that presented itself, maid's work in a Cannes hotel. It paid minimum wage, but it offered room and board, she told her mother proudly. She repacked her suitcase and caught a bus.

The hotel guests were retirees in their eighties and nineties, parked there by their grown children who'd been sold on the full meal service, the company, the sunshine the brochures touted. The glossy pictures in the brochure were ludicrous when held up against the place itself. The manager gave Françoise and the sole other maid, a timid young farm girl, a tour of their duties. He showed them how to make the beds, pulling the blankets tight over soiled sheets. The hotel's guests were prone to incontinence, strange bleedings, and other bodily emissions. The sheets were to be washed only once a week. There was a big basin outside filled with cold water. There was no soap, because soap would necessitate a second rinse. He instructed them to rub with their hands until the stains came out. When Françoise and the other girl hung the sheets to dry in the sunshine, the smell of diluted urine clung to everything.

Mealtimes were no better. The food the guests left on their plates was scraped back into a big vat to be served again the next day as a stew or a shepherd's pie. Françoise and the girl were instructed to help themselves to those same leftovers. They worked from six a.m. till eleven p.m., for fifty cents an hour.

"This is exploitation!" Françoise said to the other girl. "It must be illegal!" She needed a raise if she was ever going to make enough for a ticket to New York. If they both threatened to quit, their boss would be forced to listen, Françoise said. They'd unionize!

The girl was afraid of getting fired. Her parents would never understand.

"Just follow me," Françoise said. She went to find the manager.

"The working conditions are unacceptable," she began, her speech carefully prepared during hours of changing sheets.

He cut her off. How dare she complain, the little ingrate. There were a thousand other girls who would be happy to take her place. "Pack your bags," he said. "I want you gone by tomorrow."

He turned to the farm girl. Did she have a problem, too?

"No, no, sir!" she said. "I'm happy here! Thank you!"

Françoise packed her bags with shaking hands, willing herself not to cry. She had to call her mother to pick her up. As she waited, she braced herself for the lecture she was sure to receive.

To her surprise, Josée took her side. "You did the right thing," she said. For a brief moment, there was solidarity.

Josée helped Françoise find a job at another hotel, in the town where she lived. There was no room or board, but the pay was three times as much and the hotel was clean. Françoise moved into the guest room of Josée's summer home. She never stopped feeling she was living among someone else's strange pretend family. Her relations with Louis Guérin were strained and stiff. And although he fawned over Josée's every move, it was clear to Françoise how little respect Josée had for him. Josée loved well-educated men of strong opinions and beautiful speech, men who could match her wit and make her laugh. Louis Guérin was doting but dull. Satisfying though the pain she'd inflicted on Paul might be, with Louis himself she was bored and curt. And with Françoise, who dragged herself through the house in a bleak cloud of heartbreak, Josée fought constantly. But by the end of that summer, Françoise had a plane ticket to New York, for the beginning of September.

Here my mother's story wavered. She couldn't remember how she'd earned that much money or where she'd bought the ticket. And she acknowledged that Josée had recently mentioned having paid for the ticket herself. "So maybe that's what happened," she said, clearly skeptical.

"We got into a terrible fight one night," she told me, "and she said to me . . . she said, 'As if it's not enough that we feed you, you have to piss us off as well.' She twisted her knife into the most painful part of me. I'd had no one but her to turn to, nowhere to live, and she resented me for the *food* I ate? I left that night."

"What could you have done to make her say that?" I asked.

She was silent for a while before she answered. "I don't know."

On the table between my mother and me lay three small notebooks that she'd found in the back of the closet, notebooks she'd kept from 1974 to 1976.

"Oh, look!" she said as she thumbed through the pages. "I wrote that line down."

In clean round print, completely unlike her handwriting now, she'd written: *"Dimanche 25 août, vers 9h30—après 'Comme si ça ne suffisait pas de te nourrir s'il faut en plus que tu nous emmerde,' je suis partie."* She had remembered it word for word.

SHE WALKED ALONG the road away from her mother's house. As night began to fall around her, she realized she had no plan. She was too scared to face hitchhiking alone at night. She slept outdoors instead. She had no blanket, and the woods were cold and filled with strange sounds.

In the morning, she brushed herself clean and walked back to the edge of the road. She stuck out her thumb. She made it to Paris by early evening.

The city surged around her, Paris in August, a ghost city of closed doors and shuttered storefronts. She wouldn't go to her father's or Jean-Michel's. Everyone else she knew was out of town.

She headed for her mother's houseboat. It would be locked, the drawbridge up, but she could sleep on the grassy embankment that led down from the sidewalk. It was safer than the city's parks. She climbed over the low wall that separated the riverbank from the street and began to make her way down. She froze. All the lights in the boat were on. She heard faint music and laughter. The front door opened, framing a familiar silhouette.

"Sylvie?" she called.

"Françoise!" her sister yelled back. "What are you doing here? Come in!"

Sylvie was giggling and swaying as she explained. Josée had asked her to watch the boat once and she'd secretly made copies of the keys. They were having a party! What did she want to drink?

Sylvie presented Françoise to the assembled friends with a sweep of her hand. Françoise recognized Éric, the older of the two brothers from Ussel, with his girlfriend sitting between his legs.

Invading her mother's home uninvited made Françoise deeply uncomfortable. She wondered if she wouldn't have preferred sleeping outside.

"I'm really tired," she told Sylvie. "I'm going to bed." There were only two places to sleep on the boat, Josée's bedroom and the delicate, perfect little-girl's room, the shrine to Andrée. She chose the latter, closing the door against the music.

Minutes later, there was a knock. Éric pushed inside, his body up against hers, and closed the door behind him.

"You're all grown up," he said.

She stepped back, pleading exhaustion. But he grabbed her shoulder and pulled her to him in a kiss.

"Your girlfriend," she said.

"She doesn't mind," he said, pulling at her clothes.

"But I do," she said, more forcefully now. He backed her toward the bed.

"Shh," he said. "I know you've always been in love with me."

"The idea of you," she said. "Please, let me keep my illusions."

"You'll enjoy it once we begin," he said.

But she didn't. She kept her head turned to the side. Her eyes were on the nightstand, on her ticket to New York.

chapter five

Françoise stood alone on the sidewalk on West Thirty-Fourth Street, suitcase in hand. Her mother had warned her never to take a taxi in New York—thieves would open the door at red lights and cut off her hand with a machete to steal her rings. With about forty dollars to her name, Françoise had thought there was little danger of her taking a taxi. But the woman who'd sat next to her on the plane had insisted on giving her a ride in her cab from the airport.

On the flight over, the woman had peppered Françoise with questions. Where was she going? What would she do in New York? Did she have a job? Did she have a boyfriend? In turn, the woman disclosed so much about herself over the course of the plane ride that by the time they landed, Françoise knew as much about her as she knew about her closest friends. Françoise had been shocked by the immediate intimacy. Why would a stranger ask her if she had a boyfriend or volunteer that she herself did not? Those were private matters. But she'd done her best to answer, in her staggered English. No, she had no plan in New York, no boyfriend, no job, no permanent place to stay. She watched the woman's eyes grow wide with worry, and the reality of her journey settled around her for the first time.

The woman explained how the city worked. The avenues went up and down, even numbers up, odd numbers down, and the streets went sideways. "Except in Greenwich Village," she continued. "You *must* go see Greenwich Village! It's a little like Paris." *Why would she want to go see something that looked like Paris,* Françoise thought, *when she wanted to get as far away from Paris as possible?*

She'd circled the cheapest youth hostel in her guidebook and written a letter requesting a reservation. "Dear Sir or Madam," it began, followed by phrases she'd copied diligently from a textbook.

Now, standing on the sidewalk before it, she craned her neck and the building stretched above her, disappearing into a point, like in the movies.

Inside, a dingy hallway. Men loitered, looked up at her in silence as she passed. To the left were service windows with bars across them, like in a post office. There was no lobby. This was a strange sort of hostel, she thought. She walked up to a dour black woman sitting behind the counter. She had been practicing what she would say for weeks now; this was as far as she had planned her journey.

"Hello, I have made a reservation for a room. My name is—"

"*Whaddayawan!*" the woman interrupted.

"Hello, I have made a reservation for a room—" Françoise began again.

"*Gway!*" the woman said.

Françoise tried to show her a carbon copy of the letter. The woman glanced at it, pushed it back.

"*Notteere, gway,*" she said, shooing Françoise toward the door.

"*Euh,* I have made a reservation for tonight?" Françoise repeated.

The woman called a balding white man out into the hallway.

"What seems to be the problem here?" he said. He seemed to be the manager, and yet he was not wearing a suit. Françoise repeated her carefully rehearsed speech.

"This. Is. Not. For. Women," he told her, putting his hands on top of each other and slicing them sharply apart to punctuate the word "not." "This. Is. The. YMCA. The YMCA."

"Yes," Françoise said, pulling out her guidebook and showing him that she'd circled it.

"There. Are. *No.* Women. Here," he repeated. "No. Women. Go somewhere else."

The streets were dark. It was too late to find another hostel. She had made a reservation. "I stay *here*," she said. "I have no place to go. I can pay for one room."

"We have *one* floor for women," he said, holding up a finger, "but it is full tonight. We cannot give you a room there."

"But I *must* stay tonight," she repeated, making it true.

"Okay," he said, conceding. "Okay. Maybe we will be able to move you to the women's floor tomorrow. Tonight, we are going to put you on a floor where there are usually no women. What we are going to have to do is, we will have to lock you in the room and you cannot go into the hallway or the bathroom. Okay?" He turned an invisible key in the air as he spoke.

The manager left and returned with two armed guards. They walked Françoise down the hallway to the elevators. At the tenth floor, the manager pushed the emergency button and blocked the doors open. "Wait in here," he told her. The guards began to pace the hallways, barking orders to the men on the floor to go into their rooms, locking their doors behind them. When the territory had been cleared, the manager walked Françoise to her room.

There was space only for a single bed and a desk. A barred window looked down onto a sliver of alleyway.

"Put your suitcase down," the manager said. "I'll take you to the bathroom now."

They took the elevator to the women's floor. The three men waited outside the bathroom.

A few older women stood at the sinks. One was blow-drying her hair, which she seemed to have washed in the sink. Were there no showers? Another, dressed in rags, sang to herself loudly and tunelessly as she scrubbed at a pair of underwear with a toothbrush and toothpaste. Did they have special toothpaste in America? Did these women *live* here?

The doors to the toilet stalls ended a foot short of the floor. Françoise felt exposed. Her feet showed and the sounds she made drifted out into the room. Were all the bathrooms in America like this?

"It was like going to the bathroom in an open stall on an airplane," my mother told me. "Americans are so prudish and the French walk around stark naked, but at least we close ourselves into a room to piss and shit."

The guards led Françoise back to her room. Were they worried that she was some sort of nymphomaniac? They closed the door behind her and she heard the key turn in the lock. *Merde,* she thought, flooded with fear. What was she doing here?

I need to write this down, she thought, but her arm was too heavy to reach for her notebook. She was exhausted. She fell asleep clutching the only comforting thought she could find: *Don't worry, you'll remember this.*

And she did. When my mother told me about arriving in New York, her narration broke through a fog. Those first forty-eight hours—the manager's faded yellow T-shirt, the creaking of the bedsprings—were crisp and clear.

The next morning, the manager moved her to the women's floor and gave her her own key. There was a cot, a worn and dirty dresser, a small window that looked out on all the other windows. Lost women, each in their small cells. *What now?* she thought after she had unpacked. *Now I go outside,* she told herself. Outside, she hesitated. Right or left? She turned right and walked west toward the Meatpacking District, with its low-slung industrial buildings, toward the entrance to the Lincoln Tunnel. Turning left would have brought her to Fifth Avenue, with its huge, glossy shop windows, but she didn't know that then. The sun was fierce and sharp shadows cast the city into vivid relief. The sidewalks were wide and the streets were filled with potholes. Taxis sped down the broken asphalt, careening and chaotic. The few people she passed walked briskly, their heads down. The phrase *time is money, time is money* kept pounding through her head. Paris was a city of café terraces and sidelong glances. There, the sidewalk was a constant runway. Here, no one looked at her. She was invisible. The anonymity filled her with her power. *I could die,* she thought, *and no one would know for months.* She had spoken to no one and was carrying no ID. It would be difficult to connect her body to the room at the YMCA. She could die, and her mother would not know. She felt elated. If she chose to live, it was only for herself. She carefully retraced her steps back to her room.

FRANÇOISE UNRAVELED NEW YORK—pecan pie, the Staten Island Ferry, coffee out of paper cups, waitresses who called you "honey," and strangers who asked for directions without saying hello. She'd imagined a city like Frankfurt, smooth and modern, but New York was held together with rubber bands and Scotch tape. The subway rattled so loudly as it pulled into the station that you could scream and no one would hear you. She fell in love with the city, in all its grittiness and anonymity.

After ten days at the YMCA, she found herself a shared room at the Markle Evangeline Residence for young workingwomen in the West Village. Her roommate helped her find a job selling candy and cigarettes from a street kiosk.

The Greek who owned the kiosks was named Dimitri, but he told everyone to call him Dennis. Too late, Françoise realized that she could have picked a new name for herself here as well. Dennis showed her how to lift the heavy metal grate and work the cash register. She worked mornings, six to noon, quickly moving up from Dennis's Twenty-Third Street kiosk to his most heavily trafficked corner in Grand Central. Soon she realized she was putting her hand on the right cigarettes before customers even told her which brand. Construction workers smoked Lucky Strikes, other blue-collar workers smoked Parliaments, secretaries smoked Mores. Françoise spoke to almost no one all day long, and her powers of observation sharpened.

In the afternoons she worked in a Japanese architecture firm, making Plexiglass models. Within a few weeks, she had enough money to move out of the Evangeline into a small room in an apartment that she found through *The Village Voice*, an apartment without curfews or vigilant matrons. Her roommate was a young woman from the Midwest who taught middle school in the Bronx. She had faded blond hair and heavy bags beneath her eyes, but she appeared fairly normal at first. Over the next months, however, she became crazier and crazier.

"And today they set fire to the tables!" she would launch in the second Françoise walked in the door. "And this kid had a knife! And I went! And I told him, 'You have a knife! You have a knife! I am your teacher, give me the knife!' And he put the knife to my throat! And the other kids were all around me! And they were jumping and screaming! And they were laughing at me! And they were going to cut me! And I jumped on a chair! And—"

Eventually, Françoise would retreat to her room and close the door. She could hear her roommate outside, calling the toll-free numbers listed on infomercials and telling her story to the operators until they hung up on her.

"You should go home," Françoise would tell her. "You should go home." But her roommate wasn't listening.

The only person Françoise could express herself to was a thirty-year-old German architect named Meister, who taught at NYU; one of her professors in Paris had given her his number. Meister had an aristocratic nose and spoke perfect French. Françoise narrated her life to him once a week over lunch. When she told him how she'd arrived at the YMCA he laughed, forcing her to laugh at the story as well.

"My whole life is downhill from here," she told him one afternoon. "There's nothing left for me to discover."

"How old are you again?" he asked.

"Almost nineteen," she replied, "and I know it sounds funny to you but it's true. I've passed the climax of my life and all I can do is repeat myself."

"So when was the climax of your life, you wizened old cynic?" he asked.

"When I was fifteen," Françoise replied, "and ready to die for the right to smoke in the courtyard." This time she refused to smile at his gentle mocking.

"And now," I asked my mother, "now how would you answer that question?"

"When I became a mother," she replied without hesitation.

IN HIGH SCHOOL, I unraveled New York for myself. It did not occur to me that my mother had walked these same downtown streets that pulsed with a wild, lawless silence at three a.m. It did not occur to me that my transgressions were not revolutionary. I drank wine and smoked cigars on the Brooklyn Bridge, peeing down through the wooden slats onto the cars below. I stole brandy out of my photography teacher's supply closet and threw it up in Park Slope. I cut class to smoke pot on the piers that overlooked the Hudson River. When I stumbled home drunk, my mother gave me tighter and tighter curfews. She insisted I was asking for boundaries. I insisted I was discovering where my boundaries were.

One Valentine's Day, two friends and I convinced a man outside a liquor store to buy us a bottle of tequila. We bought limes and salt from the corner deli by my father's studio and wandered through the winding streets of the West Village, rotating the three—we'd suck the back of our hand between thumb and index finger so that the salt would stick, sprinkle it on, suck it off, swig the tequila, then bite into a wedge of lime. The bottle was finished before we knew it, and then we were staggering through an Indian restaurant, patrons staring, so that we could throw up in the bathrooms, and then we were sitting on the sidewalk, one friend bent over my shoes, gagging, and then we were in a cop car, sirens blaring, my friend throwing up all over the inside of the door. Our other friend came in a separate cop car, a policeman sitting in the back with her, massaging her inner thigh. They kept us for hours in their precinct office, one friend cursing violently enough to get herself handcuffed to the chair, the other sobbing that now she would never get into college. I refused to give them my mother's phone number.

"If you were my children . . . ," the cop who manned the phones kept saying. "If you were my children, I would whip you bloody black-and-blue with a studded belt until you'd learned a damn lesson."

We all gave them the phone numbers in the end. It was that or spend the night in a cell. Still, I trembled when the cop told us that our parents were in the other room.

"Can't see them just yet," he said, sneering. "We're showing them how to use the belt."

But when my mother saw me she hugged me, hard. She pulled me under the cloak of her fierce love and swept me out of the precinct. We piled into the car with my sleepy little brother.

"You're not mad?" I asked. "I'm not punished forever?"

"No," she said. "I think you've gone through enough for one night. And I don't think you'll make that mistake again."

Years later, I told her how grateful I'd been, and also how confused. A bottle of wine stolen from the kitchen had led to screaming fights that left us both hoarse. But about this, she had never been angry, not even the next day.

She laughed. "Your friend's father was furious with me," she told me. "In the waiting room, he kept implying that my terrible daughter had corrupted his innocent one. And I knew that maybe he was a little bit right. You hadn't simply followed along with some other girls like a sheep. You were always your own person. I was . . . I can tell you now . . . I was a little bit proud of you."

I'D THOUGHT IT would be embarrassing to go to college never having kissed a girl, the way other people might have thought it important to lose their virginity. The gay boys and lesbians were the coolest kids in my high school, with their pink and blue hair and candy necklaces. We all considered ourselves a little bit gay. Even Zane had had a crush on a boy and joked about it often, not really joking.

I was still nursing the heart he'd broken when I learned that a girl I'd rarely spoken to had a crush on me. This was a novelty for me, that someone might find me appealing from afar. She and I began talking on AIM at night and passing notes during the day. One day, we walked together down to the first floor, where the stairwell widened. She asked if I had ever kissed a girl before. I said I hadn't and shuffled my feet. I knew she had kissed many. She talked vaguely about "the right moment for things." She said, "Well then, I guess . . . I'll just . . ." The kiss shot through my body like a sugar rush.

"Maman, Papa!" I said, bursting into their bedroom one morning a few days later. "Guess what? I have a girlfriend!" They had gay friends. They had watched me mope for months. It didn't occur to me that they'd be anything other than pleased.

My father slowly folded down the top of *The New York Times.*

"How *modern* of you," he said, eyeing me coolly over the paper. My mother said nothing at all.

Wendy wore boxers and walked like a boy, which I liked,

although I also liked how small she was in my arms, how soft her lips were, how big and cartoonish her eyes became when she looked up at me. When she touched me, I discovered, through her hands and mouth and desire, a body I had not known I had. Sex with her made my thoughts stop. I walked around in a fog. I slipped into cosmetics stores just to smell the men's cologne she wore. I never questioned whether my attraction to her meant I myself had changed.

I did not come out to my friends; I simply began holding Wendy's hand in the hallways. A few people tried to ask me about it, hesitant questions filled with ellipses. There were several openly gay students, but we were the only couple. *Yes,* I said firmly. *I'm dating her.* I willfully ignored their real question.

One afternoon early on, Wendy brought me to the LGBTQ center on Fourteenth Street, where she had spent a lot of time. Under fluorescent lights in a grim upstairs room, we were asked to go in a circle and say why we were proud to be gay. My heart raced. I did not think of myself as gay. I did not see why I should be proud.

My pediatrician had her hand on my abdomen, pressing down. She casually asked me if I was sexually active. I said yes. "Are you using protection?" she asked. I said no and she pulled her hand away in surprise. I mumbled that I was dating a woman. She sat me down in her office chair and looked at me seriously, arms on her knees. "I know people who are gay," she said. "And I've known you since you were a child. You are not gay."

I suspected that this was how my mother felt as well. She rarely slipped in what she said to me, but her discomfort was palpable. I quickly learned that whenever I said I was going to see

Wendy, she found a reason to keep me home. I began to say I was seeing other friends, tossing their names out in rotation, but in truth I saw my friends less and less. Wendy loved me with a ferocity and neediness that I found bracing. I had worried that I had too much love inside me, that I would drown people in it until they pushed me away. But with Wendy, I poured and poured. It was never enough. She hinted at notebooks filled with poems written about me before we'd ever spoken. She worried that I was straight, and so I hid my own worries and reassured her. When we fought, red cuts appeared on her forearms the next day. Her parents had very little money, and she often implied that I thought she was not good enough for me for this reason. I found myself trapped in endless loops of "No, I love you more," unable to hang up the phone. We both knew she loved me more.

One evening, we were doing our homework together in my room. I heard the front door slam shut, the beleaguered *"Bonsoir"* shouted through the loft as my mother shifted her heavy backpack off her shoulders. I braced myself. Usually, I instinctively made Wendy leave before she returned. But this evening I hoped to prove myself wrong.

"Hi, Wendy," my mother said as she walked into my room, her tone far from friendly. "Nadja, can I talk to you alone for a minute?"

In the kitchen, she told me Wendy could not stay for dinner. I was to go tell her to leave right now. We fought loudly in French but I did not win. I walked Wendy to the train. When I returned, there was a note on my computer. "I just wanted to write my essay in peace (without dinner) but alas I have been booted off the island," it read. I sighed, feeling besieged from all sides, and shut the document.

"Nadja," my mother called me back into the kitchen. "When you walk her to the train . . . you don't kiss her on Canal Street, right? Please promise me you never will."

"The world has changed," I said. "It's not the seventies anymore." When my parents thought I was not listening, I could hear them discussing the phase I was going through.

"It's better not to add fuel to the fire," I heard my father tell my mother gently one evening.

In later years, I would find fast intimacy with many new friends through exchanging our coming-out stories. Their stories, filled with pain and courage, moved me deeply. My own—my father's folded newspaper, his quip—seemed cavalier in comparison. My friends often asked me then a second question, one I did not know how to answer: *When did you come out to yourself?* I told them I had not. I had felt no moments of anxiety. I had been granted—by my parents, my city, my high school—the easy fluidity of a girl raised without shame. I knew how precious it was, that freedom to fall in love with whomever I pleased, and I was grateful for it. I did not want to limit myself to categories. My identity had never changed.

But one evening in my late twenties, as I sat on the floor of my childhood bedroom, journals and diaries piled around me, I discovered a completely different narrative. There, in a diary from middle school, an unhappy entry about my crush on my best friend. There, copied out lovingly in my thirteen-year-old hand, the lyrics to a song in a lesbian movie I now remembered sneaking into a stack at the video rental store. There, in the notebook I had obsessively kept while I was dating Zane, forgotten words scrawled across two pages: *Who are you trying to fool?* I had written to myself. *YOU'RE GAY.* I tucked that version of my past back into the boxes with my notebooks. I continued to tell my story as I always had.

I kissed Wendy on Canal Street. I kissed her in the school hall-ways and on the subway. Teachers who had smiled benignly when I kissed my boyfriend now stopped to ask us why we weren't ashamed. On the subway, a group of women began to chant, "Dicks not chicks, pussies are disgusting."

"I'm sick of this homo shit," one screamed from across the train car as we continued to kiss each other.

"It's just internalized oppression," Wendy whispered to me, because these were women, and people of color. I blinked back tears and kissed her again.

One spring afternoon, Wendy and I were sitting on a down-town stoop with our knees touching, holding hands. I grinned at something Wendy said and she leaned over to kiss the dimple in my cheek. I looked up. A beautiful older woman in overalls had turned her head to stare at us as she walked past. She had long gray hair to her waist. She was beaming. I held her gaze. It was a smile like I had never received from a stranger. I didn't under-stand, and then I did. I understood what it meant to feel proud.

FRANÇOISE WANDERED ever further downtown. After respond-ing to a flyer on a lamppost, she found herself cast in a play by the avant-garde playwright Richard Foreman. She stood still for hours onstage, shifting poses only once or twice, repeating lines from novels. She had three jobs now—cigarettes in the mornings, archi-tecture in the afternoons, Foreman in the evenings. Her father lent her the key money to rent a loft in SoHo. I have her letter to him from then, the SoHo she exuberantly describes totally different from the SoHo I grew up in, with its high-end designer shops. "It's

2,000 square feet (180 m2) and $250 a month—which is *relatively* cheap," she wrote. "Some of the other spaces I visited were $400!"

Françoise's loft had been a sweatshop, and you could see straight from the set of three windows on one side to the other set half a block away. It was only barely legal to live in the abandoned factories downtown, and though she paid rent to the Italian man who owned the lumber shop next door, she kept the windows covered with cardboard at night. She had a mattress, a hot plate, and a radio. There was a big industrial sink and toilets in stalls, one of which had been converted to a shower. She left at five every morning, and when she came back at eleven each night, she set about making a new floor over the old one, with planks her landlord sold her. She was happy. She felt herself living.

"IT WAS DIFFICULT for me when you started growing up," my mother told me. "I wanted to freeze time so I could keep a baby version of you in my pocket. I remember a conversation I had with my father. He told me to be excited. He said there was a whole new phase to enter when you begin discovering your children as people."

My mother employed, over the years, a long string of recent college graduates. As I grew up, her assistants went from being breathtakingly cool older girls, on whom I took field notes in an eight-year-old scrawl in my diaries, to friends of mine, hired on my recommendation. My mother ran her children's book publishing company from the same dusty book-piled office out of which she and my father had once created their underground comics magazine, *RAW*. It was on the ground floor of our building. The machinery was still there—the massive paper cutter with a steering wheel and guillotine, the typesetting drawers, the light table—amid the new iMac computers. The furniture had barely changed since the early 1980s. My mother functioned with a very small staff, training them thoroughly, paying them modestly, resigned to letting them move on after a year or two.

After college, I took a job at a Jewish newspaper. I was unhappy there in the way presumptuous young people often are in their first jobs. I believed I could see all of the company's dysfunction and the solutions to it. Yet, despite my extraordinarily clear memos, my superiors refused to let me overhaul the organization. The offices were in the Financial District, an area of Manhattan I hadn't known well before. I disliked the constant throng of men and women in business suits, the abundance of grim, quick lunch places, the narrow streets and tall buildings that blotted out the sky. Sometimes, after work, rather than returning to my apartment in Brooklyn, I would walk uptown to SoHo, the sky opening up along an underdeveloped stretch of Broadway, and have dinner with my parents. Over Chinese food, my mother would respond to each of my complaints with suggestions that I now thought of, in my new work vocabulary, as "actionable." Occasionally she provided me with the precise tactful wording for an email while I scrawled in a notebook. She piled me high with praise. I left feeling invincible, wrapped in a glowing cocoon. But the next morning, back under the fluorescent lights of my cubicle, the feeling would inevitably fade.

A year and a half after I had graduated, my mother offered to hire me. It seemed a simultaneously wonderful and terrible idea. At the newspaper, I asked for a raise I strongly suspected would be refused. "It warms my heart to see a young woman asking for a raise," said the female editor in chief. "But no." I quit.

In comparison, working for my mother was idyllic. She loaded me with as much responsibility as I could handle. I was assigned tasks that ranged from helping to shape the stories to negotiating the price of paper in China, and I felt I was learning constantly. She listened carefully to my suggestions, praised me only when I had worked very hard, and scolded me on days when I hadn't. I had heard the complaints from friends who had worked for her before me—that she was volatile, that her anger was often out of proportion to the mistake—but I was used to these things in my mother.

There were days when the purple under her eyes was deeper than usual—when, say, all the fall books were due at the printer and, on top of it, *The New Yorker* cover was going through a last-minute change. She let out huge French huffs of frustration, slammed the table with her fist when a pen fell on the floor. The other employees became skittish. But I knew how to calm her. I spoke gently, put a cup of coffee in her hand, hugged her until we got back on track.

There were days when she pulled out my old baby clothes at morning meetings and told stories about my bowel movements, and days when she scolded me like I was fifteen for not emptying the grounds from the coffee machine. But later, privately, she listened to me and apologized. More often there were days when we sat side by side in front of manuscripts, each with a red pen in hand, riffing on each other's ideas, each of us feeling the excitement as a story fell into place. I learned a new kind of awe for my mother. She knew how to edit images with the same ease that others could tweak sentences. She would alter small details and, as if by magic, the meaning of a picture would snap into focus.

She shaped each project around each artist's strengths, so that their visions shone through and her own efforts remained invisible. She worked constantly with her hands—printing, cutting, taping manuscripts in place. She gave of herself to her projects without any sense of self-preservation. She never settled for good enough. She drew on every last reserve of her energy until each book was best-it-could-be, and knew, too, when that was. Often the staff came into the office in the morning to discover that overnight she had made entirely new designs, new layouts, new covers. She would lay out our assignments for the day, then leave for her job at *The New Yorker*. When she returned, at seven or eight p.m., she would again sit for hours, tweaking and fixing our work, always easy with her praise, always in places it felt deserved.

I began to understand why, when my brother and I were young, coming home to a dinner still unmade, a table still unset, my socks on the bathroom floor had made her explode into such fireworks of frustration and fury. I envied how few minutes she lost of each day. Even her train rides to and from her Times Square office were time she spent thinking about her work. I struggled to imitate her and yet could not stem the slipping away of my own hours into periods of blankness, lapses of mindlessness when I blinked to discover I had overspent my lunch hour on our stoop, staring into the sunshine, watching the models and tourists walk by, merely happy to be alive.

FRANÇOISE'S FATHER came to visit her in New York in March, on his way to St. Barths. He asked to meet her friends. Françoise had a party, and as the loft filled up with her new friends, she was surprised at how many there were. Paul schmoozed happily with the crowd. He radiated pride for his daughter and her space.

Her mother came to visit in June, with Louis Guérin still in tow. She was also, suspiciously, on her way to St. Barths. The second that Josée stepped into the apartment, it lost its luster. Everything—the salvaged posters and flyers, the furniture scavenged from the street—seemed to shrink. Everything seemed to be covered in dust.

"You're living *here?*" Josée said. "The neighborhood is awful. You don't even have a chair. Why don't you come live on my house boat? You'll be much better off. Don't you miss Paris?" She reminded Françoise that her return ticket was valid for only a year. Besides, Josée said, SoHo was not safe. She pointed out that Françoise had been robbed a few weeks before.

Even after Josée's departure, the magic did not return to the loft. Her mother had transformed it from an enchanted fortress into a barren foam mattress and a rusty hot plate. She didn't even have a chair. Although it would never have occurred to her to ask to move in with her mother—had never seemed that her mother might want her there—now that she had offered, the draw was irresistible. Paris glittered through her mother's words: the Seine, the quiet streets now held a nostalgia she'd never felt before. Here was Françoise's chance to have a relationship with her mother. She booked her flight home.

THERE WAS THAT CLICHÉ about how people kissed the ground when their plane landed. Josée said she had seen that once, long ago, when she was a flight attendant, bringing the first Jews from

America over to Israel: bent over in their winter furs, kissing the sticky-hot tarmac. But when Françoise landed in Paris, exactly a year after leaving, kissing the ground was the last thing she wanted to do. She felt like a magnet polarized to repel.

In the airport, Paul was waiting for her by the gate. When they reached the arrivals area, Jean-Michel ran up to them with a bouquet of flowers. "You go home with him and I'll never speak to you again," Paul threatened.

"You go home with him and I'll never speak to you again," Jean-Michel shot back.

Françoise hated being forced to choose between the two men, but it was her father, not Jean-Michel, whom she'd asked to come get her, and so her decision was made.

Paul drove her to his place. He'd invited a young surgeon, his protégé, to lunch.

"Why don't you put your things away?" Paul said, gesturing toward Andrée's room.

"Actually," Françoise told him, choosing her words carefully, "Josée offered that I could stay on the boat with her for a while . . ."

"What? You're going to go live with that bastard whore?" Paul asked, veins popping with instant rage. He ordered her to leave immediately. Françoise, too tired for emotions, picked up her suitcase again. The young surgeon offered to drive her to her mother's.

"You know," he said to Françoise in the car, "you have very beautiful eyes."

"Thank you," Françoise said.

"You really could be quite pretty if you just tweezed a bit, between your eyebrows," he said. "They're conjoined."

On her mother's boat, a luncheon party was in full swing.

Josée turned to greet her with a warm "Ah, there she is!" She explained to her friends, in exaggerated detail, how she'd saved her poor daughter from a rat-infested hovel in the dingiest part of New York City.

After the guests departed, they fought all evening. Françoise barely lasted the night. She had forgotten how few defenses she had against her mother. In the morning, Françoise repacked her suitcase and left, unsure where to go.

A friend from architecture school offered her the couch in the beautiful, light-filled duplex her mother had just bought for her. She was a gracious host, but she had just found herself a boyfriend, and the apartment had few walls and little privacy to offer. From the couch, Françoise listened to the two of them laughing in bed together. She stared up at the high ceiling and struggled to sleep, embarrassment burning hot in her stomach. She felt like an overlay on the world rather than a part of it. The small hole she had once made in the fabric of the city had been filled in without a trace. Paris had erased its memories of her.

WE WERE IN THE KITCHEN TOGETHER, my mother and I, our bodies moving in synchronicity. She stirred the pan I had placed on the flame, I cut the onions she would need before she thought to reach for them.

"Can I help?" my brother asked as he opened the fridge to get himself a glass of water. He had started college this year and I had just finished it. Each time I saw him he was more of a man. He had a beard now, torn pants that slouched low on his hips, muscles that rippled up his arms. I wondered what it would be like to become taller than my mother. I envied him that.

He sat on one of the stools where we'd eaten breakfast as children, and his knees danced up against the edge of the counter. "Can I ask you for your advice on something, Nadja?" he said as he popped his thumb into a grapefruit to peel it.

As a younger child, my brother had believed me to be the ultimate authority on a great many things. After school in our living room, my friends and I had sorted out our understanding of women's rights by lecturing him. *Do* buy her flowers, but don't hold open the doors. *Do* pay for the meal, but also let her pay for yours. Later, he'd hung on my every word as I'd explained about gay rights and trans issues, nodding along, eager to get it right. "What about *me* though?" he'd said in despair. I told him he had it easiest, but it seemed to bring him little comfort. My sweet, conscientious brother wore his straight white male privilege like an albatross.

That past winter, during a trip he and I had taken to Berlin, he had realized with a violent jolt that I wasn't the perfect older sister he had imagined me to be. I could be uncool, I could make mistakes, I could lead us both, unwittingly, into danger. I don't know which of us this hurt more. Now we were building a wary new relationship. I leapt at the invitation to give advice.

"So I *know* you're not supposed to hook up with girls when they're too drunk to say yes," he began. He explained that, at school, there had been many orientation sessions impressing upon the students the importance of consensual sex.

"But what about when I've been drinking, too?" he continued. How many drinks did she have to have before it became not okay? If she'd expressed interest before, and they went out drinking together, was that okay?

I began speaking loudly and authoritatively. I had a lot to say, and I was conscious that my mother was listening, even though her back was turned.

"You can trust yourself," I said. "It's not a hard-and-fast rule that if a girl has had a drink, she's off-limits. But there *are* many men who use alcohol to take advantage of women. Follow your instincts and don't do anything that feels questionable. If you don't think she'll remember it the next day, then wait. If she's repeating the same questions or can't walk correctly, then she's too drunk to consent."

My mother sighed. She wrapped her arms around my brother.

"Oh, my poor little boy!" she said.

"*Why?*" I said, the word coming out more confrontation than question.

"They've gone and made it all so complicated for you!" she said to him, rubbing his back as he leaned into her. "You poor thing."

My anger rose sharply. I tried to tell my mother that she couldn't possibly understand the binge-drinking culture in American universities. I tried to tell her about the many young women I'd known who'd woken up in unfamiliar beds with bruises blooming on their thighs and the knowledge that their bodies were no longer safe.

My mother and my brother were still touching, his head on her shoulder. I was still talking about frat parties and roofies and grain alcohol, but then my voice was cracking. I put down the knife I was holding. I felt aware of my own melodrama, and in equal measure I both wanted and did not want my mother to see it.

"I can't talk about this right now," I said and pushed past them. I made it to my room before I began to cry, but left the door open as I began to do so, with air-gulping, shoulder-shaking sobs.

My mother's footsteps soon followed. "Oh, Nadja," she said,

sinking down to the floor next to me, "what on earth is wrong?" I kept my head on my knees.

"Did . . . something happen to you, *mon poussin*?" she asked with infinite tenderness. She put her arm around my back and brushed the curls away from my neck. I wished in that moment that something had. It would be so much easier to explain.

She'd been admonishing me since I was twelve. Wear higher collars, say no more forcefully, if it bothers you just ignore it. All I had ever wanted was her anger on my behalf. I'd wanted that hug she gave my brother. I'd wanted that *Oh, my poor little girl*. I still wanted it, so badly.

"Sometimes you're just so . . . unfeminist," I said.

"Oh, *mon amour*," she said. "It's not that simple . . . These young girls of today . . . they allow their whole lives to be ruined. They decide that they're the victims, they decide that they're damaged."

"They *are* victims," I said. "It's a terrible crime."

"Maybe, but . . . practically? What good does it do them?"

She was looking at me earnestly but I couldn't think of anything I hadn't already said twice. I felt a gulf yawn between us and a swimming feeling, like vertigo, at the impossibility of changing her mind.

"You know," she said, after a long pause, "I suppose you could say that it happened to me once. In a sense."

"With Éric?" I asked. "Before you left for New York?"

"Oh no!" she said, surprised. "No, no. *That* wasn't . . . no," she said. "Another time."

BACK IN PARIS, Françoise returned to architecture school half-heartedly. She had rented herself a tiny maid's room in a desolate neighborhood, far from everyone she knew. She was suffocating in self-loathing. Every outfit seemed to clash. She dragged herself to parties but her thoughts drowned out the buzz of the room. No matter what she did, she couldn't escape a constant longing to be someone else, somewhere else. Doing anything was excruciating. Doing nothing was excruciating.

She continued to go to the Aquarelle, the café where she and Jean-Michel had always gone, a few streets from the Beaux-Arts. The same people were there, talking about the same things. She felt like screaming. She had changed profoundly, and they didn't even seem to notice. She needed something new, broader circles, different people. She wanted to expand Paris for herself, approaching everything with the same sense of adventure she had felt in New York. There was an old Greek man who was a regular at the café. He was in his fifties, twice the age of any of the students. He was fat and unattractive, neither quick nor witty, but the students tolerated him interjecting in their conversations from time to time. He cornered Françoise one afternoon and told her about his records. He had a huge collection of records. Come and see them, he said.

He didn't live close by, but she went anyway. It was public enough. They knew so many people in common. They saw each other every day.

He locked the door from the inside. It hadn't occurred to her that there could be a situation where she wouldn't be able to fight someone off. That was a surprise. She had thought of herself as strong. But when it became clear what was physically inevitable, she played dead. It interested him much less that way. It was over quickly.

My god, she thought, *how pathetic.* It wasn't as bad as she'd feared. It was just her body. It was easy enough to leave her body.

How stupid of her it had been, she thought later, to go to his house. Lesson learned. From now on, she wouldn't go to someone's house unless she was sure she wanted to have sex. But she wasn't going to let one unpleasant experience change her. He didn't deserve such power. It was years before she spoke of the incident to anyone.

She told me this calmly. She seemed more worried about my reactions than her own. But I wasn't reacting. I felt numb all over. My thoughts were replaced by a buzz like the low hum of a generator.

"*Mais, Maman,*" I said, "he had no right to do that to you." Even with the rest of me shut down, the words jerked out of my mouth automatically.

"It was my responsibility to know better," she replied.

"It wasn't your fault," I said. Though I wondered what good it could possibly do her to acknowledge all the anger and hurt I felt she should feel.

"Fault and responsibility aren't the same thing," she said. "It was my responsibility. It was much more traumatic when someone broke into my loft and stole my radio. That was my *space*. I didn't particularly want to have sex with Meister either but—"

"You slept with Meister?" I said.

"Of course," she said. "I admired him, intellectually, as a mentor, so it was . . . okay. It was fine. I waited for it to be over so that we could go back to talking. The Greek guy, though, he repulsed me, physically. But mostly it was just a revelation—there were people who needed to force others to have sex with them. I felt bad for him."

I could feel how stiff my body had gone and knew that I was

glaring at her. I was furious. With the Greek guy. With myself. With her.

"Come here," she said and pulled me into her arms. "I'm sorry," she said. "I'm so sorry. My poor girl."

"Why?" I said miserably. "Why should *you* be sorry?"

"Because," she said, "I'm your mother. I'm supposed to protect you from all this."

In Paris, Françoise sank into a deep depression. She spent days without leaving her small maid's room. It was dark and cramped. The ceiling was slanted. There was a twin bed, a small high window that let in a glimmer of light, and a wooden wall that created a separate area for the sink. The toilet was down the hall. She sat on the floor, staring at the wall by the sink that unnecessarily divided her small apartment. She needed open space. She needed to breathe. She could think of nothing but tearing down that wall. She sketched an architectural plan. She would turn the sink into a bathtub, install a hot plate, create a kitchen.

But she didn't own the room, she kept reminding herself. She couldn't tear down the wall.

One day, there was no longer a choice. With a hammer and an X-Acto knife, she forced a window into the wall. It looked awful. The edges were jagged and the floor was covered in splinters. The landlord would be furious. Françoise sat down in the corner, shaking. She was still holding the X-Acto knife, and she pressed it now to her wrist. Her body resisted her. She breathed deeply and steadied her arm. She pushed harder, as hard as she could, using her right hand to cut across her left wrist. A bead of blood appeared, and then another, until blood trickled across her arm. She thought about leaving a note, but what would it say? *I'm killing myself because I made a hole in the wall*? She pressed down harder and more blood came. But she was still in her head, watching herself. "Harder," she coached herself, mumbling the words. "Harder than that." But she couldn't make the knife slice through to her veins.

I can't even kill myself, she thought. She threw her head back against the wall and shut her eyes, drifting off to sleep in the splinters of her room.

My mother told me about trying to cut her wrists late one night in her children's book office, on the ground floor of our four-story building. I was still in college then and still eager to prove myself. Her voice was unwavering, and her tone resigned yet matter-of-fact. I tried to match her. I was tough, I wasn't shocked, I looked her in the eyes. I asked her if she knew then that you have to cut your wrists in a vertical line, straight up your forearm, not horizontally across. She looked at me, surprised, and said she hadn't. It was information I'd inhaled like New York City smog. How to cut your wrists, how to create dreadlocks, how to slip keys between your fingers to make brass knuckles—these were just things you absorbed in high school. I shrugged and she continued, almost conspiratorially, describing the details, the blade pushing its way through her skin. I barely flinched. But later, writing about it, my hands cramped up and I sucked in sharp air through my teeth. I paused every few words to rub away the ache in my wrists.

FRANÇOISE LEFT PARIS four months after she'd arrived. In her dreary maid's room she'd stared at the ruined wall and dreamed of her loft as it had been when she first moved in: the spacious rush of freedom, the honking of the cars outside on Canal Street, the wooden floors she'd laid herself stretching half a city block. But when she returned to New York, her loft was still the shattered illusion she had left behind: the loft as her mother had seen it. The light was gray and meager now, whole swaths of the center of the space left dark. She'd given up her job selling cigarettes, her job at the architecture firm, in the avant-garde plays. She could have tried to get them back, but she couldn't find the courage. She had a few odd jobs but she went less and less often. Instead she huddled by the industrial gas blower in her sleeping bag, trying to stay warm.

At first, her phone rang sometimes. It had a jarring, insistent jangle. She stared at it until it stopped ringing, until eventually her friends stopped calling.

She slept eighteen hours a day. She hardly ever left the house. When she was awake, she read from a dense philosophy textbook. Heidegger, Nietzsche, Kierkegaard. The letters swam and rearranged themselves. She read certain pages over and over, until ideas pierced her with astounding clarity, then left her devastated. She couldn't tell if the text had begun to make more sense or if she was beginning to make less. She ran out of food. She ate raw oats by the handful. She began to write letters, her hand moving with furious speed, letters addressed to no one, letters that she knew she'd never send.

She knew she was going crazy. *Devenir folle* wasn't just an expression to her. She'd watched her roommate go crazy; she knew what it meant. But she didn't know how to turn back.

One day, she was a triangular metal ruler balanced on its point. A woman's voice sang a wordless opera, holding her in place with its crystalline pitch. She was inside the voice, she was the voice. She knew she was hallucinating and she struggled to open her eyes. But a triangular metal ruler didn't have eyes. It lasted an eternity.

Finally, she forced her eyes open and found she was standing on a street corner a few blocks from the loft. She was between a lamppost and a trash can. She was talking to herself. People were staring. She couldn't remember having left the house.

She looked around wildly at the people passing by. Their eyes were cold and they kept their distance. The anonymity of New York reared up around her, dangerous. She dragged herself back home. She gathered her courage. She called her father. He didn't ask questions. He paid for her plane ticket home.

My MOTHER FOUND one of the letters she'd written that winter alone in New York. It was on delicate translucent paper. It was in that unfamiliar hand, the one that was no longer hers.

I am going to tell you New York—I know in advance that I can't write to you—not now—my head is lost in a storm of sensation—my notion of time reconstructs itself each second— for weeks now I haven't known how to think—I can't do it anymore—I don't know how to write a simple letter—I am going to tell you New York—Nothing that I can say makes sense—it changes at the moment it hits the paper—so I know that what I write is—will be absurd—But I am going to tell you New York—I shouldn't, but I want to write to you—I found your letter today—I just reread your letter—I line up my words—I place one word after the other—Normally that is a way to write—But all this—and the rest in general—is that

*I think I can only know that I lost—all this—thinking of
writing—could only exist if I hadn't lost time—For a few
weeks now—or months—maybe deep down since New
York—but certainly for a few weeks—In this moment—I
have only the instant—the instant from second to second,
from hour to hour, in days and in nights, up until the weeks
and the months—the instant—*

I held the letter carefully. I had recently looked up the etymology of the word "past." It was from the French *pas*, for step, from the Latin *passus*, for a stretch of the leg. In its earliest uses it meant journey. The past, then, was not a fixed place one could visit. It was not static. It was a voyage, constant motion. But this letter, with its manic present tense, reduced that journey to its smallest unit: a single step, a single outstretched leg. It felt like the closest I could get. I pretended it was addressed to me, sent by the girl I'd been searching for.

PAUL LIVED in a bachelor pad now. The apartment's wide wrap-around balcony overlooked the corner of the Seine where a small replica of the Statue of Liberty stood, facing west toward New York. In the living room there was a large zebra-skin rug and a hidden wet bar that turned out from the wall at the push of a button. Blue lights lit the undersides of the black cabinets. Françoise moved into Andrée's room. A parade of her father's girlfriends, all around her own age, greeted Françoise with tousled hair in the mornings as they made themselves coffee.

Paul was trying to lose weight with new diet pills and he

offered them to Françoise. She liked the blitzing rush of energy they gave her, how they cut through the fog. Neither of them knew, or maybe admitted that they knew, that they were taking speed. Françoise wrote manically, filling notebook after notebook. Paul was nearly always gone: at work, at the casino, on dates, on long holiday weekends. Alone in his place, Françoise felt her mind racing, and yet she was unable to outrun her dark thoughts. Everywhere she looked, she saw dead ends. She had lost New York. She had lost everything. She stood on the terrace, looking down at the street below. It was never empty enough. Or perhaps she was simply too cowardly. One May weekend, the answer materialized abruptly. The medicine cabinet. Her father's sleeping pills.

She poured the pills out into her hand. Too few would make her sleep, and too many would make her throw up. She based her calculations on how many she'd seen her father take. It was such a clean, such a comfortable, such an elegant way to die. What a beautiful gift she could give herself.

She stripped down to her underwear and went into her father's room. She pushed the button that rolled up the heavy metal grates that covered the windows. The afternoon sunlight streamed in. She lay on his bed.

Do you realize these are the final moments of your life? she asked herself silently.

I'm just lucky to have such an easy way out, she replied.

She swallowed the handful of pills and lay down on her father's bed to die. She wondered about leaving a note. But a note could be dissected, mangled, and reinterpreted. Her parents would use her words to shift blame. And she was exhausted, too tired to write.

Are you sure you have no regrets? she asked herself sleepily.

No, she thought. *The things I have yet to do don't exist. No regrets.*

She concentrated on the feeling of the covers against her skin. The sunlight seared her eyelids shut. She drifted off.

ORANGE!

Make it stop!

She was tied down. It was violently orange. It had to stop. She had to move. She could hear herself howling.

"If you calm down, we'll untie you." A nurse's gentle voice. Françoise could see her in her peripheral vision.

Make the orange stop! Françoise thrashed as hard as she could against the restraints.

"Your mother is here," said the nurse.

"No! no!" Françoise shouted. She heard the rattling of a gurney's wheels down the hallway of a different hospital, echoing through the years.

"Oh my darling girl, it's so wonderful to see you awake," Josée said.

Françoise's hands pulled against the restraints.

"I saved you, you know," Josée said. "I found you just in time."

"You killed my baby," Françoise said. "You killed my baby."

SATURDAY AFTERNOON, the day before Mother's Day, Josée had been on the roof of her houseboat, gardening. Françoise had tentatively agreed to stop by for dinner on Friday evening but had not come. Josée thought little of her absence. In those days, Françoise often made plans she didn't keep. But as Josée bent to trim a branch, she froze, the shears locked open.

"Maman!" she heard Françoise's voice calling her.

"Did you call me?" Josée turned to ask Andrée. But Andrée was downstairs in the shower.

"Maman!" Françoise's voice called again. It was crystal clear. Josée ran inside.

She pulled Andrée from the shower, her hair still sudsy with shampoo. She made her dial the number of Paul's concierge, then got on the phone herself.

"Is Françoise's motorbike in the courtyard?" Josée asked.

"Yes," the concierge said.

"Go up to the apartment," Josée demanded. The concierge had Paul's keys.

A few moments later, the concierge rang back. "There's no one there," she said. She had shouted Françoise's name into the apartment and no one had answered.

"Go back and look around," Josée demanded. She paced anxiously as she waited. She dialed the concierge again. The phone rang and rang.

"Oh, *Madame*!" the concierge said, finally picking up, out of breath. "She's not! She's not dead!"

Josée dragged Andrée to the car. The paramedics were on the scene when they arrived. There was very little time to spare, they said. Françoise had been dying since Friday afternoon.

My mother's eyes flashed with anger and disbelief as she told me this last part. I could feel her aching for an explanation.

Josée believed in the supernatural. She once told me that ever since a near-death experience waterskiing she'd had a deep connection to the afterlife. Some of her experiences were with the spirits of departing mothers who hadn't been able to say good-bye to their daughters. Sometimes, they were able to tell her their daughters' full names. Josée would call them. Invariably, she'd learn that they'd recently lost their mothers. "She wanted me to tell you she's always been proud of you," she'd say to them.

Andrée would later tell me that after leaving the hospital that day, Josée took her to a movie. There was time to kill before Andrée had to catch her train back to boarding school. They went to see Roman Polanski's *The Tenant*. "What a film to see on such a day," she told me bitterly. "What a film to show your child."

I had not seen the film, so later I looked it up. It was released in France that final week of May 1976. It begins with two people meeting around the hospital bed of a woman who has just attempted suicide. As they flirt, the dying woman, unable to communicate, screams her last. The couple leave the hospital room and go to the movies.

I believed without question in Josée's powerful magic. I was grateful to her. But I knew better than to express this to my mother.

"LAST TIME I was in France," my mother told me at our kitchen table in New York, "I rifled through a book on adolescent suicide in a bookstore." The authors had defined adolescence as the state of being ripped apart by two desires of an equal intensity: to be rid of your parents and to be loved by your parents, to become an adult and to remain a child. And suicide, suicide was the perfect paradox that allowed you both. On the one hand, it was the ultimate autonomous act. It was taking control. But after your death, your parents threw themselves on your body. You were allowed to remain a child forever.

"We've all been through that phase," Paul said cavalierly when he came, newly tan, to visit Françoise in the hospital. Her pride was wounded. It was almost as if her father was disappointed by her lack of originality. But maybe, my mother told me, maybe it was the best thing he could have said. She ceased hoping her parents would care. And then she was free.

"Do you ever . . . ," I asked, "do you ever still consider it?"

"Things change," she said with a sigh, leaning back. "I'm in much more of a . . ." Her hand planed through the air like a bird as she searched for the word. "There are people who depend on me now. I still have moments when I feel . . . lost. But never as lost as before. It's like there's a big ocean and I still fall in from time to time. But then there are all these . . ." She pressed her thumb against her fingers like a shadow-puppet duck and made dots in the air between us. "There are all these things I can catch onto."

She turned her hand against her mouth, fingertips and thumb pressed against her lips, and then allowed it to collapse. She spoke through her fist for a moment, then her hand was in motion once again.

"It's the collateral damage of the human condition," she said with a heavy sigh. "I think therefore I am. Sometimes I envy very small children. You'll see, when you have them. Until a certain age, they live purely in the moment. It's magic. All these states of the soul, this despair, all of that doesn't exist when you're in the present. When I was younger, I didn't know how to listen to the rain. I didn't know how to take hold of my breathing. I didn't know how to stop the rushing thoughts in my head. I didn't know all of these things."

AFTER SHE WAS RELEASED from the hospital, Françoise recovered, moved back to her loft in SoHo, met my father, fell in love. But although she answered all my questions about events up to that point with candor, she insisted on stopping when she met my father. There are some things I should never know, she said.

Though of course I knew the origin story of my parents' romance, had always known it in the way of things you don't remember learning. My mother first met my father shortly after moving back to New York, in the fall of 1976. It was at a dinner party thrown by a couple she'd met in the downtown art scene, part of the circle that radiated outward from her days in Richard Foreman's plays. He'd had a Jewish girlfriend at the time, a short-lived romance born from a sense of compulsion. Françoise had seen him as easily cowed and had not been impressed.

Later, she came across a four-page strip he had published in an underground comix magazine. It was black-and-white, jagged angry lines, raw emotion etched so strong and ragged it seemed strange the paper wasn't torn. It was about his mother's suicide. It was about his anger.

She called him. They spoke for hours—all night, in some retellings—ignoring the mounting phone bill. Her English was limited and speaking on the phone was difficult. But she had a pressing need to understand.

"How could you?" Françoise wanted to know. "How could you publish something so intimate about your mother?"

I don't know how he answered her questions. I could ask, but my parents are no longer the people they were then. The question would be answered the way they would answer it now, with all the filters of time and my father's ensuing fame. However he managed to respond, it was during that conversation that they fell in love.

ONCE, WHEN I was well into this book, my father told me that my mother, when he'd met her, was not the person she'd become. Yes, I said knowingly, she was not as confident then. I'd seen the photographs. I was proud that, in her twenties, my mother was not yet the striking beauty she was now. I hoped that I, too, would only grow more beautiful with age. In old photographs, there was a timid set to her mouth, a guardedness to her eyes, a face hidden behind a halo of frizzy hair. That girl wasn't my mother. My mother could get dressed in ten minutes flat for a swanky party uptown. She could make a thirty-dollar dress look straight off the runway. In recent photographs, my mother's eyes met the camera with a startling frank intelligence that made you stare.

But my father had furrowed his brow at my answer and shook his head and said *Um,* which was rare from him. "She was very . . . broken," he said slowly, then stopped, biting back more words. He'd had to raise her, he said. He'd had to guide her through an accelerated childhood. A teddy bear was involved.

"Is it true that Papa had to raise you?" I asked my mother.

"Your father is rewriting history," she said. "To his advantage. As usual."

"And the bear?" I asked. A cross-eyed teddy bear named Gladly. Gladly, my cross-eyed bear. Gladly my cross I'd bear. I remembered the pun being explained to me once, one of the first I ever understood. I remembered, vaguely, seeing it in my mother's arms, in my mother's closet.

"What bear?" she said.

"The one in your closet," I said.

"That was your bear," she said. And it's true that when I decided I was too old to keep my teddy bears in my room and yet still too young to give them away, my mother put them on a high shelf in her closet. They were still there, mixed with my brother's, the cross-eyed bear among them.

chapter six

I have always known what it means to be a character in someone else's story. My birth was marked by an asterisk in *Maus*.*
As I emerged into the fluorescent lights of St. Vincent's Hospital
in the Village (it seems strange, to use "I" for that self I cannot
remember), some other part of me fell through my father's black
tear of ink on the page. Or rather, not one page, not one asterisk,
but hundreds of thousands in books being opened for the first
time, being printed for the first time, even now. And later, in
other strips and other stories, there I was, at four, at fourteen, my
stretched face drawn straight from my high school ID card photo.

"How's Nadja's book going?" an acquaintance of my mother's
asked her once, while I was sitting next to her. "Has it been published yet?"

It had not. At that point, I had been working on it, on and off,
for nearly six years. My father told people about my project with
pride. My mother resented him for it. She became angry when
anyone asked her about it. "It has nothing to *do* with me," she told
me when I asked why. "It's your book. I have to think about it as
being about someone else, some other girl who shares my name."

*Nadja Mouly Spiegelman. Born 5/13/87.

"Not yet," my mother said to her inquiring friend. "It's a little like being on death row, awaiting my lethal injection." They laughed.

"Is that how you really feel?" I asked her later. "Death row?"

"Oh, *mais chaton!*" she said. "They treat people very well on death row. Last meals and all that."

"Having a writer in the family is like having a murderer in the family," my father told me wryly, and often, in reference to both himself and me.

My mother had told me that even in the hospital she refused to let the nurses take me from her arms. Each time they tried to slip me from her grasp—*so you can sleep*—her eyes snapped open. *I can't sleep without her.* She checked herself out of the hospital the day after I was born and never put me down. But I could not remember a time when I was small enough for my mother to carry. I didn't know how it felt to be aloft in her arms. Was that me any more real than the versions drawn and printed?

My paternal grandparents were a book. I learned to know them only in its pages. My father had closed away a painful part of his past and left it there for us, for anyone, to find. It wasn't until I read *Maus* at fourteen that I discovered that his mother had killed herself. I was sitting on the carpet in a corner of my bedroom, the house strangely quiet, each of us behind our own closed doors. I was so absorbed that I had sunk to the floor. *This is the grandmother I never had,* I thought. Here she was, in a book so many other people had read before me. My father's grief howled from the page, uncut by time. The anger and pain was as raw and unfiltered as it had been in 1972. I hadn't told him I was reading the book now. I hadn't planned to read it. I had tried several times before and slammed the pages shut.

"Would Anja have liked me, do you think?" I asked him very quietly that night as we set the table for dinner. I watched his eyes: the surprise, the rising well of tears.

"She would have *loved* you," he said. He looked away and back again. "She would have loved you."

Each time I asked my parents the origin of my name there was a different story: It worked in both languages; I'd been named for the title of a book by André Breton; they'd met an Italian tour guide whose name they had liked. But my favorite was that I'd been given the name of my father's mother, Anja, recombined.

I had had once, in an impossible past, a sprawling family tree of Spiegelmans so dense I could have disappeared in its shade. Sometimes when I believed in magic, or wondered, as I often did, why I had been chosen for this unfairly charmed life, it was this: that crowd of Eastern European Jewish faces who hovered near me, nameless, with mouths and eyebrows like mine, hair like mine, with so much spilled blood concentrated into my own. There were so many of them and so few descendants to watch over. The one I saw most clearly was Anja, whose face I knew from a single photograph, whom my father had loved and almost never mentioned. Sometimes in moments of deep crisis, I asked her for guidance. I knew she stayed closest. I thought of her often, that grandmother I'd never had.

IN JANUARY OF 2012, my mother and I went to France, just the two of us. My mother had arranged the trip so that she and I could spend two days in Paris before continuing on to the town of Angoulême, where we would meet my father.

In the past, I would have packed bags of nuts in my suitcase to preempt fights with my mother over food, would have made a list in my notebook of the hurtful things she might say to me, to pre-empt their sting. But now my notebook contained only our flight numbers and travel times. When we got to our Paris apartment, a studio in the heart of the city that my mother had purchased a decade before, I made us dinner while she plugged in her laptop and worked.

The next day, she leapt out of the bed we shared, crackling with nervous energy. I heard her on the phone with my grand-mother, apologizing in a voice that sounded young. I heard Josée's muffled scolding on the other end of the line. It was two in the afternoon, and we'd been due for lunch on the houseboat at noon. I got out of bed and tried on four different outfits, trying to smooth away my stomach with my hands. I counted the months since I had last seen my grandmother, August to February, and wondered if I had gained weight in that time. I had. My mother took a shower, then angrily reminded me we were late. We ran outside to hail a cab. I noticed my mother's lipstick was perfectly applied.

"But aren't you ravishing!" Josée said to my mother when we arrived. "As slim as ever." She looked me up and down but said nothing.

We removed our shoes in the entryway. "You'll catch a cold with your bare feet," Josée said. "Here Françoise, I bought these especially for you." She produced a pair of elegant soft white slip-pers. "Nadja, you can wear these," she said, handing me a pair of floppy gray booties with pom-poms on the back. The houseboat was difficult to heat, and it was cold. Josée had spent a rough winter, battling floods. She moved stiffly.

My mother and I immediately set to work in the kitchen. She

handed me a baguette and I sliced it. She pulled out a basket and I found a napkin with which to line it.

"You see!" Josée said, laughing, as she watched us. "Daughters *are* good for something, after all."

"When did you first realize that?" my mother asked good-naturedly, as Josée poured herself a glass of wine.

"When I got old and sick," Josée said. "When I was thirty, a friend told me we have children so that they'll take care of us one day, and I laughed at him. Children are so much more fun when they're young! But you'll see, as you get older, that it's nice to have someone to lean on. It could be anyone really, a secretary or a house-keeper even, but it's that much more comfortable when it's someone you know well." There was an undercurrent of resentment in Josée's tone, but my mother laughed easily, a casual smile in place.

Six months earlier, during a family trip to Paris in August, my mother had received an emergency phone call from Josée. She said she had just fallen and broken her hip. Normally she would have called one of her other daughters, but since my mother was here, perhaps she could come? My mother, brother, and I jumped into a cab. On the way to the houseboat, we puzzled aloud. Why had Josée called my mother instead of an ambulance? How would we get her off the boat? But when we arrived, Josée was standing at the top of her stairs, packed and ready to go. She managed to climb into the taxi and directed the driver to a clinic she liked. "*Madame*," the doctor told my anxious mother, "if your mother has a broken hip she should be in a hospital, not here." But Josée insisted she did not want to go to the hospital, and eventually she was assigned a room. She gave a sigh of relief as we hoisted her onto the bed. "It's very comfortable here," she told us. That evening, X-rays were finally taken. In hushed tones in the hallway, the doctor informed my mother that there was absolutely nothing wrong with Josée's hip—in fact, there was nothing wrong with her at all.

But my mother knew that something was wrong, even if not medically. Josée did not often ask for her help. What was she trying to communicate? My mother thought she knew what it was: Josée was too old to live on the houseboat alone and too proud to admit it. The winter chill and damp cut straight through her.

My mother had worriedly discussed solutions with everyone in the family. Sylvie and Andrée felt Josée should enter an assisted-living facility. My mother recoiled at the suggestion. Instead, my mother mused, Josée could sell the houseboat and buy herself a comfortable apartment. Josée brushed the suggestion aside.

"Of course she can't sell the houseboat," I said. "It's her life's work. It's her *chef d'oeuvre*." It was unclear who Josée would be without the boat. It was how I explained her to my friends—the Jacuzzi, the table that rose out of the floor with a remote control. It was how she introduced herself to strangers: "I live on a boat."

Perhaps she could afford to keep the boat and rent herself an apartment, my mother suggested. This, too, Josée shrugged off.

"Of course she can't rent," my brother said. "Renting is temporary. It means admitting that she'll die."

Eventually, my mother decided that she would buy Josée an apartment. My mother was proud that she had earned her living well enough to do so, but she knew that Josée's own pride was a delicate thing. She framed it carefully. She told Josée that she would like to buy an apartment for my brother and me, which Josée would furnish and live in. To this Josée agreed. She chose an apartment a ten-minute drive from the houseboat. She referred to it as

"Nadja's apartment" and complained often of the work involved in renovating it. In the years following, she would continue to spend a great deal of time on the houseboat, in constant motion, frequently dining and sleeping there. But in winter months, she would marvel over the apartment's central heat.

Now Josée would show my mother the apartment for the first time. But as it was still under construction, she'd prepared lunch for us on the houseboat first. As soon as we sat down to eat, Josée began complaining about Jean-Claude, Sylvie's husband. Jean-Claude was a mild-mannered, diffident man with an array of food allergies. He took up very little space in a room and seemed to me difficult to dislike with any vehemence. But Josée's affections were cyclical, and loving one of her two Parisian daughters meant fighting with the other. On that day, Andrée was in, Sylvie was out, and Jean-Claude was taking the brunt of Josée's displeasure.

"But you know, I was very impressed with Jean-Claude once," my mother said, and I knew exactly which story she was about to tell. She had told it many times.

One afternoon, when my cousin was young, he had fallen into the Seine. Jean-Claude had jumped right in to save him.

"He didn't even take off his coat!" my mother said, as she always did. "It was quite heroic. I was very impressed with him!"

"*Mais non!*" Josée scoffed. "The boy was clinging to a buoy raft. Jean-Claude jumped right down onto it and split his kid's lip open. Some hero!"

This was the first time I'd heard that version of the story. I looked at the two women; neither wavered. I'd been there that day, ten or eleven years old, standing on the deck of the boat. I strained to remember. I tried to see my cousin's lip, the blood dripping into murky water, but I remembered the moment as if in a movie, from behind a roving camera. I even saw myself standing there. I'd inhabited my mother's memory and lost my own.

There was a beat of strained silence. My mother shrugged and changed the topic. I knew she would continue to tell the story just as she always had.

"Nadja, I'm glad you're here," my grandmother said, turning decisively to me. "I've been meaning to talk to you."

My body tensed. With startling clarity, I knew what was coming. I'd been too busy sucking in my stomach to anticipate it. Now I saw that Josée had planned for this all along.

"When I first read what you said in that book I felt *sick*!" she exclaimed. "Sick to the bottom of my heart. And I have been sick sick sick ever since."

I stayed silent and looked at her calmly. I felt myself exit my body, the way I often did when faced with anger.

My father was in France to promote the French edition of *MetaMaus*, a book about the making of *Maus*. I'd been interviewed for the book, and in response to a question about my own relationship to the Holocaust, I had replied, "There's also my French side of the family, and what they were doing during the war. My great-grandmother got caught up with this Italian who had dealings with the Nazis, and when he died she was blamed for what he'd done, so she was in jail for being a Nazi sympathizer. Which was a very indirect way of being involved, but there's still this conflicting sense of my ancestry. Victims and perpetrators both."

Josée had received the French edition in December. She'd found the reference to her mother immediately and been distraught. My mother had mentioned Josée's displeasure to me only in passing, but I knew that my comment had provoked tension between them. Now Josée had the opportunity to confront me about it herself.

"And on top of it all, it's not even true," she said now.

"How is it not true?" I asked. My mother had told me Mina's story when I was eight years old. She'd heard it directly from Mina herself. I wrote it up for a fourth-grade project. I titled it "My Great-Grandmother, My Hero" in marker on the cover and bound it with yarn. Later my mother told me that she had gulped when she'd seen my project alongside the others in my classroom. She wondered if perhaps she'd told me a few things prematurely. But it was a story I felt I had always known, and one I was proud of.

In the French edition, my quote reads, *"Lorsqu'il est mort, elle a été tenue pour responsable de ce qu'il avait fait et jetée en prison comme sympathisante nazie."* This translates back as "After he died, she was held responsible for what he'd done, and thrown in jail for being a Nazi sympathizer." It was the word "thrown" (which I had not used in English) that gave Josée the most trouble.

"She wasn't *thrown* in jail!" she said vehemently. "She was *put* in jail! She wasn't even put in jail. She was imprisoned! How could you publish these lies?"

What was this about, I wondered coolly. Was it easier for Josée to get angry than to thank my mother for buying her an apartment? Was she jealous of the attention my long-dead paternal grandparents had received? Or was this simply a manifestation of the general French attitude toward World War II, which made discussion of anything but the Resistance taboo? I began to feel the stirrings of my own anger. I defended myself. I told her I was not ashamed of Mina's story. I told Josée I was proud of it, proud of how my great-grandmother had lived her life so far outside of society's rules for women.

"What if my friends read this?" Josée asked. "I cannot see my friends anymore. I'm embarrassed to leave my house."

"But Nadja," my mother cut in, in a conciliatory voice that crept under my skin, "listen to what Josée is telling you."

"I'm listening," I said testily. "And trying to respond."

"She only wants to tell you more about Mina's story," my mother said.

"No I don't," Josée said. "Not if she's going to twist it all into lies."

"Really, at the heart of it, we can all agree," my mother said. "We all loved Mina."

Josée snorted angrily. "If *this* is how she shows love . . ."

"I'm sorry I hurt you," I said stiffly. "That was never my intention."

Josée's blue eyes turned sharp and cold as icicles. "The only blessing is that Mina is no longer alive to see this," she said. "Just go ahead and forget your mother's side of the family entirely. You never had a great-grandmother! Erase her from your mind. If this is how you remember her, it's best you don't remember her at all."

I sighed and sat in silence for a moment. Then I stood.

"I'm leaving," I announced. "I'm sorry that I hurt you. I don't know what else I can say." Leaving was the way my father ended (and often won) arguments. It seemed to me both a mature and an effective thing to do. I went to put on my shoes.

My mother stopped me on the wood stairs that led from the belly of the boat to the drawbridge.

"Don't go," she said. She spoke quietly, though she'd closed the foyer door behind her.

"Why not?" I asked. "It's fine. I just don't want to listen to this."

"Just . . . please don't go," she said. I stood perfectly still, waiting. She sighed and said, "Don't force me to choose between my mother and my daughter."

"Oh," I said, turning. "You don't have to choose. Stay. I know how to get home."

"But why are you leaving?" my mother asked. "What is it that's making you so angry?"

The question caught me off guard. I sat down on the steps as if I had been pushed.

"I just want a grandmother who sees me," I blurted, surprised by the sob that rose up in my throat and nearly escaped.

"You're not going to be the one to change her," my mother said.

"I don't want to change her," I replied, shaking my head to clear it. I rose again to leave. "I just don't want to eat lunch with her."

Josée stepped out into the stairwell. She looked me in the eyes, her face gentle now.

"I love you, you know," she said softly. My breath caught. I had never once considered that possibility.

"But you've hurt me so deeply, oh if only you knew how badly you've hurt me!" She burst into tears. I'd never seen her cry before, but there was something strange about how familiar it felt, as if I'd always known how it would be. I went back inside.

Josée dried her tears.

"You've disgraced my mother's memory," she told me. "I'm so ashamed." I shifted uncomfortably in my seat. My mother got up to go to the bathroom. I watched her leave, eyes wide and anxious. I wanted to ask her to stay but knew how weak that would make me look. Josée shuffled around the kitchen, rinsing dishes and putting things away, as she continued explaining to me how wrong I had been.

I dug through my purse and pulled out my red notebook. I began to write down everything Josée was saying. I wrote, as always, in English, translating her words in my head as soon as they were spoken, and so, as usual, none of my quotes were exact.

I wrote: "I know it's *useful* to you to have your whole life in perfect balance. But I hate to break it to you, girl—no one in this family was a Nazi."

I wrote: "They didn't have *dealings* with the Nazis. They occasionally traded goods with the Nazis."

Josée saw me writing and became calmer. She began dictating to me, speaking slowly, glancing over my shoulder to the paper. She sat down across from me.

"Those were the happiest years of my life," she said softly. I glanced up at her. For an instant her eyes allowed me into their depths. I was struck by the feeling that this, at last, was true. But it contradicted everything I thought I knew about her past.

"Beppo, the Italian . . . he was the only father I ever really knew," she said, and was about to say more when my mother reentered the room.

"So! Let's go see Nadja's apartment!" my mother said cheerily. She clapped her hands together, picked up her coat.

Josée and I shared a look. The broken moment shimmered in the air between us. We gathered our things and followed my mother out. I put a hand on Josée's shoulder.

"I *would*," I said quietly, just to her. "I would like to hear the whole story." She jerked away from me, shrugging off my touch. But her anger felt halfhearted now. Something had opened between us.

"Nadja will be happy in this new apartment, I think," Josée said as we drove over in the car.

"Yes," I said. "Thank you."

"It's very conveniently located," she said.

"Is it near the subway?" I asked.

"No," she said. "But I never take the subway anymore."

My mother had been baffled when Josée sent her the listing. The apartment Josée had chosen was the opposite of the houseboat in every way. The houseboat was open water and open skies, new rules made only to be broken, Josée's distinctive taste in every detail. Close as it was, the new apartment was in the heart of the staid upper-class suburb of Neuilly. Boxy concrete balconies climbed the building's façade. Heavy glass double doors in the lobby instilled a sense of hush. There was a small clean elevator, a concierge, plain brown doormats in front of each door. It felt like a building for an old woman with well-coiffed gray hair and a small white dog, the kind who might carry school photos of her grandchildren in her wallet. It was difficult to imagine Josée living here.

Josée was proud of the space. She showed us the electric metal blinds that descended like storefront grates, the same kind Paul had had in his bachelor pad years ago. She demonstrated the modern light switches she'd had installed, panels of touch-sensitive concentric circles that proved impossible to control. She showed us the luxurious tiled shower, with its sliding mirrored door.

"The shower is mirrored on the inside as well," she said mischievously.

I stepped out onto the balcony. In the distance, a toy-sized Eiffel Tower marked the skyline, the way it seemed to from nearly every vantage point in Paris. Close by and yet out of sight, I could hear a playground. How strange that the sound of children playing was so universal, I thought, uninflected by language or culture.

Josée joined me. "I used to attend the school next door," she told me.

"When you were how old?" I asked.

"Oh, I don't know," she said. "Until I was six? And then of course there was the war."

I nodded, realizing how little I knew of her life. "Do you keep good memories of it?"

"Oh, only," she said. "I only keep good memories of everything."

She went back inside, but I stood there a moment longer. A little girl's high-pitched shriek sliced through the still air.

ON THE PLANE back to New York, my mother repeated a negative comment Josée had made about one of her sisters. "Poor thing," my mother said, but I could hear the guilty delight that danced under her words.

"Well, but," I said, "Josée was a bit rude to you as well."

"What do you mean?" There was the hint of a challenge, the beginnings of a defiant smile.

"When she said daughters were good for something after all, though it may as well be a secretary or a housekeeper. Don't you think she meant that to hurt you? I mean, after everything you've done?"

"Oh, Nadja!" my mother said. "You're still stuck in your black-and-white phase of good and evil. The world is more complicated than that."

I became defensive. "It's not that I care whether Josée is good or evil in any objective sense," I said. "It's just about whether or not I can love her, or even whether I have to. She's only ever been cold to me, and so cruel to you."

"Well, what about Josée's own mother?" my mother said. "Mina was cruel to Josée, you know. Can you forgive her?"

I blew air through my lips, *pfff,* the French equivalent of *I don't know, whatever.* We'd only been in France for a few days, but I always picked up the mannerisms quickly.

"I haven't even thought about Mina yet," I said.

"Josée had a difficult life," my mother said.

"So did many people," I replied. "It's not a perfect excuse. You had a difficult life, too."

My mother rustled her newspaper, shifted in her seat.

"I suppose that in learning about your life," I continued, "I've learned to forgive certain things. I understand how problematic your relationship with your own mother was, and how that's influenced ours. I see now that no matter how it felt at the time, you were always at least trying to do what you thought was best. But you . . . you? How did you forgive Josée?"

"It's not about forgiveness," my mother said. "I just stopped needing her to love me. And I don't need you to forgive me, either."

"Okay," I said. "But I do, as I get older."

"For what?" my mother asked, her tone undeniably tense.

I mentioned how she'd favored my brother. Though in a way, I said, it was a good thing. "In the end, I think, it made me stronger."

I felt proud of myself for speaking so clearly. I was cool and rational and mature.

"I hope you don't see that as a justification," my mother said. "You can't hang things in a balance like that—this hurt, but in the end good came out of it." It wasn't an apology, but it wasn't a denial, either. It was as close as we'd ever come. I should have let the matter lie, but I pressed on.

"You were tough on me, and it made me tough," I said. "In the end, I think there *is* a balance. I like who I am, more or less. I feel strong, capable, and confident. And that came from you, one way or another. As a kid, I was jealous of the attention you gave my brother—but honestly, I don't think you did him any favors."

My mother pulled away from the armrest we shared.

"Did I ever tell you about the moment when I decided to have a second child?" she asked. She looked at me sharply. I saw the hard metal glint in her eyes and knew that I did not want to hear what she had to say next. But I kept my voice light and said no, she had not told me. It had been so long now since we had fought.

"You were three and a half years old and it was your bath time. I loved your bath. It was the only moment I had to myself. And you loved your bath, too; you've always loved water. I left you to play while I had a cigarette, read a book, I don't know what. But this day, when I got up to leave, you said, 'Maman, stay with me in the bathroom!' I felt so trapped. I stayed for a minute, and then I tried to leave again. And you said, 'No, Maman! Stay with me longer!' You were on the verge of tears. I sat back down. But the violence of my emotions—being made prisoner by you, my hatred for you—it scared me. So I left. I slammed the door behind me and let you cry. *That's* when I decided to have a second child. It was to break something between you and me."

"Oh," I said. The back of my throat burned hot with shame. She picked up her newspaper and began to read. I turned toward the window. Tears pricked at my eyes. I sniffed loudly but she did not turn. We barely spoke for the rest of the flight.

THE TRIP LINGERED with me. Back in New York, I felt that I contained something new. For weeks it sat inside me and then it emerged, like sea glass shifting upward through sand. It was the first time I had entertained this thought, and yet somehow, also, I had always known it would come to this: I needed to know Josée's story.

I knew so much of my mother that I felt I could inhabit all the years before my birth almost as if I had lived them myself—every strand of emotion that vibrated along the five-pointed cat's cradle that tied the Mouly family together. And yet at the very center of my mother, a mystery remained. Perhaps I understood my mother's adolescence only because I had lived those years of my own life. My mother and I had never been closer. Yet I worried that I did not understand how she had forgiven her mother because I hadn't fully forgiven my own. Or maybe I had not yet understood how to not need her to love me. Either way, I wanted to know what my mother had done. And I wanted to be able to forgive Josée myself, for my mother's sake and my own.

But first, I had to make Josée forgive me. That path was very clear. Josée had laid out explicit demands: I must remove the sentences about her mother from subsequent printings of the French edition of my father's book. I emailed my father a new version of the text. In it, I made no mention of my great-grandmother. Instead I said simply that my French ancestry complicated my Jewish one because only 3 percent of the French had actually taken part in the Resistance, while all the others, whether tacitly or actively, had collaborated with the German occupation.

I disagree with/disapprove of/am ashamed by your whitewashing of history, my father wrote back to me.

I called him on the phone, tried to explain. "Josée was as clear as she could be without saying it outright: I remove this line about Mina, and she'll tell me about her life," I told him. "It's worth it to me."

"I'll do it," my father said. "I told you you could speak in your own words, and if this is what you want, then I'll do it. But I'm disappointed."

"I thought you'd understand," I said.

"Where do you think I would be," he asked, "if I'd left out of my books the parts that made people uncomfortable?"

My father and I rarely disagreed. His words stung.

"It's a small omission," I said, more to convince myself than to convince him. He almost never changed his mind. "It's in the service of more truth."

"It's cowardly," he said. But he sent along my text, and the future editions of the French printing were changed. He was cold to me for a few weeks and then thawed. When my father and I fought, which was rarely, it was not as wrenching as my fights with my mother. I never worried that he had stopped loving me. But he almost never gave me his opinion unbidden, and I valued it more than anyone else's. I couldn't bear to admit that he might be wrong any more than I could bear to admit that I was.

"It's not fair," I whined to my mother. "Papa didn't have to face Josée's anger. He doesn't understand."

"Oh, but he did!" my mother said. She told me that the December before, in Paris, Josée had tried to engage my father over those very lines. He'd shrugged it off and bought her a crêpe. She'd thrown the crêpe on the ground. My father had shrugged again, laughed about it later.

"Then the subject came up once more, when just she and I were in her car," my mother continued. "I opened my mouth to say that it was a good thing. The shame stops with this generation. My children are proud of Mina. She turned to me and—with all the hatred and venom I've always imagined she felt for me—she said, *'Tais-toi!'"*

I jumped back, rattled. My mother had often told me to shut up in that exact tone, though it had been years since she'd done so.

"I'm sorry," I said in a small voice, my apology automatic.

"Oh, but it was wonderful!" my mother said. "It was such a relief." She smiled with glistening eyes, her gaze forceful and direct. She was willing me to understand, trying to beam her emotions to me telepathically.

"A relief?" I asked.

"It means I didn't invent her, that version of my mother," my mother said. "It means she's still there. And for a moment I could be a child again, her horrible unwanted child!" She reached toward me but did not touch me, as if inviting me to jump into her arms or join her in a waltz.

"I see," I said, though all I saw was one more thing I couldn't yet understand.

I MADE ARRANGEMENTS to move to France for a year. I found a job in a gallery, a subletter for my room in Brooklyn.

That August, I sat by myself on the steps of the Brooklyn Museum and watched the fountain dance to no music. Groups of teenagers rearranged themselves on the steps, like seashells in a tide, Hasidic women jogged by in long skirts and sneakers, a young mother laden with bags from the farmer's market watched her daughter toddle dangerously close to the water. I had thought Brooklyn would be enough for me, a city across the river whose geography mystified my parents.

My flight loomed a few weeks away like the steep drop off a cliff. I'd been to Paris often, and yet I knew the city only the way a little girl would. I'd followed my parents from museum to bookstore to café to restaurant and understood the landscape only as a bare mental map of our personal landmarks. I had no friends there. Paris was a city in which my independence evaporated so fast I barely felt it leave. It was not a city in which I had good memories. When Americans gushed about the Seine, the *macarons,* the women, the wine, I wanted to tell them that that was not Paris. Paris was long anxious dinners with your grandparents, shopkeepers who slapped your hands for touching key chains, a concierge who scolded you for laughing too loudly in your living room on a Saturday afternoon. I knew these were things I couldn't complain about—who would take me seriously?—and yet I was scared.

My parents drove me to Newark Airport, the pulsing strobe lights of the Holland Tunnel heightening my anxiety. We said our tearful good-byes. My mother joked that she wouldn't let my plane take off. I turned around three times to wave as I moved slowly toward security. But when I arrived at my gate, the waiting area was empty. The man behind the counter told me that my flight had been canceled. The next flight was tomorrow. "Why?" I asked. There wasn't a cloud in the sky. All around me, screens flashed ON TIME and NOW BOARDING. The man shrugged.

I called my father. My mother turned around abruptly on the New Jersey Turnpike, barreling back toward the airport.

One last night in my childhood bedroom, suitcase still packed. I was drained, empty—all my emotion had flown off into the air where my plane wasn't. My father joked that my mother had used her powers to cancel my flight. I joked, too, but I knew it was true.

One more time at the corner of Canal Street and Broadway, where the fancy stores of SoHo bled into the knockoff designer bags of Chinatown. New York was my city. I knew its rules and how to break them. I knew how to weave in and out of the tourists, when it was okay to speak to strangers, how to jaywalk. This was a busy intersection, crowds shoving, but I knew it well. I knew it desolate at four a.m., taxicabs burning red lights and rats rustling through the trash. I knew it under two feet of snow, and in startling summer downpours. I rarely felt more a New Yorker than while I waited for that light to change, pushed left and right by the tourists who crowded the sidewalk. The pedestrian crossing light had a significant lag, but I knew to turn my head to catch the traffic light turning red, and I always stepped out into the empty oasis of the street thirty seconds before it signaled WALK.

Today, though, I looked down at my feet. I felt the noises of the street fade. Carved into the cement of the sidewalk, in simple handwriting that could have been either someone else's or my own, was the word NADJA. No matter how much I searched, no memory of writing it surfaced. It seemed to me a secret message, risen up out of the city itself. I shifted my stance so that my name was directly below me and stood looking down at it through the changing of two lights. The crowds surged around me, huffing, complaining, elbowing me in the sides. I did not give. I did not want their feet to wear my name away. And then, eventually, reluctantly, I moved again.

That evening, I took a cab back to the airport. I called my mother.

"Will you let my plane take off this time?" I said.

"*Oui, mon chaton,*" she agreed, wistful sadness in her tone. More and more these days, she seemed burdened by the powers that I continued to ascribe to her.

And then the plane barreled down the runway and I felt the surge of weightlessness in my stomach as the wheels let go of the ground. I flipped the pages of my book, unseeing. New York shrank to pinpoints, was swallowed by the ocean.

I put away my book and pulled out a long list of questions. "What sorts of fights did you have with your own mother?" and "When did you lose your virginity?" I couldn't imagine asking Josée any of these things. I imagined her drawing my plane forward through the sky by a silky spider string. I thought about how my mother had come to New York to escape her mother, and about how now I had set out to find her. I had the feeling I'd formed a loop, spun time around on its tail, and suddenly I was traveling backward.

My mother was eighteen when she came to New York; I was twenty-five when I left it. Perhaps a ghost of her plane crossed mine. Perhaps, for just an instant, we overlapped in the silence over the black water. Inside the cabin, in the white-noise hum of recycled air, we were both sitting perfectly still.

chapter seven

The plane hit the tarmac so smoothly that the cabin applauded. My stomach was a tight fist. From inside the taxi cab, I saw the Seine and then the Louvre, and my heart leapt despite myself. It usually made me feel French, to not love Paris, but right then I felt more American than I ever had. I leaned my phone against the window to take pictures, all blurry, all accidentally containing tourists taking pictures of their own.

In my parents' studio apartment, in the perfect geographic center of the city, I was alone. I had never lived alone before. I struggled to find the quiet reassuring rather than unsettling. I unpacked my belongings. My mother's collection of broken telephones, chargers that had long ago lost their appliances, mismatched sheet sets filled the closets. I moved them to the highest shelves.

I discovered that the apartment was filled with objects that had belonged to my grandfather, my mother's share of what had been taken from his apartment after his death. There were Egyptian artifacts, hieroglyphs carved into pieces of stone, brown leather desk accessories. There was a box filled with the artifacts he'd kept of our lives: letters my mother had sent him, magazine articles with glossy photos of her, photos of my birth, two copies of the *Teen People* in which I'd modeled real jeans for real bodies. A stack of translucent pages proved to be the faxes I had sent him as a child. I could read the strain of forced cheeriness even in my childish scrawl. *Sending you lots of kisses!* I remembered writing these, how my mother stood over me at the kitchen table, dictating, correcting my French. Every word had felt like something ripped from me. I closed the box quickly and put it away.

In New York I had a solid gold compact mirror that had belonged to my father's mother during her youth in Poland. His father had buried it, along with a gold cigarette case, at the start of the war and after miraculously surviving the concentration camps had risked his life to dig it up again. It was all that remained. Everything else, everyone else, was gone. My father had bestowed these objects upon my brother and me with gravitas. It terrified me, the power this mirror held. What if I broke it? What if I lost it? I'd opened it once and looked at my face inside. Then I buried it deep in my childhood bedroom.

The objects in the Paris apartment terrified me in a different way. I began shoving them into the boxes of stray electrical cords high in the closets. I all but threw an African fertility goddess into one of them, and at the sickening brittle crack of clay on clay felt a rush of petty vindication, as if perhaps I had broken these objects of some black enchantment. Then remorse set in. They were centuries old, these artifacts. They had seen far more than I had.

When my grandfather passed away, in the summer of 2007, a weight had lifted off me that I hadn't known I was carrying. Each time a whiff of cigar smoke or Hermès cologne sent unbidden memories straight through my central nervous system, I would remember with relief that he was not in Paris waiting for me but nowhere, nowhere, he was gone. But here he was now. His leather briefcase. A carved piece of ivory. He'd been waiting for me after all. I put his majestic red glass ashtray in the center of the table and told myself that it was not my grandfather. It was a beautiful object and nothing more. I stubbed out a cigarette butt in it to prove it. I had a lot within myself to unpack, I realized, but maybe this was a start.

I WANDERED AIMLESSLY in an ever-increasing radius from the apartment. I thought I knew the city well enough, but I soon discovered that my childish mental map had always been upside down. The Seine was south of the apartment, not north as I had assumed. I confused east for west for months.

Days passed where I spoke only to shopkeepers and café waiters. I discovered that I could wake up at one in the afternoon and no one would know. America was still sleeping. I became afraid of disappearing. Major construction work was being done on the building, and I lay in bed with my hands over my ears while the walls shook, jackhammers pounding into my skull. Men stood on scaffolding outside my second-story windows and shouted to one another as they ripped the bricks out of the walls. I became afraid of going crazy. I threw myself into a whirlwind of drinks and coffee dates with every tenuous connection I had to a friend of a friend. I had been warned that Parisians ran in tight-knit circles, that it would be very difficult to meet anyone. But when I said I used to live in Brooklyn, people's eyes lit up. "Brooklyn!" they sighed wistfully. The rooftops, the speakeasies, the artisanal hamburgers! Why would I come here? I asked questions constantly—about slang words, the names of streets, why the waiters were so rude—and my new friends answered eagerly, talking over one another. I soon learned that in France it was rare to admit ignorance on any topic. My open naïveté was a novelty. And I, in turn, enjoyed having my accent and customs gently teased. "*Très* Brooklyn," my friends would say, impressed, when I served them glasses of water in jam jars I had rinsed. I found myself completely comfortable in my new identity as an outsider, more comfortable than I'd ever been before.

FINALLY, I COULDN'T put off calling my grandmother any longer. I paced my apartment as the telephone rang. "I'd like to come over," I told her, my voice squeaking.

"But of course!" she said. "I'll make you a little lunch."

"I thought, perhaps, you cook so well, maybe you could teach me a few things?" I said. "Cooking lessons?"

"Cooking lessons?" she said.

"Yes," I said, "and to see you, also. And to talk a bit, maybe, about my mother. About your childhood. I'd like to know."

"Ah," she said. "I don't know what I can tell you about Françoise. But we'll see all that when you get here. It will give me great pleasure to see you."

The day of the visit, I looked at myself in the mirror. I smoothed my dress over my hips. I tried to see myself as my grandmother would see me, but instead I saw only my mother scrutinizing herself, the expression I'd seen on her face so many times.

On the subway, I made a game of the things my grandmother might say to me. Ten points if she told me I'd gained weight. Fifteen if she insulted my sweater. But when I arrived, she hurried to the door to embrace me.

"Look at how beautiful you are!" she exclaimed. "Paris must suit you. You've melted away."

She took a white-fleshed fish from the fridge and had me place it in a bouillon she had already prepared.

"Your fish is delicious," she told me as we ate.

"But it's the bouillon that's good," I said, embarrassed by the wave of pride that flushed my cheeks. I asked her if I might record our conversation.

"Would you like my tape recorder?" she said. "I brought it down from my closet for you; it's right here."

"Oh!" I said, startled. "Um, thank you. But actually, I can do it on my phone."

"On your phone?"

"Yes, see? It's recording now."

"Well don't put it there. It'll catch all the vibrations of the table. On top of this book is better. Doing interviews was my job for quite some time, you know."

I looked up at her in surprise, eager for her to continue.

"I was a ghostwriter for many years," she said. The word for this in French is *nègre*, and for a quick moment I wondered if she was being racist. She enjoyed being provocative, her comments sometimes so shocking that it was difficult not to laugh. "Look, black and yellow have made a little bumblebee," she said once, as we passed an interracial couple and their child.

"Do you have the books you wrote?" I asked her.

"Oh, I've put them well away, under my bed. You have to get down on all fours to reach them. The first was about the legion-naires. It's very difficult to make those men talk. But still, it was exciting. Every experience they described, we had to try ourselves to make sure it was possible. If they said it took so much time, carrying so much weight, to get down to the riverbank, then we timed ourselves doing it," she said. "I even got my mother to help."

I tried to imagine Josée and Mina running down a steep embankment with heavy loads on their backs. It seemed to me an apt metaphor.

"What tricks did you learn to make people talk?" I asked.

"Looking at them," she said with a charming smile, then pursed her lips and looked at me, batting her eyelashes. I noted that my grandmother understood the power of a small simple answer, and most likely, too, its ability to be accurately transcribed. My mother, by contrast, spoke in paragraphs rather than sentences, and while sometimes her responses wound toward an increasingly precise answer, they more often unfolded in directions that surprised us both. I nodded at Josée, waiting for her to continue.

"And always here!" she said, gesturing to the bar in her kitchen at which we both sat. "So many secrets have been told at this bar. It must be located on a karmic center of energy. Here, this is a good trick. You offer them some wine, some *saucisson*, some tea. They sit like this." She slumped back in her chair, letting her arms fall wide and lazy on the table. "They come out with all sorts of boring things about their family for hours. And then all of a sudden they tell you the interesting things."

"It's the things about family that I'm interested in hearing," I heard myself say, because the opening was there.

"Yes," she said, "the tables have turned. Would you like some more tea?"

I held out my teacup for her.

"What was my mother like as a girl?" I asked.

"So," she said evenly. "When you pass something, like a cup, you always pass the plate underneath as well. Like that. You give it all. It's much easier for the person serving. She aims and you don't move. And it's more refined."

"Okay," I said, surprised that she'd rebuked me in a way that didn't sting.

As I was preparing to leave, pleased that our first session had gone so well, I noticed a black-and-white photo propped against the wall by the table. Josée was beaming, her cheek pressed to an odd, soft object in her arms. My mother, aged eight or nine, stood behind her, her face transformed by a radiant smile. I picked it up. This was not the childhood my mother had told me about. I asked Josée what she was holding in her arms.

"It's a pillow with an embroidery of a dog," she told me—a pillow Françoise had made for her. It was so sweet, so dear to her. But after the divorce, my grandfather had sold it to the auction house, along with most of Josée's other belongings.

"I bid on eight or nine lots of pillows, just to try and get it back," Josée said, laughing. "But it wasn't in any of them." She took the photograph from my hand, looked at it, and replaced it carefully against the wall.

From the houseboat, I had a long walk back along the Seine to the subway station. I called my mother immediately, breathless with triumph. Josée had not disdained all of my mother's gifts after all. My mother had forgotten the dog pillow. The dog pillow had been loved. This might fix everything, and so easily.

"Well," my mother said eventually, with a sigh. "If she'd really loved it, she wouldn't have left it behind."

I stifled my disappointment, and we talked of other things. It wasn't until later, listening to the recording, that I noticed how few of the questions I'd asked about my mother Josée had actually answered.

I STUBBED OUT another cigarette in my grandfather's ashtray, which held a great many butts now. I wondered about the fate of the dog pillow, if the person who had bought it had thrown it away. Very few physical traces of my mother's childhood remained. Josée had told me, without a hint of shame, that she had no photographs of my mother between the ages of six and nineteen.

There was, in the apartment, a large oil painting too big to fit in the closet. My mother had taken it from Paul's apartment because she'd remembered it from her childhood home. It was in the French pompier style and it depicted, in fact, a raucous firemen's picnic. Drunken men slumped against trees, gave goblets of alcohol to children, groped women's rears. It was garish, but the frame was nice. I had put it on the floor behind the dining table, but now I worried for its safety. I hung it above the bed. It looked stately, if you didn't examine it too closely.

THE FIRST TIME it happened, I was eight years old. I'd gone to Paris by myself, to visit my grandparents. Even then, I'd wanted to prove I was old enough—old enough to travel alone, old enough to have experiences that were mine alone. I was to spend the first half of the week with Josée and the second half with Paul.

On the houseboat, Josée scolded me for washing dishes incorrectly, for stealing the lumpy cane-sugar cubes from the silver sugar bowl at night, for eating too much bread with my meals. "It expands in your stomach," she said. I slept on a mattress in the room that doubled as her massage room. One day, the masseuse came and my grandmother lay naked on the massage table next to me, moaning.

I had never felt so homesick before. But there was also an afternoon when Josée taught me how to fly a kite, and an evening when she told me, in front of her friends, that my dress made me look "as skinny as a string bean." There were ducks that made their nests on the houseboat, and Josée showed me how to throw them stale bread out the kitchen porthole. Behind a plant by the Jacuzzi I found a baby duckling that had died the spring before. Josée had had it poorly taxidermied by a friend. I fell in love with the soft still thing, cardboard jutting from its neck, and she told me I could keep it. I took it with me when I left.

One of my aunts drove me from the houseboat to the luxury apartment building on Avenue Foch where my grandfather lived. In honor of my visit, he had made his small office into a room just for me, with a rosebush in the window. He had hung a painting of two terrifying white kittens on the wall.

My first night, he took me down to dinner in the lavish restaurant on the ground floor. After dinner, a man rolled a cart of desserts over to our table and I politely said I was full. But my grandfather must have seen my eyes go wide at the *île flottante*, a meringue floating on vanilla cream, and he insisted I order it. When I'd scraped the last of the cream from the plate, I looked up to see him watching me with horror.

"You fat little pig," he said. "How could you have eaten all that?"

That night, I sat on the bed in my room as I listened to him on the phone in the living room.

"It's not just a bubble in her stomach that's going to pop and go away. We need to do something about her," he said.

He didn't come to say good night. I fell asleep staring warily at the ominous blue-eyed kittens. Hours later, I heard the door to my room open and my grandfather come in. I was lying on my stomach on top of the blankets, my face turned toward the wall. He sat down at the foot of my bed. He gently lifted my nightshirt. He began to stroke my butt. I kept my eyes shut so that he wouldn't realize I was awake. I don't know how much time passed. Eventually, he left.

The next morning, he told me to eat plain nonfat yogurt with artificial sweetener for breakfast. He had filled the fridge with it just for me. When I bathed, he remained in the bathroom. At eight, this was something my mother or grandmother might have done with me as well, but his presence made me uncomfortable without my knowing why. I noted it in my diary, in a childish scrawl. "I know he's my *grandfather*," I wrote, "so it's okay. But I just wish he'd leave me alone."

I didn't tell my mother. What would I have told her?

IT WAS YEARS before anything happened again. I kissed my grandfather on the cheek when he bought me too-expensive Christmas presents, just as I was supposed to. His skin was strangely, worrisomely soft, but I remember very few of the actual moments I spent with him. Mostly my brother and I sat quietly on his brown leather couch, or didn't sit quietly and were scolded. Then we sat down to elaborate catered meals—plates of oysters, lavish cakes—and I was inevitably reprimanded for eating incorrectly, or too much. His girlfriend was a marquise who wouldn't marry him in order not to lose her title. Once, I was invited to her castle, where the stairways were tight, winding stone affairs and I slept in a princess bed with a red velvet canopy. At high noon, all the children were locked into a cabin filled with bunk beds and made to nap. Through the windows we could see the adults drinking cocktails by the pool in the sunshine. The other children did not see this as a grand injustice, but I tried to argue my way out and was spanked by the woman who was minding us. This I did tell my mother, my voice trembling with outrage. I liked the marquise, but she told me gently that I could not call her *grand-mere* because she already had too many grandchildren of her own. I had no memories of my grandfather from that visit beyond one breakfast, when he lectured me on butter knives.

Then I was fourteen, and the way his gaze and hands lingered on me made me uncomfortable. But I was often uncomfortable in my body then, and there were many men who made me feel that way. My grandfather had invited the family out for dinner. I hated the mannered extravagance of those meals. My grandfather flirted with the waitress outrageously. He slipped an enormous bill into her hand as a tip. I felt her discomfort acutely. The conversation was strained, with both my aunts trying to convey their polite dislike for the marquise, whom they suspected of being after their father's money. I went to the bathroom to have a moment alone.

The bathroom was very small. There was a vestibule with a sink and a mirror, perhaps two feet wide, then two doors that led to toilets. As I was washing my hands, my grandfather came in. I backed up against the wall to let him pass. He stood facing me, pushed up against me. He touched my stomach.

"You stick out here," he said. I put my head down. I could smell the stale cigars on his breath.

"But not as much as you stick out here," he said, putting both his hands on my breasts. I laughed politely and pushed past him, out of the bathroom.

At the end of the meal, my mother said, "Thank your grandfather." I kissed him on the cheek and thanked him.

Back in New York, I told my mother. I told her about the bathroom and that night when I was eight years old, and the vague discomfort I had no name for. I was leaning in her doorway, watching her get ready to go out. She was wrapped in a towel with her hair dripping wet, applying lipstick.

"But he's a plastic surgeon!" she said. "You don't understand. He's just used to touching women." She turned back to the mirror, clipping earrings on her ears.

"It's a professional deformation," she said. "It's just the way he is."

"Okay," I mumbled and went to my room.

THE LAST TIME it happened, I was nineteen. My mother wanted to go have lunch at his apartment once more before we left. She wanted me—me specifically, though my father and my brother were also in Paris—to come along. Your grandfather is dying, she said. This might be the very last time you see him. This possibility seemed sad to me only in the most maudlin, abstract way. But when my mother decided that I was going to do something, it was very difficult to alter that path.

My grandfather had been on the verge of death for three years and would go on to live another two. He had bladder cancer and he wore diapers. He refused to hire a nurse, preferring to have Sylvie and Andrée change him. It was made clear to my mother that she was the delinquent daughter, the one who was not doing enough.

His maid had procured lunch for the three of us. I used the oyster fork incorrectly. After we'd finished eating, my mother went into the back room, the office still decorated as my bedroom, to talk to the maid in private. My grandfather got up and stood behind my chair. He put his hands on my shoulders, his grip surprisingly firm, and pulled me upward.

"Well, let's have a look at you," he said.

My mother came back into the room.

"We've got to run, thank you so much for the marvelous lunch, Papa," she said, giving him a hug.

"Yes, thank you," I said as I leapt for my coat. "Good-bye!" I waved and walked quickly down the hallway to the elevator. My mother and grandfather stood in the doorway to his apartment.

"Not even a kiss good-bye?" he asked, calling out to me.

I hesitated, shifting my weight, trying to think of something to say that meant no but sounded like a friendly joke. My mother said, "Come give your grandfather a kiss," so I walked back.

As I leaned in to kiss his cheek, my grandfather grabbed my breasts. Then he grabbed my shoulders and held me at arm's length and stared at my chest.

"You're much too round," he said.

"Okay," I said. "Bye." My mother and I walked to the elevator.

As the doors closed, my mother laughed.

"What was *that*?" she said, grinning as if we'd both just been through a wacky caper.

"*That's* why I never particularly want to see my grandfather," I said. I wasn't smiling. I was annoyed.

Her smile faded. "*Ohhhh*," she said. "Oh." We were both silent as we left the building.

On the street she asked, "But why did you never tell me?"

"I did," I said.

"Of course you didn't," she said. "I would remember."

"I did," I insisted. "You said he was a plastic surgeon and that's just how he treats women."

"But he's your *grandfather*," she said. "He's not allowed to do that to *you*."

"Yeah," I said, "I guess I know that." But I hadn't known it, really, before then.

MY MOTHER WAS UPSET, but when she told my father, he was furious. It was a surprise to me that this should make anyone so angry. I felt very cozy beneath the black blanket of his outrage. I have always felt at my safest around anger directed at someone not present.

"You don't ever have to see that asshole again," my father told me.

"Really?" I said. I looked at my mother. She nodded confirmation. I felt as if I had received an undeserved gift.

In conversations that happened behind their closed bedroom door, my mother asked my father to talk this out with Paul. My father refused, saying that if he saw the man it would only be to break his jaw. My mother begged him to call Paul on the phone in that case, and find a resolution man to man. Instead, my father wrote my grandfather a letter. I never read it, but I know my father's anger when it turns into words. He faxed it from New York. A few weeks later, one of my aunts called. My grandfather was very wounded. He couldn't understand why I'd invented such outrageous accusations. I must be crazy, he'd concluded. Which was no surprise, considering.

We sat on my mother's bed as she told me about my grandfather's reply. That my grandfather had accused me of inventing the story disturbed me deeply. Ever since the disappearing food in high school—those weeks when I'd allowed myself to become convinced that I was doing something I had no memory of having done—my hold on my own past had felt tenuous. When we watched the film *Gaslight* in a college course, my whole body trembled. Later, in seminar, I had blurted out, "My mother used to accuse me of willfully throwing away all her spoons," which was true. "I did *not* throw the spoons away," I continued forcefully, though we were talking about Barthes and no one had appeared to doubt my innocence. I did not know then that the film had been powerful enough to become a verb.

"I'm so glad it happened in front of you," I said now to my mother with a huge exhale of relief, because I still felt a nagging worry as to whether anything had happened at all.

"Yes," my mother said. "Well." She pulled her earrings from her ears and gazed at them in her hand. The circles under her eyes were deep and she looked infinitely sad.

"It's not easy for me, all this, you know," she said.

"I know," I said, though I hadn't until then.

"He's still my father," she said. "The only one I have. And he's dying."

"I'm really sorry that I've made it so complicated for you," I said with genuine remorse, though I knew in a textbook way that it was considered incorrect for victims to blame themselves.

"It's not you," she said. "It's your father. If only he had called him instead of sending that letter."

WE DIDN'T TALK about it much after that. I suppose we no longer had Christmas lunch with my grandfather, though getting out of it must have raised considerable tensions within the family. I do know that I never saw him again. When we were in Paris, my mother saw him on her own. I stayed behind with my father and brother. I felt as I had on the rare days when a thermometer had miraculously displayed a temperature high enough to keep me home from school.

Two years later, my mother called me sobbing to tell me that Paul had died. I was working as a counselor in a summer camp for people with developmental disabilities, as a way of trying to push my extreme and somewhat debilitating desire to be of service to others to its breaking point. I was nearing it.

My father was not going to Paul's funeral, of course, my mother told me on the phone. I sensed that she didn't want to face it alone. I offered to leave the camp a week early and go with her.

The funeral was held in Paris. Though my grandfather had never been a religious man, he had hedged his bets at the end and called a priest. The service was Catholic, with Latin chants and a censer that spewed aromatic smoke. The church was filled with women I had never seen before, women of all ages in pearls and flamboyant black designer dresses.

"I loved your grandfather *so much*," they came one by one to tell me afterward, "*so much*." Their voices wavered, but their faces were so taut they could barely shed a tear.

Later, a much smaller party went to the internment in Ussel. My memories of that trip are all tinged gray, though it was July. I'd been curious to visit the town where my mother had spent her summers and boarding school years, imagining folkloric country cottages, but it was all grim, short buildings of a claustrophobic sameness. My mother told me several times how grateful she was to have me by her side. At the cemetery, the coffin was pushed into a mausoleum. My mother squeezed my hand tightly. I cried along with her, though less for the grandfather I had known and more for the grandfather I wished I'd had.

———

IT SEEMED TO ME now suddenly possible that they were the same person. I was learning that adults look very different through the eyes of the young. My mother had mentioned, over the years, her great grief that she had never had a moment of reconciliation with her father. My aunts had. They loved him now, with a simplicity they could not manage before. "He was a different person at the end of his life," Sylvie said. "We talked honestly, about a great many things." They did not hide this from my mother. It was their prize, for having changed his diapers, and her punishment, for living in New York with her crazy lying daughter. I knew that my mother didn't blame me for this, and yet guilt weighed on me all the same. It was one of the many reasons I'd come to Paris. It was why I'd called her so breathlessly to tell her about Josée's photo of the pillow.

I went to a shelf of the studio apartment that was lined with my grandfather's collection of old medical books. They were mostly from the 1700s, their spines golden and red, and they crumbled to the touch. I opened one. A photograph slipped out and fluttered to the floor. My breath caught. I bent to pick it up. But it was only a glossy color snapshot of my grandfather and some other old men in a banquet hall, wearing name tags. A surgeon's conference, sometime in the 1990s. This wasn't a fairy tale, I reprimanded myself. The books didn't contain answers.

I was struck with a visceral childhood memory of how much I had once wanted to touch all the forbidden objects on my grandfather's shelves. I ran my fingers along the books gratuitously, touching for the sake of touching, and picked out another. It was a small book, with the words DICTIONARY OF MEDICINE barely visible on the spine. It was stuck to the three books beside it, their spines fused. I pulled all four out together and something rattled. The books were a box. The top two opened away from the bottom two. Inside, set into a leather-colored compartment, was a small crystal decanter and three shot glasses. There was a hole for a fourth glass, but it was missing. Was this from the 1700s as well, or only designed to look so? I had no way of knowing. I opened it, closed it, opened it, removed the shot glasses and decanter and lined them up on a shelf. It was exactly the sort of object I had always loved, with its hint of the untoward. I had had a book that contained a flask, far less elegant than this one, in my Brooklyn apartment. I twisted the stopper out of the decanter and smelled it: a faint whiff of alcohol. *Sillage,* I thought. It was a French word I had recently learned. It had a beautiful sound, *see-yaj.* In its first definition it meant the wake left behind by a boat in the water. But it could also describe the perfume that lingered in the air after its wearer had left the room. I sniffed the decanter again but the smell had dissipated. There was little of my grandfather left to forgive, and perhaps, I thought, this was all I would ever find: the ripples in the water, the lingering smell.

A FEW DAYS LATER, my grandmother called. "Do you like Hopper?" she asked. The Edward Hopper show was the event of the season. Two-hour lines snaked outside the Grand Palais even on weekday afternoons, and the young people I knew all talked about how they were going or had been. Hopper's work had been relatively unknown in France until then. I loved him like he belonged to me. It was in front of a Hopper painting at the Museum of Modern Art, my father talking to me quietly about how the image worked—the lines that guided your eye, the way light entered the room like a person—that I had first felt moved by a painting.

"Yes," I said. I had a sense that interactions with my grandmother were as strategic as chess games. When she was a ghostwriter, she picked her subjects up at the airport, brought them straight to her boat, interviewed them for two or three weeks straight, and only later let them leave to see the Eiffel Tower. I wished I could do the same to her now, but Paris wasn't my city.

"I've reserved two places for us," she said. My grandmother belonged to an association of ex–airline stewardesses, the Broken Wings, which organized group outings and cultural events. Usually she placed Sylvie and Andrée in competition for the tickets, doling them out as rewards for cleaning her Jacuzzi or helping her winterize her boat.

I met Josée at the houseboat for lunch, and we took her car to the museum. As she drove, she told me about how she'd been pulled over the day before.

"This young cop signaled at me to buckle my seat belt and I just . . ." Josée wagged her finger no with a coquettish smile. "He tried two more times, then shrugged his shoulders—*You're asking for it*—and pulled me over. I showed him my doctor's dispensation—he'd never seen anything like it!" she said. "I thought his eyes were going to pop out of his head. He called his friend over to show it to him." She laughed gleefully. Her seat belt was buckled around the back of the driver's seat so that the car's warning mechanism wouldn't chime. It didn't actually hurt her to wear it; she just didn't like being constrained. Her doctor's dispensation was her grand prize for surviving breast cancer, ages ago.

"I'll use my cripple card to get us past the line," she told me, getting out of the car. "We'll have to pretend so that nobody causes a fuss." As we approached the museum, Josée's walk became a limp.

"Give me your arm," she said, leaning her weight on me and

coughing pitifully as she shuffled forward. As we walked past the line of people who stood in the rain, a smile broke across the feigned concern on my face. I'd always been a terrible actress.

I was surprised to discover that we were early. The rest of our group hadn't yet arrived. This never happened with my mother. I left Josée on a bench in a window and went off to find the bathrooms. I passed the museum cafeteria and considered buying Josée an espresso. She usually had a coffee after lunch, but today she had said we didn't have the time. *You're only opening yourself up to punishment,* I scolded myself silently as I washed my hands. But as I walked back past the cafeteria, I got on line.

I came back balancing two plastic espresso cups in hand.

"What a genius idea," she said, her eyes lighting up. "*Quel amour!*"

She sipped. "I think this is the best coffee I've ever had." Very little brought me more pleasure than having somebody appreciate a gift or a gesture. Those were the moments I held on to, turning them over in my mind like sun-warmed stones. Could Josée know me so well already?

"Do you know the happiest moment in my life?" she said into the comfortable silence between us.

"No, when?" I asked.

"When you and your mother were pulling me through the ocean a few years ago, each of you on one arm. I just floated on my back and you were like my two dolphins, my two mermaids. I had such a feeling of comfort and well-being. I could have died happily right then."

Yes, I thought, *better even than I know myself.*

The airline stewardesses were easy to spot, even among the many other older women gathering for tours. They were slender and elegant, with fur coats and impeccably coiffed hair and face-lifts. Josée introduced me as her granddaughter from New York, pride in her voice.

I found comfort in Hopper's paintings of New York, the glimpses of familiar architecture out the windows, the bright rays of sunlight that I craved in that gray Parisian winter. But it was a painting of Paris that held me longest. The title was *Soir Bleu*, always in French even when it hung in America. I'd never seen it before. It was different from everything else. Hopper's paintings were often of empty rooms and empty streets. But here, the painting was of a crowded cafe terrace: a sailor, a prostitute, a bourgeois couple, a sad clown all in white. The space itself was only barely described—two strips of blue, light and dark, defined land and sky—and the Chinese lanterns that dotted the top of the painting cast no light. I was surprised by its lack of emotional depth. Hopper painted it in New York, four years after his return from Paris, the tour guide told us, and then I understood the painting differently: perhaps, I thought, it was of the exaggerated archetypes people become in your memory, and how large and flat they then loom.

"There you are," Josée said, having left the group to find me. She glanced at the painting. "You like this one?" There was some skepticism in her voice.

"It's not the most beautiful one," I said cheerily, and I slipped my arm through hers.

The afternoon went by quickly. Josée made me laugh with her asides about the other museumgoers. Her commentary on the paintings was reserved but invariably astute. She dropped me off at home and gave me a hug, her blue eyes warmer than I'd ever seen them before.

"It's so good to have you in Paris, my little dear," she said.

chapter eight

How is it going with your grandmother?" my new Parisian friends asked me. I didn't know how to answer. Things were going well. They were going almost too well. I had had a script in mind—she would be cruel to me, I would persevere. After hours and hours together, I would eventually uncover the sweet doting grandmother I had always wanted. But here she was already, that woman I'd longed for, taking me to museums, showing me off, praising me. It was almost too easy.

My first months in Paris unfolded in a haze. There were days when I did nothing, all of my energy consumed by navigating the city. I had fluency in the language, but I was surprised to find how much of the culture evaded my grasp. I did not know then that I must say "bonjour" before asking for directions, when entering a store, to each cashier, that not to do so was as inexcusable as not saying "thank you." Cashiers slammed my items into shopping bags, people turned away from me without a word. My differentness radiated off me, profoundly irritating to others, my French too fluid to excuse it. There was a special harshness older French women reserved for younger women who did not meet their expectations. Rarely a day went by when I did not find myself scolded by a stranger. I braced myself and yet still often found myself fighting back the sting of tears.

"I'm going to forget all this. I need to write it down," I wrote in a notebook I kept during those months, but I wrote little else. I let days blend into nights and back into days, sunrise hitting me like a racing pulse. When I tried to remember the day before, it was only streaks, like a watercolor caught in the rain.

My whole life, I'd lived in a city that reinvented itself as constantly as I did. New York was a blur of rising skyscrapers and changing storefronts. But Paris held time like a lake. It piled on like sediment, in geographical layers, invisible striations up the unchanging façades. I visited all the places my mother had once lived. On Rue Dauphine, in the heart of the Left Bank, I slipped into the interior courtyard of the building where she and Jean-Michel had once shared a studio apartment. I counted up to find her windows, half expecting to see the ghost of her young self peering out from behind the curtains.

I was often lonely, and to be so in Paris felt new. One afternoon, my mood heavy, I wandered the city tentatively. I longed to see the water and so I denied myself that. I went into an artist's squat on Rue de Rivoli, its doors thrown open to tourists, and climbed the graffiti-covered stairs. I found myself in a corner that had been piled thick with scavenged objects: a plaster cast of a hand, a taxidermied monkey, empty birdcages filled with spray-painted plastic bottles. Handwritten signs dangled from the ceiling on strings. YOU KNOW YOU'LL NEVER BE ABLE TO FEED THEM, SO WHY DO YOU HAVE CHILDREN? one read. I snuck out again, ignoring the artists who beckoned to me from behind their drafting tables. I walked a few more blocks toward the Seine.

Almost there, I ducked into one of the many pet stores on the

Right Bank. Perfect puppies and kittens pawed at the Plexiglas of their small cages. A young girl Rollerbladed down a corridor of fish tanks. At the back of the store, where there were fewer children, I stopped to look at a fat golden hamster. She stood slowly and beneath her I saw a mass of babies, pink and larval, their eyes still hidden beneath bulges of gray. The hamster scratched at the straw lining of her cage, burying the babies deeper, pushing them into place, then sat again. Only a few small pink limbs escaped. An American boy near me screamed, "Look, Mom, the mouse is using his wheel!" I knew I should share this with him, or with his mother who smiled serenely at her son's manic joy. But I did not. I kept the secret for myself.

I left the store and finally I allowed myself to walk out over a bridge into the middle of the water. The limestone buildings turned rose-gold as the sun set and shards of color scattered across the Seine. But as I sat, hugging my knees in one of the bridge's stone alcoves, all I smelled was urine, all I saw were the flashing cameras that imperfectly captured the night. My mood did not lift. And I felt Parisian at last, still sad in the face of all that beauty.

Shortly after I moved to France, my mother came to visit. It was prearranged, a business trip whose timing she couldn't control, and while I might have been annoyed at this push-pull freedom (my dramatic departure, our tearful good-byes, seemed ludicrous now), I was relieved to see her. I ran to the bakery before her arrival and prepared a spread of croissants and fruit and cheese. I made her a cappuccino and then, when I saw how her eyes drifted shut, coaxed her into taking a nap in my bed. I felt peaceful, working in the early-morning light while she slept. It brought me a deep pleasure to coddle my mother—*la chouchouter,* as they said in France. When-ever I managed to slow my mother down long enough to indulge in sleeping or eating, it alleviated my guilt at my own slow pace.

With my mother by my side, there were no obstacles. Every-thing sped up. Each day she spent in Paris was filled to the brim. Time was no longer quicksand, it was an ice pick with which to dismantle the world. On the first day of her visit, she gave a radio interview, bought me a coffee machine, saw a friend for lunch, met with an artist about his *New Yorker* covers, gave another interview to a print journalist, called the mayor's office about the brothel our neighbor was opening on the ground floor, negotiated the details of the ceremony later in the week where she would be given the French Legion of Honor, showed me how to scrub the toilet bowl white and oil the wood counters, then sent proofs of the latest children's book she was publishing to the printer in China. Each night I fell gratefully into the bed we shared and slept soundly.

One afternoon, we briefly parted ways. I went into a shop, intending to buy a gift for a friend. The male shopkeeper followed me to the back of the store. He hovered near, commenting on my body, his hands almost touching, then touching, my shoulder. I left empty-handed, blushing and upset. When I told my mother later that day, she listened with a sympathy she'd rarely shown before.

"I know it's hard," she said. "But you have to find a strategy. Tell yourself that this is what you wanted, even if it isn't true. Tell yourself you make yourself pretty for a reason. Tell yourself you win each time, because otherwise it feels like losing—and I never want you to feel that way." I heard her advice, and it was useful. It marked a turning point for me. Now when I walked through groups of men who had watched me coming from half a block away, I did not bow my head. I looked them in the eyes. I dared them to speak. I wanted them to. They never did.

On the eve of her birthday, my mother visited Josée alone. She told me she needed a moment with her mother. She spent the night on the houseboat and came back looking soft and vulnerable.

As we walked through Paris the next day, she insisted on avoiding the main boulevards. We ducked instead through small streets and covered passageways, winding our way toward each destination. It seemed to me she was avoiding the streets she knew too well, the streets where time stood still.

The alleyway we had taken dead-ended into a private court-yard. I sighed with annoyance. My mother said softly, "I feel like a piece of paper when I'm in Paris." As we turned around, she looped her arm through mine.

"I have no weight here," she said. "I could blow away at any moment. Everything in this city, it's . . . it's as they say in English, it's 'heavy' here."

We cut down another small street and came across a small Korean restaurant bustling with customers. "I don't think I've had Korean food before," she said as she pushed open the door. The restaurant was loud, and yet, as usual when we were just the two of us, my mother and I slipped easily into intimate conversation.

"Last night," she said, "Josée asked me if my father had ever . . ." She paused. I waited. "What was the word she used?" my mother asked herself. "It was very specific. *Inconsiderate . . . immodest . . . indiscreet!* She asked if my father had ever made indiscreet gestures toward me."

"As in . . . sexually?" I asked, trying to make sense of this.

"Yes. I told her no. But she didn't seem to believe me."

"Why would she ask?" I said. My mother shrugged. She seemed more perplexed than perturbed.

"I told her that, well, it *had* made me very uncomfortable that he used to walk around our house naked. But Josée said she used to walk around our house naked, too, which is true. Both my parents have always been nudists." In fact, as they'd been having this conversation, Josée had been naked in the Jacuzzi. My mother was getting undressed. Josée remarked that Françoise had developed a gut and warned her that at her age any pounds she gained she would never lose. My mother seemed more upset by this comment than by Josée's earlier question.

"But what did she mean about your father?" I said, steering her back.

There had been some moments of awkwardness with her father, my mother said. Though nothing like what Josée was hinting at. When my mother was nineteen, Paul brought her to St. Barths for a vacation. My mother remembered standing in the doorway of the hotel room. There was only one room, only one bed. Paul slept naked.

"Papa, I don't want to share a bed with you," she'd said. He'd asked why.

"I don't know," she'd said. "It just makes me very uncomfortable."

"But it doesn't bother me at all!" he'd said magnanimously, as if he were excusing her for something.

My mother laughed. It was on that same vacation that the two of them had been seen together by a friend of Josée's. The friend later reported to Josée that she'd seen Paul with a very young girlfriend.

"Oh, no," Josée had corrected her. "He was with Françoise. That's his daughter."

"No," the friend had insisted. "The way they were together, the two of them, the way he touched her . . . I don't believe that that was his daughter."

It was this last that Josée had told my mother in the Jacuzzi, this that had led her to ask about the indiscreet gestures.

I said, "But it wasn't? . . . it wasn't . . . the way he was with you . . . it wasn't disturbing to you?"

No, my mother told me. What disturbed her were his very young girlfriends. *That*, she said, made her very uncomfortable.

"Was that all that made Josée suspicious?" I asked. "That her friend had mistaken you for your father's girlfriend?"

No, she said. Around the same period, in her early twenties, my mother told me, she had spent some time assisting her father at the hospital. His secretary had later reported to Josée that the two kissed on the lips in the break room.

"Was that true?" I asked.

"I don't remember it," my mother said. "We might have kissed on the lips, but it wasn't in a way that should have made anyone uncomfortable." What she remembered of that time, she said, was fainting over and over at the sight of blood and her father forcing her to keep trying. She resented that.

We'd finished our drinks. She suggested another round. I suggested that we go home, drink wine, and continue the conversation privately.

At the apartment, my mother lay down on the couch with her feet on my lap. She closed her eyes, wineglass aloft.

"We don't have to keep talking," I said softly.

"No, no," she said. "I'm just resting my eyes. I'm not going to fall asleep. What were we talking about?"

"*Les gestes indiscrets,*" I said.

"Right. Well yes, then Josée said that when I was living in my father's apartment, I'd slept with him in his bed. I told her no, I slept in Andrée's room. But she insisted, she said, the suicide, she said, I found you naked in his bed." My mother sighed and propped herself up to drink.

That was only for the suicide attempt, my mother told me now. And it was true, she acknowledged, that perhaps there had been something strange about this, about how she had lain down on her father's side of the bed that morning. But she didn't want to die in Andrée's bed, where she had often been miserable.

"And you think it was only that?" I asked in a small voice.

"Well *of course* Freud would tell you otherwise," my mother said.

She was silent a moment. Her lips twitched. She looked scared. She put her fingers to her mouth and pulled out a shard of glass. She looked at it, glistening between her fingers, and stood up to throw it away. She rinsed out her glass and poured herself more wine.

"You want the same bottle?" I asked. I let myself hope that the shard had somehow come from the bottle; that it hadn't been, from the start, in the wineglass I had handed her.

"No point opening a new one," she said. "But you shouldn't buy this brand anymore."

She sat back down by me on the couch, her arm over my shoulder as I leaned against her chest.

"No, clearly there was something . . . something strange," she continued. "But I remember what was in my head at the time. It had nothing to do with my father. I got very close to throwing myself off the balcony. I was just too scared." She turned to me with an apologetic grimace, as if embarrassed by this cowardice.

"Of course," I said reassuringly. "But—the decision to be in your underwear . . . ?"

"My last moments were precious to me. I thought, *Well, merde, this act is for myself. I might as well be as comfortable as possible.*"

"So you took off your clothes?" I asked.

"I slept in my father's bed when he wasn't there. And I slept in my underwear. And my . . . I didn't really have pajamas. I did when he was there, and not when he wasn't. And it was . . . it was May, and the windows looked out over the Seine."

"Okay," I said, "okay." We lapsed into silence. At last I said, "But so, Josée, she found you like this, and so she thought . . . ?"

When my mother spoke next, she mimicked Josée's accusing tone. "'*Because you were always his favorite*,' she said. '*Because he loved you so much and you were always his favorite.*'"

"*Oof*," I said. "She has a way with words."

My mother laughed.

I said, "Do you think that Josée ever thought, *Oh god, I need to protect my daughter from this?*"

"It didn't even occur to her," my mother said immediately. "No."

I sighed.

"Then why? Why did she wait to talk to you about this? Why did she bring it up now?" I asked.

"She's brought it up a few times, recently, on the phone," my mother said.

"A few times? Recently?" I asked. "Because you've gotten closer?" But their closeness wasn't recent. They'd been speaking on the phone every Sunday for years now. What was recent was my presence in France.

"No," my mother said. "I think she'd like to bury, somewhere in this story that she's creating . . . '*In conclusion, ladies and gentlemen,*' *what a great thing I did by divorcing that old pervert. Oh how I suffered.'* If my father raped me, then no one can accuse her of being a bad mother."

I exhaled sharply, in shock.

"And then, of course, I mentioned you," my mother continued, and I sat up, pulling myself away. "I said, 'Paul did act very inappropriately with Nadja.' And Josée said, 'Oh, but he just groped her a bit, he was a plastic surgeon, that's just how he was with women.' Can you believe it? She just dismissed it like that . . ." My mother snapped her fingers, incredulous. I let a beat of silence pass before I spoke.

"Maybe," I said lightly, "it's just par for the course in France? Maybe there's a trope of the dirty old grandfather here and they consider it normal."

This launched my mother into another story, and though I was still reeling, here it came.

"Maybe!" my mother said. "Who knows how they are in France! Because of course there was that whole thing with you and Vinchon . . ."

"Who's Vinchon?" I asked.

"Your father didn't talk to you about this?" she said, surprised. "Well then, maybe I shouldn't either. Vinchon was an acquaintance of ours, whom you met in the South of France one summer . . ."

"You had many strange friends," I said, "who often acted inappropriately with me." I tried to check the note of accusation that crept into my tone.

But my mother said simply, "It's true. You were never particularly well protected by your father, or your mother either, for that matter . . ." The admission was unexpected and gave me pause. I felt myself begin to relax, albeit uneasily.

After meeting our family, Vinchon had sent my father an email. My mother forgot the exact wording, but the email said how nice it had been to meet my father, and wasn't his daughter sexy and wouldn't it be great to fuck her. It was something along those lines, rather explicit. It was a French joke, perhaps, but a strange one.

"I can't believe Papa never talked to you about this," my mother interrupted herself to say. I *mmhmm*ed, but it seemed rather clear to me why he hadn't.

My father had shown the email to my mother, amused and perplexed. My mother had been furious. "How dare Vinchon put you in the same group as himself!" she'd said to him. "Because what are you supposed to respond? 'Yeah, I'd like to fuck her, too'?" But my father didn't react, my mother told me. He didn't threaten to break the man's jaw, like he had with my grandfather. He just never wrote back.

Later, my mother had talked about the email with one of her closest friends, an Italian woman who lived in France. "But it's just a joke," the friend had assured her in her heavy accent. "It's just male bonding. You know how they are in France!"

"No, tell me how they are in France!" my mother had said, this being the punch line to her story. She laughed. I forced myself to join in.

"Your father didn't even defend you," she repeated. "He never even had a discussion about it with you!"

"That's how a real man shucks oysters," my grandmother said to me over her shoulder. "I bet your father doesn't know how to do that."

Thierry tossed the empty half shells out the porthole above her sink. He was a handsome man who lived a few houseboats over. Josée used a mixture of her charms and lavish lunches to entice him into fixing her television or setting up her new smartphone. She leaned over him as he worked, sucking the scraps of flesh still stuck to the shells and playfully scolding him for letting them go to waste. The day before, Josée had called me to verify that I liked oysters. I was touched—she'd never asked me what I liked to eat before. Now, when she told me to set the table, I tried to find my way around the ancient Japanese cabinet that housed her plates, not asking where anything was, trying to preserve our new intimacy.

"Oh no!" she said, when she looked over at the table. "*Oh la la*, we need oyster forks, Nadja, not regular forks. And steak knives for later, not regular knives! And we use small plates for the appetizer, and the big plates for the main courses. Americans! Did your mother never teach you any of this?"

Over lunch, the etiquette lessons flowed into a lecture on which seasons to drink which wines. Such lectures had seemed hopelessly irrelevant to me as a teenager, back when I would happily drink any wine available. But now I felt I'd found precious arcane knowledge with which to amuse my American friends at dinner parties. "One must only drink Pinot Noir between February and June," I would tell them, and we would marvel at the old rules of the Old World.

A plate of six oysters was placed before me. After the third, my stomach locked tight as a fist. I wanted to finish them all—I always finished what was on my plate, more from pathology than politeness—and I had, some time ago, convinced myself to like oysters. But my body was actively refusing now. I fought my way through a fourth, then distributed the remaining two to Thierry and Josée.

Lunch poured its way through a full bottle of wine and the beginning of another. My grandmother served a beef stew. Thierry told me about his psychic connection with animals. My grandmother served cheese. As the meal wound down, I tried to clear our plates. "But really, they're barbaric these Americans," Josée exclaimed. "Don't you know it's rude to clean while the guest is still here?" I sat back down, blushing.

When Thierry left, I tried again, but my grandmother insisted we both go lie down. A nap in the late afternoon! It was a luxury I wouldn't have dared suggest to my mother.

The rental unit in the front of the boat was currently vacant, and I occasionally spent long weekends at Josée's, sleeping there. I slid shut the Japanese paper doors and lay on the mattress on the floor. Light streamed in through the round windows and I could hear the splash of oars as rowers passed. The book I was reading was very boring and I had it open on my chest as I drifted off.

I felt a pang of nausea. I knew my grandmother's boat was too big to rock, and the Seine too calm to rock it, but I was thinking of a memory. I was very young, on a small boat on the ocean, wearing a big straw sun hat. I had been sick. I had been carried down into the captain's cabin belowdecks to lie down. That was all I remembered. But just a few days before, my mother had mentioned a trip my grandfather had taken us on. She'd been telling me how he tried to buy affection, how it always ended badly. He'd chartered a small motorboat to take us out over the Mediterranean. I'd thrown up and he'd been furious at me and my mother, his gift unappreciated. She'd taken me belowdecks, away from his anger. I asked how old I'd been. Three, said my mother, and it felt reassuring, solid, to be able to point to the exact place in time where my first memory lay.

The waves of nausea came stronger now. I leapt to my feet and began to run toward the bathroom. I threw up as I ran and changed course for the kitchen, which was closer. Someone had placed a wooden cutting board over the sink. I had no time to move it. I bent over it, heaving. Timidly I knocked on the door to my grandmother's apartment, stomach still churning.

"*Oui mon chat!*" she called cheerfully. I opened the door and stood there, embarrassed. She'd changed into a kimono and was straightening some papers in her living room.

"Do you need something?" she asked.

"I threw up," I said, feeling childish.

"On the carpet?" she asked.

"A little bit," I said. "Mostly in the sink."

"Let's see," she said, and led the way. There was a small trail of vomit on the cream-colored carpet in the living room, spatters that stretched about a foot and a half long.

"Like a sick puppy," she said, laughing.

There was a huge puddle of vomit on the cutting board in the sink. She picked up the board and threw the whole thing out the window into the Seine. "Well, that's one thing taken care of," she said, brushing her hands briskly against each other. She fetched some blue powder and a strange hard sponge and I knelt down and started to scrub.

My stomach churned. This time I made it to the toilet. When I came back out, I returned to scrubbing the spot on the carpet. Josée put a bowl on the ground next to me in case I felt sick again. The stains began to disappear. Visions of oysters swam sickeningly before my eyes.

"Feeling better?" she asked as I stood up.

"A little," I said. I got myself a glass of water. I could feel her watching me, waiting for an explanation. I wanted to save us both the embarrassment of my ungrateful stomach.

"It must have been all that running around last week when my mother was here," I said quickly. "I got used to not eating."

"Of course!" she said, the tension flowing out of the space between us. "With the way she goes, nonstop, never a break, you must have worn yourself out trying to keep up."

She went next door to make me tea. I went back to the bathroom and threw up the glass of water.

"I'm leaving your tea here on the table!" she called to me. "I'm going to bed. Tomorrow, we'll have to call your mother and tell her what she did to you."

The next morning, we ate a simple breakfast of toast. I drank water out of a wineglass. My grandmother owned no water glasses. She never drank water because, she said, she knew what was in it. The night before, while I'd been sleeping, she'd thrown her broken office chair, a huge ergonomic contraption on wheels, into the Seine. I'd thought she was joking until I saw that it was really gone.

"Stress is terrible for your health," Josée told me, "and Françoise refuses to relax even when she has the chance. She must have deaths on her conscience. We'll have to tell her what she did to you."

She buttered another piece of toast for me, against my protests. "You have to eat," she said.

By evening, the story had changed. At dinner, Josée told my aunt, "Nadja's been partying too hard! When she arrived at the boat for lunch yesterday, Thierry thought that she was a destitute woman seeking shelter. He almost had to carry her down the stairs. And then she drank so much wine at lunch that she threw up all over my carpet. So, slowly now, Nadja! No wine for you." They laughed at me. I considered arguing—I'd shown up in my best dress! Only had two glasses of wine!—and instead I stayed silent and forced a smile. But that morning, my grandmother and I had found common ground. I'd happily accepted another piece of toast and let the story be about my mother.

I SAW JOSÉE OFTEN, nearly every week. She took me to museums and to plays, even though she herself hated the theater. She gave me a handbag made of cheetah fur that one of her boyfriends, an explorer who had introduced the Western world to Easter Island, had gotten made for her in Africa. She asked me questions about how I spent my days, and when I felt at ease enough to tell funny stories, she listened, delighted. She showered me in compliments. *Of course you made friends here,* she told me, *you're so charismatic and beautiful,* she told me. *You're melting away,* she said, each time she saw me. *Only a few more pounds to lose, not even.* And still, I fought with my distrust. We each had ulterior motives, I thought, and we danced around each other carefully. Josée was a seductress, I told myself; I must not get seduced. And yet here was the woman before me: so sweet, so attentive, so increasingly frail. Here she was, lighting up whenever she saw me. Here were the meals she so carefully prepared, here were the presents she gave so easily. Was she secretly a monster? Or was I, for projecting that possibility onto her?

One afternoon, she answered the door more quickly than I had expected. I hadn't had time to prepare myself for the transition from the self I was when I was alone, drifting around my body with loose grand thoughts, to the little girl I became when I was with her, compact, passive, polite. The first few moments between us were often strained, and this was part of why I never arrived empty-handed.

"I brought you clementines and pears," I said, thrusting the bag between us.

"Wonderful," she said. "Go put them down in the kitchen." She didn't tell me then that she hated pears. Later I would learn that they'd been left to ripen over one of the beds of her childhood, and that the smell made her ill to this day.

"I'm starving," she said. It was four in the afternoon, and though I'd told her I couldn't make it at two as she'd requested, she'd waited for me for lunch.

"But first I have a small project for you," she said, as she often did. This time it was to rehang the kitchen clock, which had fallen off its hook. I used a step stool to kneel on the kitchen counter, groping the back of the clock until the nail found the hole.

"There you go," I said. "Easy."

"You see," she said. "It's the simplest things I can't do for myself anymore."

"Well, I'm always happy to do them," I said.

Sylvie often helped Josée with these things, but they weren't speaking right now. I wasn't clear on the reasons why. "She came over for lunch, and I said, I don't know what, 'Pass me the salt,' maybe, and she said, 'I'm not your damn servant!' and she stormed out!" Josée said with wide-eyed innocence. "You know how she is, Sylvie. She's so volatile. No one can understand her."

I *mmhmm*ed and set the table.

I knew all too well how good Josée was at deflecting my questions with answers to questions I'd never asked. She often took us on detours into the safer, better-traveled grounds of the past, but today I was determined. "How did my mother change when she became an adolescent?" I asked as we sat down to eat, switching the voice memo app on my phone to "record."

"What do you mean by adolescent?" she said.

"I don't know—twelve, thirteen."

"Oh, well yes, those were the years that Sylvie was gone. We all breathed a huge sigh of relief. Françoise was happy then, she finally discovered herself. Before that, the house was a constant terror with those two girls fighting. We all lived in fear of their arguments."

"Sylvie and Françoise?"

"It was constant! The whole house was dominated by them. And Sylvie was a terror. She hit your mother. She was very strong. And when she left, we could all finally breathe again. I think those were very happy years for Françoise, her adolescence."

"She described it as a difficult time," I said.

"Oh, it was horrible!" Josée said.

"But I mean . . . ," I said. "Even after Sylvie left . . ."

"What year are we talking about?"

"1966 or 1967?" I guessed.

"Ah, but that's exactly when Sylvie was gone!" Josée exclaimed.

"She told me that her relationship with you wasn't easy," I said carefully.

"I don't know what she's talking about," Josée said. "She was doing very well in school. That's when she discovered she was nearsighted and went and got contact lenses. We did yoga together, and judo. And May 1968, that's when she discovered the rest of Paris. That's when the world was unveiled for her."

"But didn't you fight sometimes?"

"She and I? No. I don't remember ever fighting with her. There weren't many motives. Perhaps I scolded her for letting the bathtub run and flooding the neighbors? But otherwise no—she was obedient."

I persisted. "She told me you sent her to get an encephalo-gram? Because she was crazy?"

"*Euhhh* . . . an encephalogram." Josée thought. "Ah, yes. That was when she was fourteen. That was because she was too smart! It was beginning to worry us. A psychiatrist recommended we get an exam done on her. That wasn't because she was sad! *Au contraire.* We didn't know that we had an overly gifted daughter. There wasn't a word for it then." Josée gave me a sweet, remorseful smile.

I pushed on. My mother had told me about being so unhappy when they fought that she'd scratched her own face, made herself bleed.

"That's the first I hear about it!" Josée said. She'd seen no such thing, she insisted. It was Sylvie who'd done all the scratching. "But . . . from thirteen until when, did you say? What years does she claim she was miserable?"

I hesitated. *I remember these things geographically, not chronolog-ically,* my mother had said. "Maybe between twelve and fifteen?" I hazarded.

"*Ahh!*" Josée said, excited by a new revelation. "I think I see, maybe, what she's alluding to. What she had at the time, which must have perturbed her very much, were her *crises de tétanie!* That was a lack of calcium. It made her roll on the floor. *Ah voilà!* That must be what she's talking about. And yes, in fact, I think that's why we sent her to get the encephalogram."

Josée's relief that this matter had been squared away was pal-pable. It was difficult to find in myself the desire to continue.

"Actually, she told me there were two separate things," I said. "The *crises de tétanie,* yes, but also a certain hysteria when you fought. When she scratched her face."

"Well no. Hysteria! Maybe when she fought with Sylvie. But

never with me." And then something came to her. "Oh! I know what she's talking about now! Yes, I see. That was around the time when she discovered a passion for Andrée, and she took care of her as if she were her own child, her own baby. I thought it was strange, and I told her to ask her friends about it—at thirteen, fourteen, I think she had at least one friend. And perhaps I talked to a psychiatrist about it as well. And so I forbade her from spending so much time with her sister. It wasn't healthy. Françoise hadn't liked that one bit—that must be what she remembered."

"Because Andrée was calling her *maman,* right?" I said, hoping to find neutral ground.

Josée gave me a wide-eyed double take. "*Maman?* No, Andrée was seven years old then. I should hope she knew who her mother was!" She laughed.

"So," I said, "you don't remember the *crises de nerfs?*"

"Well, perhaps that's what we called the *crises de tétanie,* before they were diagnosed. But that she mutilated herself . . . No, I'm sure that didn't happen. Or perhaps I just didn't notice. You see, I am a bad mother after all." Josée smiled at me ruefully. But behind the smile, I saw the exhaustion in her eyes. I let the conversation drop. What was I trying to prove?

ANOTHER TIME, I asked Josée if my mother had ever cooked as a girl. When she said no, I asked if she remembered the lemon pie.

"Oh yes, no. That's not quite the story," she said. "Paul didn't fetch a chain saw. A handsaw maybe, or a very big knife." She told me the story again and it was much the same. Except for the ending, which was completely different.

"She set the pie down on the table, and we were saying *Ai-ai-ai,* how will we even cut it. And just then, an extraordinary thing happened—a thing that saved us all. An avalanche. It exploded the window in the girls' bedroom and came all the way into the kitchen. It stopped short right at our feet." I set my fork down and stared at my grandmother amazed.

"And we all said—*oof!*" she continued. "First of all because we weren't dead and second of all because we wouldn't have to eat that pie! And then we must have told that story ten, a hundred, times to all our friends. And because she has a very poor sense of humor, your mother, and a lot of pride, it stayed on her stomach. The pie, luckily, did not stay on ours, because we never ate it."

"But it's incredible," I said. "How stories change. How differently we remember."

"Your mother must agree that was the very first recipe she ever tried!" Josée was instantly combative.

"Yes, of course," I said. "But she never—"

"She says she tried to cook again after that?" Josée interrupted. "No. That's just not true."

"No," I said. "The avalanche! She never mentioned the avalanche."

"Oh!" Josée said. "Everyone remembers it that way. Ask Sylvie!" I saw my mother's memory as I had always imagined it—the family seated around an elegant wood dining table, forks raised, the yellow pie illuminated by cool winter light. And then I saw the image fill with snow.

"Look at what I found the other day," Josée said to me.

She handed me a white plaster cast. It was the face of a young girl. Her closed eyelids were barely delineated from her cheekbones, as if they had never been able to open. The nearly straight line of her wide mouth was now a smile, now a frown, depending on how you looked—a Rorschach blot of emotion.

"What is it?" I asked, turning it over in my hands. It felt both heavy and fragile.

"It's your mother," Josée said. "I was learning to make plaster casts for your grandfather's practice, and I tried my hand on her. Don't you recognize her?"

"No," I said.

"Look at her eyebrows—you can see how hairy she was," Josée said, laughing. "They nearly touched."

I held my mother's face gently in my hand, reverent. On her cheek there was a circular crack where the plaster had broken and been glued. I traced it gently with my thumb.

JOSÉE CAME OVER for lunch. It was a rare occasion; she hated driving into the city center, where there was often traffic and no parking. I cleaned the apartment from top to bottom. I put on some soft jazz and set the Ikea table carefully, forks on folded napkins. It was midwinter now, February, and a cold gray light streamed in through the tall windows. I had made a chicken cashew curry, which I hoped was foreign enough that Josée would find its quality difficult to judge.

"You've transformed my cheetah bag into a couch accessory," Josée said, noticing that I'd draped it over the armrest. "You should put a pillow inside it," she said. "I have one, I'll give it to you."

She exclaimed over the curry and I listed the ingredients for her, trying to sound casual. Then I attempted to ask questions that would pull us into her past, but once again we kept sliding forward in time. The windows were open against the dry heat of the radiator, and a breeze filtered through. I let go of my agenda and allowed her to lead. She gravitated to the moment of her divorce. It was Paul she wanted to talk about today.

"Those were the most difficult years," she said. People she'd trusted told outright lies in court. Paul had taken Andrée away from her and then, right after, he'd thrust the girl into boarding school. The women she'd once believed to be her friends turned their backs on her. They thought she must be crazy to leave her handsome rich doctor husband and go live on a boat. And at forty! Several of the acquaintances she'd had as a married woman were surprised to run into her years later. Paul had told them all that she had died.

"I left with my hands in my pockets," she told me. "I didn't ask for a cent." Which, I was fairly sure, was not entirely true. But it was a phrase she had repeated to me so often, sliding her hands over her own pockets as she did so, that I had a clear image of young beautiful Josée, strolling away, whistling.

When the divorce finally went through, she'd stood on the roof of her boat and dropped the pages of paperwork into the Seine one by one, then watched them float off. It had been the worst moment of her life, that divorce. Worse than her breast cancer the year following. Many women develop breast cancer after a contentious divorce, she told me parenthetically, and I wondered if there was anything terrible that wasn't somehow Paul's fault. It had been worse, even, she said, than the very difficult moments her daughters had put her through.

"Which difficult moments were those?" I asked.

"Your mother, she left me. I bought her a plane ticket for New York and she disappeared for a year, no news. When she came back, she went to live at her father's. And then there was her suicide attempt, of course. I saved her life and she spat in my face."

And then Josée told me the story of that day as she remembered it—the telepathic cry of "Maman," Andrée pulled from the shower with shampoo still in her hair, the rush to Paul's apartment, Françoise's anger the day after. The details were surprisingly similar to my mother's version. Then I realized that my mother had been unconscious and had had only her mother's version to tell.

"Why do you think she did that? Tried to kill herself?" I asked, wondering if this would be the question that would at last allow me in.

"She said it was a love pain, that a boy had broken her heart," Josée said. "But I . . . I don't think so."

"Then what?" I said softly.

"I think that your father . . . he conducted himself very badly with her." Josée leaned back from the table and refolded her napkin carefully. It was common in our conversations for her to slip-slide through the generations, referring to my aunts as my sisters and my grandfather as my father. Often she did not catch herself and I did not correct her, though the effect these incorrect words had on me was strong. "His secretary told me they kissed on the mouth in the break room, and you know, in a hospital, everyone is naked under their scrubs. He had such an adulation for Françoise," Josée said with a heavy sigh, her voice measured and low.

"You think that there was something . . . unhealthy about their relationship?" I asked.

"Oh, more than *unhealthy*. I hope he didn't rape her. I don't know. It wouldn't surprise me. Your mother, she'll never talk about it. And him, he's dead now. He was sexually attracted to her, yes, that much was clear. Because for him—he was such a narcissist. And in Françoise he saw himself as a woman. It was the ultimate fantasy. He'd re-created himself in her and then sacrificed her, consumed her whole. It's why she left for New York, I think, to escape him. I've spent a very long time analyzing all this, you know."

I put down my fork. I could feel my body shutting down, organ by organ. Even later, writing this, my hands at first refused to move.

"You asked me why she tried to kill herself. I think it was that," Josée continued. "She had gotten into his bed, after all. There must have been something sexual. I hope that it didn't go all the way. But I don't know. I'll never know."

She leaned forward, low to the table, and looked into my eyes. "I think that we must never talk to her about this," she said. "The most awful thing for Françoise would be to suspect that we know."

I swallowed. I nodded, almost imperceptibly.

"Of course," Josée said, leaning back again, "it is possible that she herself doesn't know. The very difficult things, sometimes you create a hole in your memory, to protect yourself from them. Like when murderers don't remember having killed people."

Josée and I had seen a French thriller with just this premise the week before. She had found it interesting, and I had hated it—not simply because of the stale male fantasy at its core, the middle-aged professor aggressively besieged by attractive young women, but because those swirling black holes disturbed me profoundly. It had happened to me once, the unexpected resurgence of a difficult childhood memory. It had made me feel I was losing my hold on reality. It terrified me, already, that I was composed of a past that was so lonely, that was made up of memories and narratives no one else in my family could agree upon. It was too much that it might be unknowable to myself as well. I wondered often how many other memories lurked within me, dark and alien as cancers.

I believed my mother's version of events. In later conversations, she would repeat to me, her voice hard as steel, that her father had never done what Josée suggested. He had not crossed any boundaries. Her eyes flashed; she did not waver. I had no doubts. Still, I knew that my grandfather had not respected certain limits. When one of my aunts was a teenager and very beautiful, he'd taken her to nightclubs and told her not to call him Papa. But that was a far cry from Josée's suspicions—*Rape! Incest!*—that did such violence to me as I wrote them. They carved this fragile complex history into mountains I barely recognized.

"Anyway, he was an inveterate skirt chaser, your grandfather," Josée continued, her voice playing from my computer speakers now. "He fucked like a goat."

It was months before I could bring myself to transcribe this recording. I knew I had to force myself to place the words on the page, if not because they were *the* story then because they were one of the stories, but I fled. I slammed my computer shut. I scrubbed my shower until it sparkled and my knuckles bled.

"Yes," I heard myself saying in reply. "He didn't seem to understand the limits."

"It was *him him him*," Josée said. Said, *Fucked like a goat*. Said, *It wouldn't surprise me*. Said, *We'll never know*.

"With me," I must have said, because there it was in the transcript I eventually made, "there were certain things that were . . . not clear and clean. He didn't always know what was acceptable, especially with his family."

"With you? But you weren't his type," Josée said. "You don't look anything like your mother! And lucky for you. He would have devoured you as well. He was a vulture, voracious. Yes, and I, I chose *that* man as my procreator!"

Later, Josée would mention that afternoon we'd spent together quite often. Not because of the content of our conversation, but because I'd insisted upon scooping the rest of the curry into a Tupperware container and pressed it upon her when she left. "A 'doggy bag,'" she told her friends in front of me, so clearly charmed by both my thoughtfulness and my foreignness. "She gave me a 'doggy bag'!"

For me the afternoon lingered briefly, like a mirage, then disappeared from the edges in as soon as it was over. My only vivid memory was of Josée leaning across the table—*We must never talk to her about this, the most awful thing for Françoise would be to suspect that we know*—and my nod in response, the pact signed and sealed, as if in blood.

Though of course I had already talked to my mother about it, *glass in her throat,* and I believed her. Wasn't this something I could just skip over and leave in the past? But here it was. It had been placed in my story and its weight dented the pages. The heavy red crystal ashtray sat beside me as I worked, steadily filling with cigarette butts.

WIND FILLED MY BACK like a sail and propelled me down the wide avenue toward Josée's apartment. The world had a hazy, unreal quality to it this morning. I'd seen friends the night before with whom I always drank heavily—vodka tonics, white wine, a sweet liquor whose name escaped me but whose cloying taste lingered.

"*Bonjour mon petit chat,* here take off your . . . thing . . . get comfortable." I was wearing a long sweater as a coat. I took Josée's lack of direct comment about it as a good sign.

"I went to war against all the women of Paris to get us a roast chicken on a Sunday," I told her. "None of the butchers would sell them until one on the dot and five minutes later there wasn't a bird left on the whole street." I'd prepared the sentences on my walk from the train.

She laughed distractedly. "So this storm!" she said.

"What?" I said.

"There are fast winds tearing through the north of France," she said. "And even here." I listened and heard the wind whistling into her kitchen, saw the trees swaying outside.

"Oh," I said. I hadn't noticed the storm. I grasped for something to say.

Around Josée, I had two ways of being, neither of which was myself. Most of the time, I spoke to her in my squeakiest polite-little-girl French, shy and eager to please. Occasionally, often after returning from a trip, I was brash, so excited to have something to say that I spoke too loudly, with little confidence that I would be listened to, and choked on my words. I sensed that Josée preferred the quiet version and that was certainly how I felt myself to be today. Small and buried deep inside, like a child in a huge winter coat. Lines from a letter I'd recently found, from a thirteen-year-old Françoise to Mina, taunted me. *I would so like always to remain the Françoise I am with you,* my mother had written to her grandmother. *It would be so much more agreeable for everyone.*

I carved the chicken, trying not to use my hands. Carving was a man's job. Josée had taken pains to show my brother how to do it one Christmas, her hands guiding his. I'd watched attentively, doubly eager to learn any task not meant for me, but I still hadn't figured out how to use the knife to seek out the soft cartilage between the bones.

"We have an excellent cheese for afterward," Josée told me, lips pursed, not commenting on my carving. "I had to put it on the windowsill."

On the ledge outside her window, a half-moon of cheese floated in water.

"Oh! He got rained on," Josée said. "We'll have to dry him off." She drained and unwrapped the cheese, and an intense odor filled the room, sharp and bodily. My stomach flipped.

"Your mother sent me that new book about her," Josée said. "It's terrible. I called her to tell her right away."

"That new book" was a biography of my mother written by comics scholar Jeet Heer. I hadn't seen the finished book but I'd read most of the text in manuscript and found it smart and competent, although I'd had to push aside the selfish desire that my mother be my subject alone. The last time I'd spoken to my mother, she'd told me that Josée had criticized the cover and said the book was printed on bad paper and full of typos.

I was surprised Josée hadn't liked the book—I remembered the four scant pages on my mother's childhood as being filled with praise for Josée.

"She says that she was an unwanted child," Josée said, "which isn't true at all! Of course she was wanted."

"But . . . you didn't mean to have a second child so soon," I said.

"She wasn't planned, but that doesn't mean she wasn't *wanted*," Josée said.

"But also, you'd hoped for a boy. I think that's all she was trying to say," I said.

"No, she was wanted. She was loved. She was our little *chouchou* when she was born."

"But it's in context," I said. "The book says she 'made her

unwelcome entrance into the world.' She's only trying to say that she was unwelcome in the moment."

"*Non!*" Josée said in a burst of anger. I looked up at her. "*I* was the unwanted child, not her." There was that brief lull in conversation, the silent pause.

"And then it says that she ran away to New York because she and I fought all the time. And that, really, no! We had one fight that I remember, but other than that . . . No. I don't remember ever fighting with her. It just isn't true." And she launched once again into her familiar narrative of those years, of her daughters fighting like wildcats and herself at wits' end, struggling to keep the peace.

In a later conversation, Josée criticized the book again, this time claiming that Françoise had called her a frustrated housewife and nothing more. When I offered to go get the book to remind her of the actual text, she replied that to set eyes on it again would make her feel sick.

Here is what the book says: "While [Josée] would eventually reinvent herself, with great success, as an art book dealer, real estate agent, ghostwriter (with at least one bestseller to her credit) and interior designer—an unusual career arc that would also inspire Mouly—mother and daughter had an occasionally nettlesome relationship. (Spiegelman says that when he first met his mother-in-law, she took him aside to make fun of Mouly for lacking sufficient cooking and domestic skills.) Mouly needed to get away from France."

I picked anxiously at my food, thinking about "occasionally nettlesome," thinking about the book I was writing.

"This chicken is delicious!" Josée said, even though it was too dry. "I had a feast. You see, I hate speaking when I'm eating and look at how much I've just told you."

The only other mention of Josée in the book reads, "Mouly says now that her appreciation of beauty is very much tied to her sense of her mother as a 'truly beautiful, graceful, elegant and glamorous person.' Even as a child, Mouly wanted to create art beautiful enough to suit [Josée]: 'A lot of my early memories as a kid have to do with making objects and paintings for her.'"

In my own book, I knew, I would complete that sentence—the vase that leaked, the gifts tossed aside without a glance.

I felt queasy. It wasn't just the cheese, which tasted even more powerful than it smelled, or my hangover. It was watching Josée smile at me beatifically and urge me to take another bite, how cozy it was in her kitchen that day as the wind howled outside. I could only imagine how angry with me she would one day be.

AFTER LUNCH, I took the coffee Josée made me to the living room. I'd brought an external hard drive with home movies that my mother had had digitized. Most were from my own childhood—endless footage of my brother and me tearing open presents and eating cake. But there was one file, mysteriously named "*Cahiers du cinema*," that was copies of old Super 8s from the late fifties that showed my mother taking her first steps, Sylvie on a high beam at the beach, a glimpse of Josée in a thick fur collar.

Josée peppered me with questions as I tried to get the files up and running. I plugged the drive into one of the USB ports on her fancy new flat-screen TV, swapped out the batteries on her remotes, and began switching through inputs. I felt Josée's admiration on me like a heat lamp. In a rare moment of physical intimacy, she put her hand on my shoulder and rested her forehead against mine.

"I just have such confidence in your intelligence," she said, her voice a purr. I rocked on my heels, my shoulders pulling back.

The first images flickered on. Five-year-old Sylvie slid down a long white pole in a playground by the sea. My grandmother staggered in front of the screen, crying out.

"Ah! That's Sylvie! That's Deauville, where we spent the summers. There's my friend Catherine! She's dying now. Oh! And there's your mother! Look, she's trying to keep up with her sister. Aha! Even then. Look how happy and full of life Sylvie was!"

Black spots licked at the screen. Sylvie, all in white, ran away from the camera into blinding white light. The TV let out a textured whoosh of static silence. It was the quality of film often used in contemporary movies to signify the past, and it was hard not to see every instant imbued with the poetry of its own degradation. Features, faces, whole bodies disappeared into the soft blur. A few days earlier, I'd watched *"Cahiers du cinema"* alone in my apartment. I'd hoped for a clear, unfiltered window into those moments of my mother's life, but the camera was so present—everyone looked at it, everyone smiled. It felt more like a mirror, like I was being watched and watching in self-canceling measures, until nothing was seen. But now I sat and watched Josée watching. She stood rooted to the ground in front of the TV, electrified and transfixed. She narrated every instant to me.

The clips were out of order; my mother bounced between two and five years old. In one scene, a hand offered her a bottle of milk, then pulled it away as she tried to grab it. My mother smiled slyly, grabbing it firmly the second time.

"There's your mother, that air in her eyes! I recognize her, that's exactly her. Do you recognize her?"

I didn't. My mother looked like a boy. She moved like a boy. Her cheeks, which were now gaunt under her high cheekbones, puffed out in perfect chipmunk circles. She had a men's haircut, so short her curls didn't show. She wore a blue striped polo shirt with a collar.

"Maybe you never knew her like that," Josée said before I could answer. "Oh my Nadja, you've made me so happy! What pleasure you've brought me!"

She stood a few feet from the TV, rocking from foot to foot. I urged her to come sit by me on the couch and she backed up toward me, hands outstretched behind her, refusing to turn her head from the screen.

My grandfather flickered into being. He was in a field, in a tan-brown sweater that looked expensive even through the poor quality of the footage.

"You never knew him like that, did you? Back when he was handsome," Josée said, laughing happily.

I watched as he picked up Françoise, who was three or four in the clip, and began nibbling on her ear, his hands on her stomach. This was the first of several such scenes on the tape—my grandfather holding Françoise on his knee, kissing her neck, chucking her chin, bopping her small nose with his finger. In contrast, Josée rarely touched either of her daughters, and when she did, did so brusquely, tugging a shirt back into place. My grandfather's image startled me. He had been so invisible behind the lens, operating the camera, that I had nearly forgotten he was there. *Ghost,* I thought. But they were all ghosts, I realized, that happy faded family, that laughed and talked and tumbled silently on the screen. There was so much I would never know.

"You see?" Josée said as Françoise and Sylvie held up dolls nearly as large as themselves. "They weren't so badly loved after all, my two poor daughters."

THERE'D BEEN NO PROGRESSION, no narrative, and thus there was no warning when the video ended abruptly and the screen snapped back to a list of files. Josée gave a small cry of pain. To fill the void, I quickly scrolled back up and played a movie titled "Fall 1987, Nadja, Françoise, Josée, Mina."

Suddenly I exist. I am six months old. My parents have stopped in Paris on their way back from Auschwitz (its own surreal home video, me in a stroller in the ruins of the camps). Morning sun streams in the houseboat windows and paints my sleep-rumpled mother and grandmother with streaks of gold. My mother bounces me on her knee. My grandmother holds a pot of yogurt toward the camera.

"You want some?" she says in a charming French accent.

"No thank you," says my father's voice, softer and more polite than I've ever heard it.

"You don't like it," Josée says.

"No, I liked it," my father says. "I just wanted a taste."

"If you want, there is some without fatness," Josée says.

"There's a fat-free version," my young mother translates happily, her accent thicker than I've ever heard it.

"Fatness," Josée repeats, nodding solemnly at the camera, yogurt still outstretched.

"No, I wasn't even watching my weight. I just don't want any," my father says.

Josée turns away dismissively and begins speaking to my mother in rapid French. My father trains the camera on me, then out the window. "Where's Mina?" he asks eventually.

"She's taking a bath," my mother says.

"So you won't take her," my grandmother scolds playfully. My mother laughs.

"I can see you knocking on the door and Mina—*oooOOoo*." My mother feigns girlish modesty, her hands at her mouth and across her chest.

"I just want to get all four generations on tape," my father says, annoyance creeping into his voice.

The camera cuts out and back on again. My mother is balancing me on her knee, her hands under my arms so that I am drawn to my full length.

"She's a big girl now, aren't you? You're a big girl," she tells me.

"She's a big *chieuse*," Josée says—the word translates roughly to "pain in the ass." She takes a carved wooden duck off a shelf and flies it gently toward my face. I gape at it and reach with chubby fingers, trying to guide its beak into my mouth.

Mina appears in the doorway behind my mother. She must be eighty-one or so, a few years younger than Josée is now, but she looks much older than Josée ever has. She is shrunken and vulnerable in her large pink dressing gown. My mother hands me to Mina, who looks surprised and takes me awkwardly.

"She's going to drop you!" Josée cries out in the present, right as Josée on the screen says, "Don't worry, it's okay if you drop her. Babies are very soft and there's a carpet."

"Josée, could you go stand by Mina?" my father asks from behind the camera. "I'd like to get a shot of all four generations."

The women arrange themselves in the doorway. For a single instant, we all look toward the camera.

"I forgot about the coffee!" Josée exclaims, and she and my mother rush offscreen. Mina watches them go, then turns to my father with a smile and a shrug as if to say, *Those girls!* Then the smile slips off her face and she stands awkwardly rooted in place, me in her arms, my father still filming her. She shifts her weight self-consciously. She looks warily from the baby to the camera and back again. The other women don't return. The camera switches off. The scene changes.

I WAS EIGHT when Mina died. I'd been swinging on the wood and rope trapeze in my bedroom. My mother came in, her eyes red and raw. I dug my feet into the ground to stop the swinging and stood very still to listen. Mina was wrinkled hands, the smell of roses and baby powder, the terrifying medical noises of a nursing home. *I know someone who has died,* I thought to myself with solemn pride and drew the new weight around my shoulders.

"What was Mina like?" I asked Josée one evening.

"Physically?" she said, then changed the subject.

"Did you fight with your mother when you were growing up?" I asked another time.

"No, never," she said.

"What do you know about your mother's life?" I asked a few weeks later.

"She kept her past for herself," she said. "I would never have dreamed of asking questions like you do."

One day, in the front of the houseboat, I found a folded paper bag inside a cabinet that Josée had asked me to help her sort. On the bag, in thick red marker, there was a note in Josée's hand.

We only really think about the past when we have no more future. [Mina] knew the bitter sensation of evoking people unknown to those to whom we're speaking. She had, with her usual valiance, turned the page. But I! I should have interrogated her, given her the feeling that her past was my own. I should have wanted to know, for love of her, but I showed no curiosity out of modesty.

I held it carefully. I showed it to Josée. She could not remember having written it. "Out of *modesty*," she said pointedly, reading it over. "Which you should show more of."

When I asked my mother about Mina, she became flustered. "I want to be able to evoke her for you," she said, "but I just don't know how."

She had been sketching me as we talked, starting over and over. A pile of pictures grew beside her, charcoal pencil on cream-colored paper. I was not recognizable in any of them individually, and yet somewhere in their overlap there was a likeness of me. As I watched my mother draw me, I thought about how crystal clear a metaphor this action was. My mother had told me once that her life felt like literature to her. It was filled with resonances and symbolism. I had always felt similarly, and I wondered now if everyone did. The acts of omission and inclusion we made in our memories were creative acts, through which we authored our lives. Perhaps this, I thought now, was why we were taught in high school to find the meaning of the green light in *The Great Gatsby*: so that we could find it in ourselves.

Now she turned the pad toward me and began to draw a floor plan of Mina's house: a series of scribbles for the rose garden, question marks filling rooms whose purpose she'd forgotten, the exact position of an armchair sketched into place without explanation. She told me that Mina didn't like cooking but loved to cook for her. She told me how happy she felt, reading beside her in the sunshine as Mina pruned the roses. She told me how proud she had been, to have a grandmother who worked. Mina was elegant, she said. Mina was quiet, she was kind.

My mother reached the end of her memories and wracked her mind for more. She couldn't remember any specific things Mina had said to her. She held her head and sighed heavily in frustration.

The next morning, she told me she hadn't been able to sleep. She'd found it painful how difficult it was to share her grandmother with me.

"Somehow, I think the best story to describe Mina would be the story about the doll," she said.

"What story about the doll?" I asked.

"I must have told you this," she said, but she hadn't.

One day when Françoise was two or three years old, Josée took her to play in the park with Sylvie. She had her favorite doll with her and was playing at throwing her up in the air and catching her. She was standing under a gazebo and, on one magnificently high toss, the doll got stuck. She asked Josée to get it down. Josée reached up but could not grab it. The doll was not far away—even my mother could see her clearly. She expected Josée to remove her shoe and throw it, to fetch a chair, to call the park guard, to phone the police. But Josée simply declared the task impossible. She scolded Françoise and told her she should not have thrown the doll in the first place. She dragged her home by the arm. Françoise sobbed the whole way.

"But Mina," my mother told me now. "Mina would have gotten the doll down. Even if it had taken all night."

And so for a while, this was all I had of Mina: the story she was not in, the doll left behind in the rafters.

ONE NOVEMBER DAY, in Paris, Josée took me to see Mina's grave. Yellow and pink flowers from All Saints' Day dotted the cemetery so that it looked strangely colorful in the silver light of the overcast sky.

"When the girls were young, I used to bring them to cemeteries to play," my grandmother said. "People said I was crazy but I've always liked cemeteries."

She and Sylvie had planted daisies at the grave site just the weekend before, but they were slightly wilted now from a heavy rain. Josée had me dig them out of the planter so that we could replace them with the hyacinths we'd bought en route. As she stood by and watched me work, I felt the muscles ripple in my arms. The dirt pushed up under my nails. Mina was buried here, and Mélanie and Beppo. But etched into the stone were names I'd never seen before, their real names, different from the names everyone I knew had always used. Moss had rendered the letters blurry and soft.

Josée talked to me as I worked, pointing at things I had to stand up or crane to see. It was very difficult to get a spot in this cemetery, she said, but here in this tomb there were three more places. She would take one, her estranged half brother another. She'd invited Andrée to take the final spot. I wondered if my mother would have wanted to be buried here, had she been invited.

Only a few years before, I had become tormented by the thought of my mother's eventual, inevitable death. I had, of course, worried about it as a child, every time she'd left me overnight with a babysitter. But now the thought was unavoidably realistic, and it crossed my mind often. On a business trip to Versailles with my mother, I'd burst into tears about it, in her presence. We'd been put up in a palatial hotel room overlooking Marie Antoinette's gardens. Maybe it was something about how beautiful everything looked, and how futile and petty and selfish that beauty had been. As my mother kissed me good night, I'd tried to memorize the sensation of her body in soft pajamas, the smell of her hair and perfume. I was trying to build a memory vivid enough to revisit forty years in the future. Then I started crying, so hard I couldn't breathe. My mother was confused but gentle when I tried to explain. She stroked my back and promised me that she would never die.

Over the course of that year, the fear of my mother's death was replaced by a fear of my own death. The terror I felt at these thoughts was so intense, and so divorced from any actual danger, that I began to wonder if perhaps these were not really the things I was afraid of at all. Perhaps I wasn't afraid of my own death but of the loss of my youth. Perhaps I wasn't afraid of my mother's death but that I would be able to keep living without her.

Here in the cemetery, my hands in the cold, wet earth, I felt in full bloom. A few years ago, Josée was telling me, the cemetery management had put up signs on the neglected plots. If no one claimed them within a year, the tombs would be repurposed. No one did. The bodies were dug up and reburied in a mass grave. The plots were sold to new people.

"Will you come visit me here sometimes so that they don't dig me up?" she said.

"Of course!" I said. "And not just for that reason." Josée beamed, a large, broad smile that I'd never seen before. Her smiles were usually a tight turning up of the corners of her mouth that highlighted her cheekbones. But this smile touched every part of her face.

A few plots away was a man with a power hose. Josée asked if he could clean off Mina's grave, then efficiently negotiated the price down by twenty euros. She had me cover the planter with a tarp to protect it. The man sprayed bleach over the stone, then turned on the hose. The pressure ripped the moss from the stone and sent huge jets of water up against the sky. The stinging smell of bleach electrified the air. The water fell down around us. And then it began to actually rain, water spreading through the whole sky. I felt the rush of being wildly, defiantly alive.

The man finished, packed up his hose, and drove away. The tomb sparkled white and the letters were crisp and clear. I knelt down and planted the hyacinths.

"*Voilà*," Josée said when I'd finished. "Do you like that?"

"Yes," I said. "It looks very nice."

She laughed and hit me playfully on the back. "I was talking to my mother."

chapter nine

Josée's earliest memory was from inside her mother's stomach. There was a violent rattling. The warm body in which she lived was rejecting her. She could feel her mother urging her to let go, to leave, to die. Even then she was stubborn. Even then she held on. Only much later, she told me, did her mother tell her about driving in circles over the cobblestones of La Défense, trying to shake her loose.

"What I didn't do to make you let go," Mina told her. "And oh, how you held on!"

Josée was born in 1930. I often wondered if the roundness of that year contributed to the precision of her memories. Her age had always been easy to calculate. Nine years old in 1939 when war was declared, fourteen in 1944 when the Americans marched through Paris. Her name, at the time, was Josette—a little girl's name, the "ette" permanently diminutive. It was the name of a baker or a shopkeeper, not a name that was destined for greatness. When she married, she became the bourgeois-sounding Marie-Josée, and then simply Josée.

When she'd asked her mother about her name, Mina told her, "It's *not* Josette." Josée, in telling this story, turned her head to the right and looked coldly down the bridge of her nose as she quoted her mother. "It's *j'ose être*."

I dare to be.

ANOTHER TIME JOSÉE told me that her earliest memory was of watching her mother through a window of her grandparents' house in Nanterre, the commune in the western suburbs of Paris where Mina's parents lived. Josée was not tall enough to see through the window from the garden, so she stood on the dog. She watched her mother dip a cotton wick in alcohol and light it with a match. Mina held the burning wick in an overturned glass cup that looked like an empty yogurt pot. Alfred, Mina's father, lay on his stomach on the bed. Mina placed the heated glass on his back and the vacuum sucked his skin up into it, bulging and purple. After a few moments, Mina popped the glass off with her thumb. A welt remained, the capillary vessels flowering at the surface. With a small scalpel, Mina made a quick *x* in the raised flesh. Blood spurted. Alfred lay gasping and bald. His hair, Josée noted with a jolt, was sitting on the nightstand. She got down from the window and flung herself against the dog. Who were these people, she sobbed into its fur, who bloodied each other's backs and cut off each other's heads? She never wanted to see them again.

But it was a very good treatment, she told me in the same breath, very good for clearing out the pulmonary tract. It dated from the time of Louis XIV, and we would perform it still if only it weren't so complicated.

It had been difficult to get Josée to talk about the past, especially her earliest past, but gradually she had begun to venture there with me. Still, her stories took strange, insistent turns. She recoiled abruptly from any condemnation of her mother.

There was only one event that Josée resented openly, and she mentioned it several times. On those same visits to Nanterre, when Josée was two or three, Mina pressed the blood from raw steaks into a glass. She took Josée on her lap, pinched her nose, and poured the blood down her throat. "That is why I never eat red meat," she told me, though she was eating prosciutto while she spoke. What she meant was that she never ate meat that appeared bloody.

It was the men in Mina's life who marked her, Josée said—Mina's little brother, who died when he was nine; Mina's father, Alfred, who died when Josée was three; and Mina's son. Josée didn't include her own father in this list. She herself, she said, had always been much more attracted to women—for confidences, to talk and to laugh. Perhaps, she told me, that's because in the beginning she wasn't desired by men. In fact, she wasn't desired at all.

"But that was before you were born," I said. "Afterward, when she held you in her arms, Mina must have felt differently." I had a firm belief that biological love manifested itself in women the instant they'd given birth.

Josée told me that it seemed to her she could remember the warm, sweet smell of her mother's milk, the gentle bobbing as her mother switched breasts. "You have to love a baby for that," she said. "It's not like she had nothing else to do."

TOGETHER, we often drove near the street where she'd spent the early years of her life, on Rue du Marché. It was between the houseboat and her apartment, in the same small neighborhood where she still lived. Once, she told me, she'd seen a For Sale sign in the window of their old building. But by the time she came back the next morning, the sign had disappeared. "I would have loved to buy it," she said.

"You have happy memories there?" I asked.

"Oh no! Horrible!" she said.

When she was four or five years old, Mina would send her out to buy cigarettes. At the café-tabac on the corner, little Josette would ask for "*des chameaux*." That was a happy memory, she told me. She'd felt like she existed then. She was grateful to be considered useful. The café was still there, the street was still there, the building, the floor. It's all still there, she told me. I'll show you, she said, but she never did.

Josée lived alone with Mina. Her father, Eugène, paid for the apartment. He visited occasionally, during his lunch hour, to "*tirer un coup*," fire a shot, in Josée's mischievous slang. Sometimes he took the time to balance Josée on his knee. "Have you brushed your teeth? Have you been to the bathroom today?" he would ask her, always and only those two questions.

One evening, at a friend's house, Josée made an incredible discovery.

"Did you know that there are papas who are home at night?" she told Mina. "How come my papa isn't here at night?"

"It's none of your business," Mina replied. "You're too young to understand." Eugène spent his evenings in his own home, with his wife and his sons.

Josée's most vivid memories of Mina were of her leaving. Once, she hid in Mina's steamer trunk, packed for Greece, in hopes of being smuggled along. Mina traveled often, unaccompanied, on vacations paid for by Eugène. In a photograph of her on a ski slope in the 1930s she looks debonair in trousers and a sweater vest. Her stance is wide and confident, one hand in her pocket, her black beret tilted jauntily to the right. That, my mother assured me, was not what most women were doing back then. When she wasn't traveling, Mina went out. She was don't-touch beautiful, Josée told me, she was so glamorous. During those trips, those nights, Josée stayed home with her own grandmother, Mélanie. The two of them watched from an upper-story window as Mina stepped out onto the street below, a shimmering vision in a sheer orange organza dress, turned a corner, disappeared.

When Josée was three, Mina sent her away to live with Mélanie in Nanterre. I could not understand this. I returned to it continuously. How could a mother send her young daughter away? Why? Mina was thirty, Josée told me with a shrug. She was busy. She had her own life to lead.

We came across a photograph, Josée at five years old in her school uniform, holding Mina's hand.

"Ah so," she said. "This is when I attended that school next door. So I did not go to Nanterre until I was six, perhaps."

Still, I did not understand. Still, six is young. One day, Josée said in passing, "When I was hidden away . . ." and then the pieces fell into place for me. Even though a man who was not Mina's husband paid her rent, her bills, her vacations, the illegitimate child was a mark of shame too great for Mina to bear.

In Nanterre, Mélanie and Josée lived in a small cabin on the property of a woman Josée called Aunt Lucy, but who, she told me, was not her mother's sister. There was no running water.

There was an outhouse. Mélanie and Josée shared a bed with a thick red duvet, the bed above which pears were left to ripen. Sometimes, Mina and Eugène made the short drive to visit her. They came on Saturdays, since Eugène spent Sundays with his family. His fancy car was out of place in Nanterre. The other kids caught on quickly. "Why don't you live with your parents?" they taunted Josée. "Why don't your parents have the same last name?" They honed in quickly on the word "bastard."

Still, Josée had two friends, two young sisters who walked her home from school each day. They didn't ask too many questions. *Finally,* she thought, *I am liked.*

"You think those girls are your friends?" Mélanie asked her one afternoon. "They only come because I buy them ice cream. You'll see."

The following afternoon, when the ice cream man passed with his cart and bell, Mélanie did not buy three ice creams. And Josée saw. The girls no longer walked her home.

Mélanie taught Josée many things. She taught her how to live in hiding without growing bored and how not to like sweets. Mélanie would often threaten to take Josée's dessert away as punishment, and so Josée trained herself not to want dessert at all. Ice cream, in particular.

Mélanie was a big, solid woman. To young Josée she looked like a balloon, with two small arms and two small legs and a pretty little head in porcelain with a bun on top. But of her personality, Josée could tell me only that she had none. Mélanie was simply a presence, a being with whom she always was. She obeyed authority, first her husband's, then, when he died, her daughter's.

My mother's memories confirmed this portrait: Mélanie was a

blank, she was a zero, she did nothing at all. When Françoise spent her weekends at Mina's home, Mélanie sat, enormous in her armchair, and never moved or even stood. She did not read or watch television. She did not speak. The only movements the woman made were to spit great wads of snuff into a spittoon she kept nearby.

At Mélanie's funeral, in 1961, a relative told Josée, "But you must be quite sad. Because, in the end, it was your grandmother who raised you." It hit Josée then for the first time, and she felt a pang of sadness. But the thought had never occurred to her before.

Josée's most tender memory of Mélanie was that she turned her back and pretended not to see when Josée picked the bits of bacon out of the vegetable stew on the stove top.

"And I remember," Josée said, her voice growing soft with what sounded to me like a forced nostalgia, "when she got into bed next to me. Her body was warm."

AFTER JOSÉE LEFT, Eugène moved Mina from the Rue du Marché to a nicer apartment on Boulevard Inkermann. There was a room there for Josée, and once a week Josée and her older cousin biked the five or so miles from Nanterre to Mina's to spend the night. One evening, Josée decided she would make her mother dinner. She chopped the store of radishes she found in Mina's kitchen, sautéed them in a pan, then served it beaming with pride. Her mother took one mouthful and spat it out.

"It's far too salty!" Mina exclaimed. "It's inedible." And it was. Josée had never cooked before, and she'd added a handful of salt. Her mother scraped the food off her plate into the trash. Josée stayed at the table and stubbornly finished every bite.

AT EIGHT YEARS OLD, Josée was sent away to boarding school in Chambon-sur-Lignon, in south-central France. With today's highways, it's a six-hour drive from Paris, but back then it took much longer. She had grown too thin in Nanterre. She was ill. Whatever the reason, she did not question the transfer. Little girls did not ask questions.

The school was coed. Between the genders, it was an all-out war. The boys picked the girls up by their arms and legs and dropped them in a shallow stream. Already, Josée had learned from Mélanie that boys were dangerous. She grew adept at climbing trees, high enough that the boys could not follow. At mealtimes, she refused to eat. She pretended, shoved her meat into the cracks in the table when the monitors turned their backs. Something was wrong with her stomach. She gave off a terrible smell. The girls in her dorm complained. Even the cleaning woman complained. But rather than be teased, Josée declared a farting competition. She farted the loudest and she won.

In the summer, she returned to Paris and lived once again with Mina. It was then that she devised a plan for revenge. At school, there were lottery tickets sold to raise money for various charities. There was a national lottery, too, for which adults bought tickets in the hopes of winning millions. There was something to be done with this, Josée thought to herself. When her mother's friends stopped by, she sold them tickets to her own private lottery. Her tickets were expensive, the equivalent of five dollars, but she declined to mention any charitable cause. "With me, you'll get something for your money in all cases," she told them. She promised them a free theatrical performance on the day of the drawing.

For the performance, Josée dressed as the moon. She put talcum powder on her face and wore a white dressing gown. She had always, as a child, felt an affinity with the moon that reflected light that silently slivered itself until it nearly disappeared. It was to be a one-woman show, put on from behind the big double curtains of the living room. The adults gathered. *"Le soleil a rendez-vous avec la lune,"* Josée sang. Charles Trenet's song, in which the sun stood up the moon, was a current hit. The performance was soon over. The adults clapped and she waited for the applause to die down. "Unfortunately," she told them, "the lottery cannot be drawn. I was unable to sell enough tickets. It's not even worth it." The adults erupted in *tsk-tsk*s and *poor dear*s. They patted her on the head and told her it had been a very good idea all the same, she'd sung beautifully. She thanked them in turn. "At least you had the kindness to buy a ticket," she told each. "The others . . . I can't say the same for them."

But in fact she'd collected an enormous amount of money. It was 1938, the war had not yet begun, and the adults had given freely. Adults were idiots, she realized gleefully. They weren't the masters she'd been led to believe. Even she, a child who'd spent her life hidden away, even she could manipulate them all.

THAT FALL, she was sent away again. Mina declared Paris unsafe for Josée, even Nanterre, and sent her back to Chambon-sur-Lignon, this time with Mélanie in tow. Because Josée was now with her grandmother, she could not be reenrolled in the boarding school. Instead, she attended the village public school, and the two women rented a room in the home of the school's sole instructor. It was right before the Munich Agreement, Josée told me, and the adults were afraid war was going to break out. Later, in my apartment, I returned to this with some confusion. The Munich Agreement led France to breathe a sigh of relief, believing war with Germany averted. It was signed on September 29, 1938. But Josée remained hidden for a full year, until the following summer.

"Well of course," Josée said. "They weren't going to bring me back to Paris once school had begun."

At the village school, the instructor assigned his students to bring in their favorite proverbs.

"You must always want what you can't avoid," Josée offered when she was called upon.

"Where did you hear that?" the instructor asked.

"I invented it," Josée said.

"And what does it mean?" the instructor asked.

"If you want it, then it can't hurt you," Josée said. "We're all going to die, so we must decide to want our own deaths. If war comes, then we must want war. If someone slaps you, you tell yourself you like being slapped. That way you're always happy."

The instructor looked at her with horror. At dinner that evening, he raised the incident with Mélanie. He was concerned that Josée might be suicidal. Josée squirmed, unsure what she had done wrong. Perhaps, she thought, she had not expressed herself clearly.

That summer, Josée and Mélanie returned once more to Paris. They were still there on September 3, when France declared war on Germany. Though the war wouldn't begin in earnest until May of the following year, fears ran high. Mina and Mélanie locked up the apartment, convinced they would return to find it looted and destroyed. The women took their jewelry. Josée took her Bébé Claude, her life-sized celluloid doll, with his brown velour underpants.

Eugène piled them all into his car. He had already moved his other family. The streets were jammed with traffic. People ran between the cars. To nine-year-old Josée, it looked like some vehicles had entire homes strapped to the top. She had never seen adults so afraid.

In the backseat, Mélanie explained to her that the Germans were approaching Paris with great long strides. They ate little children, she said. Sometimes Mélanie got confused and referred to the invaders as Prussians. Mélanie was born in 1875, and as a girl she had heard vivid stories of the Paris Commune, the city under siege. They might have to eat rats, she told Josée. The Prussians speared children on their spiked helmets, she said.

Eugène hit the brakes hard, and Mélanie fell on top of Josée and Bébé Claude. She weighed nearly two hundred pounds at that point, though later she would weigh far more. Her impact broke one of the doll's legs. Now Josée finally began to cry. *So this is it*, she thought; *these are the casualties of war.*

EUGÈNE LEFT the three women in Bernay, in Normandy, where he had rented them a small room to share. Josée was enrolled in the local school. When she got into mischief or broke things, she was delighted to discover that the adults were too distracted to scold her. The Belgians came through, fleeing the German invasion. There were waves of them, bedraggled families carting all their possessions. She fetched them water, let them in to use the bathroom. She was again pleased to be useful.

And then there were no more Belgians. Her father reappeared with the car. The Germans were coming, he told them. He drove them to Brittany, to a town as far northwest as you could go before hitting the ocean, and left for Paris once more.

In Brittany, they lived on a farm. Here, Josée was disappointed to discover there was no discussion of school. The farmer's wife sent the children out to pick the potato beetles off the plants. The beetles were thick and yellow and clung to the undersides of the leaves. Josée hated the task, but she liked the end of the day, when they brought a full jar to the farmer's wife. She would set the beetles on fire and let the children watch them burn alive.

"Look," she told them. "We're burning the Germans."

One day, there was a commotion.

"Hide under the table!" Mina commanded. "The Germans have arrived." Josée hid. She trembled with terror, ready to be eaten.

But instead she heard young men's voices raised in a chant—*ba bum bababa bum bababa bum*—and the rhythmic tramping of feet. She rushed to the window. Young men marched four abreast, their legs in perfect synchronicity. They wore sports shoes, not heavy boots, light shorts, not military uniforms. They were just young men getting some exercise.

"But they're very good-looking!" Josée exclaimed. She expected the adults to register the same impressed surprise and relief. But Mina's hand flew, smacked her hard across the face.

That's it, Josée thought. *I'm through trying to understand.*

They stayed on the farm perhaps a few months longer. It was there that Josée saw one of the most atrocious sights of the war. They killed a pig in front of her.

"The Germans?" I asked.

"No," she said somberly. "The French." In the town, there was a big celebration and a feast. Perhaps it was Bastille Day or perhaps it was a wedding. Josée didn't ask, because little girls didn't ask questions. They slit the pig's throat. The pig screamed. The blood ran everywhere. The pig screamed even with its throat slit.

It was a terrible sound. The adults were happy and drunk. They gathered the blood for sausages. Josée watched it pool on the ground by the nearby well, swirling pink into the muddy water. *This is war,* she thought to herself; *this is the blood and horror of war.*

The following winter, the winter of 1940–1941, was one of the coldest on record. Eugène brought them back to Paris too early. Others were still trying to flee the capital. The road in the opposite direction, leading away from Paris, was jammed with cars. German planes swooped in low formations. At the staccato of automatic fire, everyone stopped their cars. They threw themselves into ditches and kept their heads down. Josée was afraid, but also she thought, *At last.* She kept her nose in the dirt and waited for the planes to pass. When they returned to their cars, bodies remained on the roadside.

THAT YEAR, until early 1942, Josée and Mélanie lived with Mina in the apartment on Boulevard Inkermann. Eugène and his brother owned a company that sold animal feed. The business did well during the war, and the family was relatively comfortable. Paris was emptied of automobiles, and the remaining inhabitants, French and German alike, relied heavily on horses. But Eugène did a beautiful Resistance, Josée told me emphatically. He was a Freemason. He hid parachutists.

When I asked a sampling of young French people what their families had done during the war, two of them told me that their ancestors hid parachutists. The other three told me that they didn't know and changed the subject quickly.

At eleven years old, Josée began her seventh new school. She was eager to learn all she'd missed. In the evenings, Mina brought her to ice-skating lessons, where Josée, thrilled by the attention, sped around the rink as her mother watched. She was tall and gangly as an asparagus then, all thin long limbs and knobby knees.

One afternoon, when there were no adults supervising, Josée convinced her only friend that they should trim their eyelashes short. She believed that trimming hair made it grow longer and she was impressed by her own brilliant plan. Oh, Josée told me, how she was punished when Mina discovered what she had done.

"Look," she told me, leaning close across the brightly lit kitchen table of her apartment. "They never did grow back." She fluttered her blue eyes down and I saw the short line of lashes that I had never noticed before. She stayed that way a moment, eyes downcast, waiting for me to speak. I felt a surge of extraordinary tenderness. I knew she was showing me a small flaw in the armor of her beauty. I traced the curve of her lashes with my gaze. Here was that gangly eleven-year-old girl; now I would be able to find her each time I looked.

Josée and I often spoke over long dinners and lunches, a series of meals that ran together in my mind into one long moment. She disliked speaking while eating, but I had difficulty with the formality of the times when we sat on her couch, my notebook a barrier between us. Each time I arrived at her home, the kitchen was fragrant and the food already prepared. One time she made me lamb chops that leaked red when you cut into them, another time soft-poached pears. One afternoon, I brought her a bag of mini-*financiers* from the boulangerie. When I returned a few days later, she told me proudly that she'd finished the pastries in a single afternoon. I'd taught her how to like sweets again, she told me.

"But I suppose that's what old age is, in the end," she said. "It's a return to the simplicity of childhood."

JOSÉE'S BRIEF PERIOD of normalcy was short-lived. In February 1942, another evening of intense turmoil descended, this time within the confines of their home. After a fiery argument, Eugène had locked them into the apartment. Mina threw their clothes into suitcases and threw the suitcases out the window in a fury.

"He locked you *in?*" I asked. "What kind of apartment door can't be opened from the inside?"

"I don't know," Josée said. "I didn't ask questions. It wasn't like you here with your tape recorder, bombarding me."

Mina called the upstairs neighbor, who managed to break open the door. Mina fled, Josée and Mélanie in tow. She brought them to a small dark apartment with ugly moth-infested furniture, a twenty-five-minute walk away. A handsome Italian man awaited them there. Mina fell into his arms. He introduced himself to Josée as Beppo, but his face was already familiar. Josée remembered him from the edge of the ice at the skating lessons. She remembered it all now: his face next to her mother's, her mother's coquettish laughter as Josée whirled round and round.

"Your father wants to take you away from me," Mina told Josée. "I need to hide you." Josée packed her bags and moved yet again. She went with Mélanie to Viarmes, a sleepy suburb in the north of France. There was no school because Josée could not risk being found. They lived in a hotel with room and board. There was nothing to do. Mélanie warned her not to speak to the other children. Her father was searching for her all over France, she said. Anybody might be a spy. Josée's days dragged on in endless boredom. On Saturdays, the hotel doubled as the town cinema.

Those afternoons were the only bright moments of these long months, the reels of film spinning her into places far away.

When Josée and Mélanie returned to Paris that summer, Beppo and Mina had rented an opulent apartment on the Rue du Conseiller Collignon, not far from the Place du Trocadero, with its palace and grand fountain. This was in Paris's wealthy sixteenth arrondissement, framed on the west by lush greenery of the Bois-de-Boulogne. High-ranking government officials lived there, alongside France's old money.

The new apartment had a small garden out front where Mina could tend the roses. Finally, Josée belonged to something that resembled a family. There was a papa who came home each evening, a mother who was there in the mornings. There was a room for Mélanie and one for Josée. Beppo gently gave his new mother-in-law lessons. He taught her how to hold herself at the table, how to speak to the help. Still, Mélanie suffered terrible indigestion that year, her stomach unaccustomed to so much rich food.

"And you?" I asked my grandmother. "How did you react?" But nothing surprised young Josée. She took what came to her in life, accepting the ups with the same resilience as the downs. "I wanted to taste all the sauces," she told me. Mina and the chauffeur took her out to the shops in a horse-drawn carriage. They dressed her head to toe in Hermès and Lanvin. Beppo, eager to please, hired a Russian governess who brought Josée to near grade level over the summer. He taught her some Italian. He gave her pocket money in exchange for her good grades, which had never been looked at so attentively. Still, Josée insisted on walking to school. It wouldn't be well received by her classmates, she said, the chauffeurs and fancy cars.

On Thursdays, Josée visited her father. His secretary (who was also his new mistress) let Josée into his office through the ground-floor window. Josée waited patiently while Eugène sorted his mail. He took Josée to lunch in a nearby restaurant. He took from his pockets a wrapped parcel and slipped it to her under the table. It was white bread. Bread in Paris in those days was black, and white flour was very difficult to come by.

Eugène had shaved his head—in despair, he told Josée. "How could your mother leave me?" he wanted to know. "After everything I've done for her."

"But wasn't your father trying to steal you back?" I asked. "How could you go see him at lunch?"

"Oh, I think he and my mother came to some understanding—she told him I was living with her, enrolled in school, and shouldn't be uprooted again," she told me. But a few minutes later, she said, "My mother and my father never talked in those years." And then added, as I opened my mouth to ask, "except, of course, to come to that agreement I just told you about."

On her bike one afternoon, Josée's stomach began to hurt. Blood ran down her leg. She hurried home in terror. She had damaged her internal organs. She was dying. Mina explained in only the vaguest terms. The next day Josée went to school clutching the word "ovaries." She traded the knowledge with the other children, but even after consulting the dictionary, they only pretended to understand. The mystery was no more clear when Mina explained, a month or two later, that Josée would soon have a sibling—that a baby was growing inside her stomach.

Josée's brother was born in September 1943. Mina and Beppo, thrilled new parents, rented the apartment across the hall for their son and his nanny. One afternoon, Josée read to me from a notebook. "Secrets of a Big Sister," it said on the cover.

I cannot accomplish my role as big sister because the nurse doesn't want me to approach him out of fear that I give him microbes. Maman is the recipient of all his smiles, she is very proud of him. I am not jealous and I am very happy about it. I would also like to have a sister but I am not giving up hope.

"I hadn't given up hope!" Josée said, laughing. "Well, I always was very optimistic!" We were sitting on her bed on the houseboat, and I peered over her shoulder at the perfect looping little-girl script.

"I found these notebooks in Mina's house after she died," Josée told me. "But I haven't had the time to look at them until now."

I only really suffer at night, Josée read from another entry. *I cannot sleep despite the Gardenal that Maman gives me. Every night, I obligate her to get up, poor thing. Despite myself, of course, but still I cry or whimper so much that she insists on comforting me, becoming cold and shivering by my side. And I, like the egoist that I am, I let her console me. Truly, she is the pearl of all mothers. There are few like her and I love her. She told me the other day that I do not show it enough. So now, I show it*, Josée read, then huffed, "Oh, this is all boring! Enough." She closed the notebook and put it aside.

"No, please," I said. "I'm interested." She sighed and opened it again, reading silently ahead.

The saccharine sweetness rattled me. Her diary read like a diary in a sentimental film, pitch-perfect to the point of the surreal. For a second, I caught myself wondering whether the notebook was an elaborate forgery. I shook my head quickly to dismiss the thought, dismayed at the depths of my own cynicism. As Josée continued to turn the crumbling yellow pages, reading on with steady interest, I rested my head carefully on her shoulder. Was it possible that my grandmother was once this little girl, with all of her effusive innocence and sincerity? I tried to feel her presence in the woman beside me. The image flickered in and out of focus, unsteady.

"Oh ho!" she exclaimed. "Watch out! Now I'm really getting started. So!"

I no longer see my flirtation, Josée read with salacious delight. *Naturally, and I don't regret it. I only saw him in the mornings and coming home from school. I saw him only once on Tuesday. He is not a crush. We don't know each other. Except there is a look between us when we meet each other. But once, the last time we saw each other, he looked at me deeply, as if he wanted to ask me something. But he surely did not dare, as I was accompanied by Marie-Claire and Nicole* ["Those were my friends who walked me to school," she interjected] *and even if I had been alone, I would not have answered. I would have pretended to not pay any attention to him. Perhaps that would have made him suffer a bit. Good. Maman taught me that we must not be dominated by men, it costs too much agony. That is why I have already begun to avenge Maman. I've already had quite a few conquests. Little ones, but it's better than nothing. I avenge my mother and become war-hardened for later. I think I am on the right path.*

The little girl beside me solidified and grew bright. This Josée I recognized: she was the woman over whom many men would later suffer.

Maman is a dear and I love her more and more, she continued. *It's true that since Christmas I have been very mean with her. She is very annoyed and very tired. She won't be long in falling ill herself. I must get better quickly so that I can relieve her a bit. Maman just went and got me a bonbon. Poor Maman. She doesn't know what to do to make me happy. The candy that Mamina gave me is delicious. When I was sick this winter, she bought me roller skates and a rubber ball. What an adorable mother I have. I must finally leave you. Who is this "you" destined for? As it's very tiring, to write for so long.*

"Did Mina read your diaries?" I asked.

"No," Josée said. "She wouldn't have bothered."

The final entry read: *Wednesday I went to have lunch at the office* ["My real father's office," Josée clarified.] *In thinking about it hard, I like Papa, but I prefer very much Beppo and Maman. Perhaps because they are raising me rather severely and surely because they give me the impression of loving me more. Maman told me not to write Papa too many letters as he could take me back at eighteen with the letters written by me as proof. This bothers me very much. I would like to stay forever with Maman and Beppo.*

There was a blank page and then a single line:

It's been a year since I've written. Beppo died May 31st, 1944.

IN THE NIGHT, Josée could hear Mina shuffling in the bedroom next door. She heard her walk to the bathroom and back, many times. As soon as morning presented a reasonable hour, Josée went into the master bedroom. It was a room in which she rarely stepped foot. Beppo was in bed, as he had been nearly constantly during the months of his long illness. Mina was in the bathroom.

Josée stood by Beppo's bed. He looked up at her and hiccupped three times. She did not know then about the death rattle—how a dying person might gasp, his head lifted with sudden energy from the pillow, eyes and mouth wide in the astonishment of death.

"Don't worry, he's doing fine, Maman!" Josée called out with the pleasure of all children bearing good news. "He just has the hiccups."

Beppo looked up at Josée, looked deep into her eyes, and then he died.

Mina rushed back into the room. "He's dead," she sobbed, "he's dead."

The doorbell rang. Josée went to answer it. Marie-Claire and Nicole were there, come to walk her to school.

"I cannot go to school today," she said with perfect composure. "My father just died."

chapter ten

L ess than a week after Beppo's death, on June 6, the American army landed in France. The city exploded in celebration. But Mina, Josée, and Mélanie drifted through the hallucinatory scene in mourning.

When the Americans rolled through the streets in August, Josée remembered, Mina pushed her up onto the tanks, making her take what she could grab. I had at first imagined her as young in that scene, on her mother's shoulders. But as I began to plot the whirlwind of anecdotes against a timeline, I realized that she was fourteen.

"To those soldiers," I said, "you must not have looked like a child."

"No!" she said. "I was a young woman. That was what was so uncomfortable to me. They all wanted to grab me and kiss me. And they were dirty. And I had rarely seen black people before."

"And for Mina, that was okay? For you to be grabbed and kissed by soldiers?"

"Well, she pushed me up onto the tank," Josée said. "But there were cigarettes and chocolates and chewing gum, which we discovered only then, and cans of corned beef. None of which I liked at the time."

She told me how the Americans' falling bombs looked like fireworks against the nearby Bois de Boulogne, and how the evenings spent crowded into the building's underground shelter crackled with nervous energy. "You bombed indiscriminately, you Americans," she said. "You bombed from so high above." But all of it was only a backdrop for the far more personal and poignant dramas of adolescence. Even witnessing a German sniper shot off a roof, his body landing in the street a few feet away, was marked by the memory that she had had her hair professionally styled that afternoon.

She was in love. A young boy her age named Gerard had moved into her building with his mother and brother. His Jewish father had been deported.

"Had Gerard also been deported during the war?" I asked.

"I don't know," Josée said. "He appeared at the end of the war." It was possible, she told me, that his family had lived at that address before the war and been removed during it, but she didn't ask.

They met in secret, on prearranged routes in the park where he walked with his tutor and she with her governess. In the afternoons, when she knew the coast would be clear, she played Beethoven's "Pour Elise"—"Für Elise"—on the piano. It was their signal. That night, he would climb up a ladder to her bedroom window. They would steal out into the service courtyard and kiss. Before each encounter, Josée took long bandages from the medicine cabinet and tightly bound her breasts. *If he feels my breasts against him*, she thought, *who knows what dangerous state he might enter.* She still didn't understand how children appeared in women's stomachs, and she didn't want to take any chances.

For a time their encounters were kept safe under the veil of blackmail. The concierge's husband was having an affair with

Gerard's maid, and though both had glimpsed the young lovers, they had each other's secrets to keep. Josée told no one, not even her friends, sure they would be scandalized. One day, however, the affair was revealed. Mélanie surprised them in the act. Or perhaps it was Mina. Or maybe they were not surprised in the act at all but seen by a neighbor who tattled. Regardless, Josée remembered Mina's fury vividly. Mina slapped her, *un aller-retour*, making a return-trip backhand across Josée's face. Mina slapped her daughter often. Which is not to say that she was an abused child, Josée added quickly. It was a different time, and Josée was much better off for this severity. But the crime of kissing a boy merited far greater punishment than just a slap.

Mina brought her by the scruff of the neck to a run-down boarding school back in the Normandy countryside, in Alençon. She made it clear that the school had been chosen as punishment. The other students all came from small neighboring villages, the daughters of peasants and agricultural workers. Josée's mere arrival was enough to earn her a terrible reputation. What could she have done, the other girls wondered, to have been sent to such a remote place? Was she a murderer? Even on weekends, even over the winter holidays, when the other students went home to their families, Josée stayed on in the dorms. It was so cold that the buckets they had been given for bathing iced over in an hour.

Josée wasn't upset in the slightest with her mother. The punishment was perfectly reasonable, and in any case not a thing that should be questioned. She didn't come from a generation that judged their parents. But she did gain weight at Alençon, a place known for its heavy food, seventeen pounds before the end of the year. And she caused trouble at school.

"I screamed at them that it was unacceptable to have such cold water," Josée told me. "But it was after the war, there were restrictions, it wasn't their fault, poor things. I invented a shower, hooking the bucket up to a tube or some other such thing . . . I remember this now only because I found a letter, recently, that I'd written to Mina about it," Josée said.

"Oh, I'd love to see that letter!" I said.

"I burned it," Josée said.

"What?" I said. "When?"

"A few months ago. Mina had kept everything, every letter I sent her. I burned lots of things, letters from Beppo's family, all of it."

"Why?" I asked.

"I didn't think it would interest anybody. I wanted to make it simpler, when I die, so that you and the girls wouldn't have so much to sort through."

"Please don't burn anything else," I said quickly. "It's just paper, it doesn't take up much room. I'd be happy to go through all of it now, with you."

"No," Josée said. "I need to put it all in order."

Months later, she did let me see her papers. It was then that she showed me the diary, "Secrets of a Big Sister," and a book in which her friends had written funny quotes at the end of one summer. There were no letters.

"*OH MAMAN, tu es la plus belle du monde,*" Josée sang to herself one afternoon as she cleared the table where we'd eaten our lunch. "I used to sing that song to my mother," she said, looking up at me with a sweet smile.

"My mother told me she used to sing that song to you!" I said.

"No," Josée said sharply. *"O mama, tu sei per me la più bella del mondo,"* she sang again. "It was in Italian," she said. "Luis Mariano. It wasn't of your mother's time."

"Are you sure?" I asked. "She remembers—"

"No," Josée said. "It's impossible."

"In what moments would you have sung it to Mina?" I asked.

"Oh, I don't know," Josée said. "Perhaps when she was bringing me to boarding school at Alençon for my punishment. But kindly."

Again, I looked up the dates when I got home. The song was recorded by an Italian singer in 1958, then in French by Luis Mariano a year later. Josée would have been twenty-eight, married and no longer speaking to her mother. And yet I thought back on the way Josée softly sang the words to me, the way her face glowed with nostalgia. Somehow, in her memories, the song her daughter had sung to her had become the song she used to sing to her own mother. And through the haze of overlapping generations, the unrequited love was real.

ONE EVENING IN 1998, when Josée was sixty-eight years old, she was having dinner with a woman who was complaining about a man. He had been married and had a child when they became involved, and then she had fallen pregnant as well. He divorced his wife, but not for her—he married a third woman, had a third child. "That's men," Josée agreed. The vast majority of her friends were divorcées. But as they continued to talk, it became clear that the man in question was her Gerard. She arranged to pass a note to him through the woman's son. She wrote "Pour Elise" on the back of her business card.

"He'll know what it means," she said.

He came to the houseboat for lunch. From the window, Josée watched him arrive. He was a man now, macho and tan from skiing, with a confident swagger. These were qualities that generally attracted Josée. She made him scallops on a hot plate and they talked until eight p.m. He fell back in love with her quite quickly. Her houseboat was flooding, and eight days later he offered for her to come live with him. But Josée refused. He had three ex-wives, four kids, and too much money. Besides, all of his wives had been much younger. Besides, she would never abandon her boat.

But a year later, her boat again flooding, Josée reached out to him for help. He installed her in his apartment with its view of the Eiffel Tower and gave her the master bedroom while he slept on his son's small bed. He ran her baths, took her to the fanciest Japanese restaurants, bought her a music box that played "Pour Elise." Josée told him about how she'd bound her breasts, and he admitted to her that he'd worn several pairs of briefs during their encounters, terrified she would feel him pressing against her. They returned to the building in which they'd lived as children and, giggling, convinced the concierge to allow them inside. But the courtyard they had imagined as vast and endless was small and ordinary. The ladder they had remembered was in fact a staircase of three steps. They laughed. The scene was a hollow vessel, far too small to contain their past.

Mina, who had never liked Gerard, must have been watching from the heavens that day. Josée had a nasty bout of sciatica, and Gerard had to all but carry her around their old building.

"Let's have a honeymoon," he said. He wanted to meet her grown daughters, have her meet his sons. Josée refused. She wondered why she had gone looking for trouble. She had already known too many men.

"Let's go to Venice," he said. It was what he'd promised her when they were young. They went for eight days. He rented them a luxurious hotel room on the canal. They went to palaces, ate in fine restaurants. They went to Verona and he climbed Romeo's ladder. A photographer snapped a picture: Josée on the balcony, Gerard's lips lightly meeting hers. They shared a bed, but they never made love. Each time he tried to kiss her, Josée saw Mina's face looming between them and recoiled. Soon after they got back, Josée pulled away until he understood it was through. She didn't want to fall back into all of that.

"Anyway, he's dead now," she concluded, as if to settle the matter. There was a beat of silence.

"They're all dead," she continued, much more softly. "Every man I've had a relationship with, friendly or romantic. They're almost all dead."

It was not until her return from Alençon, in the summer of 1947, that Josée first learned of the horrors that had taken place in the concentration camps during the war. She went to the movies with Gerard and his brother to see *Nuit et brouillard*, the documentary that revealed the genocide. The whole theater howled with shock. Gerard and his brother clung to each other. It was then that they first understood that their deported father would never return.

"Is it possible that you saw Gerard again once you were married?" I asked.

"No," Josée said. "Why?"

"*Night and Fog* came out in 1955," I said.

"*Ah non!*" Josée said. "It most certainly did not."

"Is it possible you saw a different documentary?" I asked. "Or a newsreel?"

"No, it was that one, with the scenes from abandoned camps," Josée said. "I remember it very vividly. No one in France had known what was happening during the war. We were all in shock."

"Okay, but then . . . perhaps you saw the documentary later? With Paul then and not with Gerard?"

"No," Josée said, "I saw it with Gerard and his brother. The whole theater was screaming."

"But that documentary was released in 1955 . . . ," I repeated.

"No," Josée said firmly. "It wasn't."

"It was the war," Josée said often, with a finality she knew I could not challenge.

"I didn't have time to wonder about whether or not I had a good relationship with my mother," she said. "There were far more important things to worry about. It was the war."

"Of course I would consider my childhood difficult," she said. "But not through any fault of my parents. It was the war."

I pushed Josée hard for details, but all I got were stories about food rations and candles, bomb shelters, the car trip back to Paris when she'd hidden in ditches, the embarrassment of having a chauffeur in 1942. My cynicism took over, despite myself. I began to hear the phrase as shorthand for avoiding the questions she found too difficult to answer. I thought often of my other grandparents and I bristled. But I knew that in the hierarchies of history and pain, I had no right to judge. I had never seen a dead body. I had never even seen a pig killed.

AFTER A YEAR at Alençon, Josée was sent to a much nicer boarding school, one intended for the children of diplomats, at Versailles.

"Why?" I asked.

"Because my punishment was over!" Josée said. "Alençon was a terrible school with a pitiable level of education. I wasn't going to stay there forever."

"No, I mean why didn't you just go live with Mina?" I asked.

"Oh . . . ," Josée said, and paused for a minute. When she spoke again she'd slipped into a little-girl voice. "I suppose I could have. Maybe my punishment wasn't quite over."

"Was your brother ever sent to boarding school?" I asked.

"That would have made Mina sick to her stomach," Josée said. "She couldn't bear to be parted from him. He was *l'enfant roi,* the little king. He was a boy, first of all. And he reminded her of her one great love. He looked just like Beppo. Mina had a visceral love for him."

"Oh," I said.

"That's enough for today, don't you think?" Josée said, pressing her palms against her knees to stand. "You've exhausted me with all this talking."

AT THE BOARDING SCHOOL in Versailles, Josée flexed her powers of rebellion. When a teacher read her roommate's diaries, Josée was outraged. She had a fierce sense of privacy and she never rifled

through other people's affairs. And she was in love with the roommate, who was voluble and Russian—a love she described to me as
romantic though undeclared, unrequited, and unconsummated.
She never would have protested her own rights, but for this girl she
was ready to go to the ends of the earth. She hit her fists against the
classroom doors, chanting, *"Formez le monôme!"* and all the girls
streamed out to join her in the hall. They went through the school
chanting, their numbers growing larger with each classroom they
passed. *"Formez le monôme,"* they encouraged each other, a chant
with its own melody and rhythm, as they gathered outside the
doors of the *directrice*. Which is why, Josée told me, she was never
angry with Françoise for her own later rebellions. She had done the
same, in her day.

"What's a *monôme*?" I asked her.

"I don't know," she replied. "It's just what we said." I looked it
up later in the dictionary: a parade of students.

Near the end of the year, in May, there was another incident.
On a school outing to a concert in Paris, Josée slipped away from
the group to have dinner with a boy. When the time came to return
to Versailles, the chaperones were unable to find her. The fourteen
other girls missed the last train back to Versailles and were forced to
sleep in a hotel. Josée, meanwhile, caught a late bus and made it
back to the boarding school that same night. The teachers were
furious, but when they threatened to call her mother, Josée threatened to call all the other parents and tell them how lax the school's
supervision was. "Do you want the Congolese ambassador to know
his daughter spent the night in a hotel in Paris?" she asked. A few
days later, Josée was called in from lunch to see the *directrice*. The
other girls watched her march off, surely to her doom.

"Do you like the author Claudel?" the *directrice* asked.

"I find him too religious," Josée answered. It wasn't a religious school, and so she could say such things.

"Turn," the *directrice* said. "Walk. Stop. Turn. Walk back. Very good." She looked Josée up and down.

"How would you like to play Joan of Arc in the school play?"

JOSÉE OFTEN RETURNED to Paris on the weekends, and it was on one such Saturday a few days later that Mélanie met her with the news.

"Your mother is in prison," Mélanie told her. Mina had been taken on Thursday, but no one had contacted Josée at school. Presumably there had been some warning: a summons from the police, a trial, lawyers. But this was the first Josée heard of any of it, and Mélanie presented it to her without explanation.

The jail's visiting hours were on Thursday afternoons. Josée was to go see Mina herself, to get instructions on how to run the family's finances and care for her four-year-old brother. Mélanie was seventy-two years old and so fat then that she could barely walk. Josée asked a family friend to write her a note to excuse her from school the following Thursday, saying that she had a doctor's appointment. Of course she could not let it be known that her mother was in jail.

"How was it when you went to see her?" I asked.

"I wasn't terrorized," Josée said. "When you've been a kid who's known the war, who's seen so many terrible things, nothing impresses you. This was just one more difficulty like all the rest. Life went on."

She and her mother sat at a table together with their hands in plain view, under the eye of the matron.

"I wonder now," Josée said, "if perhaps there wasn't a glass barrier between us with a microphone? No, I don't think so. I think we sat just like this."

As she spoke, I watched the glass barrier rise and fall in my mind. Isn't that something you would remember, whether or not there was glass between you, whether or not you could touch your mother?

"Everything that's painful, thank God, erases itself from your memory," Josée continued, as if in answer. "Details like that, you see, I . . . I just don't know."

As Josée understood it, after Beppo's death his two business partners had gallantly offered to name Mina as the managing director of their enterprise, which sold boot-legged liquor to the Germans. Mina was unclear on the nature of the businesses but she was proud of her competence as a secretary. She had readily accepted. And then, within months, the war was over and the new French government began to investigate those who had profited. Mina was not a collaborator. But the government asked for repayment of the money earned, a sum far greater than Mina and the failing business could ever pay. And so, Mina was sent to prison for debts that were not hers but were now in her name.

"What did you talk about, during those Thursday visits?" I asked.

"She told me about her life there," Josée said. "She had a job in the nurse's ward. She saw abominable things—people who wanted to kill themselves, people starving, people dying of dysentery. Women who suffocated their newborn children beneath them."

"What?" I asked. "Why would they do that?"

"Because they didn't want to bring kids into that world? I don't know. She saw these things, she told me these things. It made me feel . . . As much as she had told me nothing at all when I was younger . . . But it did her good to get these things out."

Later, on one of the many occasions when Josée denied that Mina had ever told her anything personal about her life, I mentioned this.

"Oh, no," Josée said. "Mina didn't tell me all of that."

"Then how did you know about it?" I asked.

"Perhaps Mélanie told me, perhaps Mina had confided in her," Josée said. "But anyway, years later. Not when I was seventeen."

From that moment on, whenever I asked Josée what she and her mother had talked about in prison, she always gave the same elusive answer.

"I don't remember," she'd say. "She told me how to run the house. Important things. We didn't have time for chitchat."

"Did you tell her you'd been cast as Joan of Arc in the school play?"

"No," Josée said. "We wouldn't have talked about that."

"And did she tell you about the things she saw in the nurse's ward?"

"No," Josée said, "I already told you no. And enough questions. I can't talk while I'm eating, I swallow too much air."

At home, I returned to our first conversation. In my transcript, the ellipses in her speech seemed to me a proof of honesty, her voice staggered by unexamined pain, and this was how I had remembered her tone to be. But when I replayed the recording itself, Josée's voice was captivating and confident—as if, perhaps, she'd wanted to shock. She listed dysentery, suicide, all the horrors in a crescendo, as if she felt that each alone was perhaps not enough.

Why had Josée retracted this? Perhaps she did not want to betray her mother's confidences, however disturbing they had been. Or perhaps she'd realized, belatedly, that in this anecdote Mina had allowed the roles of mother and daughter to reverse, leaning on her daughter in a way that others might condemn. Everywhere on Josée's houseboat were photos of Mina. I noticed that she spoke more softly and carefully around them, and even occasionally glanced toward them. It was difficult not to feel, during many of our conversations, that Mina was listening.

I LOVED DISCUSSING the supernatural with Josée. I felt that these conversations were often our most honest. They had the unintentionally revealing quality of other people's dreams.

She told me in detail about her near-death experience, her NDE as she called it, pronouncing it *en-day-euh*. She said that most people saw their lives play out from birth to death, but she'd seen hers backward, from death to birth. She told me that, in those moments, you saw your life not as you yourself had experienced it, but as other people had. You became the other people in your life and felt, as they had felt it, all the times you'd brought them joy and all the times you'd caused them pain. Much of it was very surprising, she told me, and not at all what you would expect.

I asked who she had hurt and she told me only Paul. In the end, she said, it was only those you'd hurt intentionally that counted.

She told me that after her NDE, she'd become involved in a community of people who'd experienced the same thing. With the help of a spiritual leader, she underwent rebirthing sessions. She relived the primal scream she gave as she entered the world. It was very telling, your primal scream. Hers had been filled with rage.

She told me her NDE had left her with the ability to see auras.

I asked her the color of mine. She told me that the skill had faded over the years, and that only certain people's were strong enough to see.

She told me about her past lives. She'd been a man in many of them, which, she said, explained a lot. In one, she had been stabbed in the back with a pitchfork by her cheating wife. She had bled out over three days in a cow's trough, which was why she'd always hated hay. In one, Mélanie had been her sister, and this explained the affinity they had always had.

She told me that Paul had come to visit her after his death, and that they had settled their scores once and for all. She had awoken to find her pillow soaked with both of their tears and he had never come again.

And she told me that she often felt Mina close by.

"I keep telling her to go up," Josée said. "Go up, Maman, go up go up go up! Go do something else! Because there are many things you can do after you die, you know, you don't have to stay here. You can be reincarnated. But she won't go. It does make me happy, though, having her near. Every time I hear the squeal of brakes behind me, or I almost trip and catch myself, I say 'Merci, Maman!'"

"So after you die, you can choose whether to be reincarnated or to stay close to earth?" I asked.

"Well, you don't choose," Josée said, as if this were obvious. "It depends on your karma, and on the life you lived on earth."

"If you live a good life, you get reincarnated?"

"You reincarnate yourself until you're satisfied. Or until others are satisfied with you. But Mina stays near us."

"You think Mina watches over *me*?" I asked, my voice betraying how much I cared.

"*Oui!* Of course! But during that time, she doesn't do anything else, either."

"She can't both watch over us and be happy?"

"No. It's one or the other. She's stuck," Josée said sadly.

"So why does Mina stay close to us?" I asked.

"I don't know," she said, annoyed at my questions that went in circles. "I didn't judge her while she was alive and I'm certainly not going to judge what she does with her death."

THE FINAL TWO MONTHS of Josée's spring semester were difficult. She told no one of the burdens she faced back home. She often missed school. She commuted back to Paris twice a week to provide food for her grandmother and brother, which in those postwar years still involved standing on long lines for rations.

But in the small portions of time that remained her own, she devoted herself whole to the play. At the end of the year, she appeared as Joan of Arc, resplendent in her white shift. It was the crowning gesture to her staggered education. I imagine her onstage, her fists raised high in the passion of martyrdom. Neither Mina nor Mélanie nor her father were in the audience, but Josée had long grown used to such things. I see her youthful beauty casting arcs of light that illuminate the whole room. And, even then, I see her hardening.

ON ONE THURSDAY, she had lunch with her father before going to visit her mother. She told him she had to hurry—it was a long train ride to the prison, involving at least two transfers.

"Take your time," he told her. "I'll drive you there."

She ate more slowly. But when the hour approached to drive her, her father told her he no longer had the time. Josée was forced to rush to the subway. There were five minutes remaining in the visitation hour when she arrived. Mina was called. She came to the doorway, but she did not approach the desk. When Josée took a step toward her, Mina held out her hand to say stop. She disappeared back into the depths of the prison. The following week, Josée tried to explain that it had been Eugène's fault. But Mina was still furious and refused to accept her daughter's excuses.

"There, I think," Josée told me, "my father did that just to hurt my mother. Or perhaps he simply lost his courage at the last minute. It wasn't an easy thing, to go in front of the prison." She was silent a minute.

"Still," she said, "it cut me very deeply. You know, little things like that, they hurt you more than all the rest."

Though they had never lived together, Josée and her father were close. When she was born, Eugène had legally declared his paternity, which other men at the time might not have done. He slipped her small presents, tickets to the circus, whenever he could. Of the papers Josée had kept in well-hidden boxes on her boat, the vast majority belonged to her father.

After Eugène's death, neither his wife nor his three sons were particularly interested in what he had left behind. Josée took upon herself the task of emptying his office and his home. She kept his old date books, the many letters sent to him by his uncle during his service in World War I. She kept his slippers and his robe, all the signs of her father that she had never had at home. I was uninterested in these. I cast them aside, digging and digging for Mina.

But Josée proudly showed me each small scrap: his expired driver's license, a medal he had won.

She put in my hands his date book from 1930. On the day of her birth, in pencil, he had made the small notation "J.E."

"He couldn't even bring himself to write my name," she said.

MINA WAS RELEASED from prison the following Christmas, after eight months in jail. Difficult as that time had been, the only real hardship Josée alluded to was her mother's return. Mina immediately reclaimed her control of the family's affairs. Josée, used to her independence and new responsibilities, did not take it well.

Josée spent a month in Italy by herself, then returned to Paris and finished her final year of high school through correspondence classes. She took a quick course to become certified as a secretary. The family's finances were severely reduced, but Mina was adamant that they stay on in the home she and Beppo had rented. Both Mina and Josée found positions as secretaries. Josée took phone calls and dictation for a lawyer. The pay wasn't much, but she was proud to be making any money at all.

The morning after she'd received her first paycheck, Josée went to the florist by her office and spent a quarter of the money on an azalea plant in full bloom. It was a gift for her mother. Her boss saw her come into work—I imagine her staggering, her face hidden behind an explosion of pink flowers—and offered to drive her home. Josée accepted. It would be far easier than carrying the plant home on the city bus, and this way her boss would see her impressive front doors. She climbed into his fancy American car.

Mina was out front gardening when they drove up. She stood very still as Josée got out with the flowers.

"Don't you have any shame?" Mina said as Josée reached her, her voice trembling with anger. Josée was confused. She came forward with the flowers, and Mina slapped her.

"How dare you drive up here in that man's car," Mina said.

"But . . . he's my boss," Josée said. "I bought these flowers for you. He offered to drive me home so I wouldn't have to carry them."

"Of course," Mina said. "That's what they all say." She went back inside, leaving her daughter on the doorstep sobbing into the azaleas.

Josée's eyes filled with tears as she told me the story. "You see? It affects me even now," she said.

"Did she ever apologize?" I asked.

"Oh, no. Mothers never apologize to their children. I don't think she ever apologized for anything," Josée said. She quickly launched into another topic.

"Oh! It hurts, that story!" I said, interrupting her with a pained laugh, my hand over my heart.

"Well, you know, when you're that age, you take everything so seriously. Your first salary, your first gift to your mother. But now I see . . . she was only trying to protect me from the mistakes she herself had made." The subject was closed and she refused to say anything more.

I HAD ALWAYS ASSUMED that Josée and Paul had met on an airplane. It seemed befitting of the grand scale of their turbulent romance, and Josée's stories of her days as an airline stewardess loomed large in her telling of her past. I'd imagined her in her sharp blue uniform and matching cap, wings pinned on her chest, catching Paul's eye as she walked down the aisle demonstrating safety procedures. I'd imagined my grandfather as I'd always known him: a cigar in hand, expensive shirt buttons straining slightly over his stomach and broad hairy chest, a lascivious twinkle in his eyes. But the truth was they met at a dinner party in a small apartment when Josée was a secretary and Paul a medical intern. Josée had been invited by her boyfriend's sister. There didn't seem to be much more to tell to their meeting, other than that the boyfriend had been quite annoyed with his sister, Josée said laughing. But, she said, when Paul wanted something he went after it, and he went after her. And she'd liked him, loved him even. He was charismatic, at ease being the center of attention, and he was sturdy and masculine and handsome. He made her laugh, bantered easily, made declarations of love in grandiloquent French.

"You must be the only person," my mother told me with awe when I recounted this, "to whom Josée has ever admitted that she once loved my father."

Paul was twenty-eight when Josée met him, and she was nineteen. She spent her twentieth birthday in tears.

"Why?" I asked.

"Because nothing was happening," Josée told me. She'd waited her whole life to turn twenty. It was to be the beginning of her glorious emancipation. But instead she lived at home, with Mina, Mélanie, and her brother, and she sobbed as she blew out her candles.

"I was also crying because of the dog," she added.

Paul was studying bone grafts, and he did trials on abandoned dogs. He'd left the most recent one with her. Josée knew she wasn't supposed to become attached. She helped Paul with the trials. She held the dogs as they whimpered during the operations, and she knew what any attachment would later cost her. But this dog was sweet and vulnerable and feeble. It limped around in its plaster cast. The dog died on the morning of her twentieth birthday. Her father, who had come by to wish her a happy birthday, had thoughtfully taken its body to burn in the large industrial ovens of his business. Which only made Josée more distraught—she realized too late that Paul would be furious, that examining the corpse had been the whole point.

When Josée told me this story I felt my temples vibrate and expand, a feeling I had always associated as a child with being in the presence of magic. I pictured time bending as the image of my mother crying over her dog's corpse folded to overlap with that of Josée. I had never seen either of these women, so formidable in the incarnations I knew, cry such unself-conscious tears as one would shed over an animal. And maybe there are dead dogs in every story. Certainly there were parallels between their lives more striking than this one. But this image made my whole body buzz. In some place outside of time, both young women mourned all they had failed to accomplish, not knowing, as I did, all that they would.

JOSÉE HAD SEVERAL ABORTIONS in the first few years she and Paul were together, she told me. It was the only solution to pre-marital sex. Only soldiers had condoms, and she had never seen one.

"No one used contraception?" I asked, shocked. "But what did your friends do?" In America, condom use was so widespread that, by 1950, vending machines had been installed.

Some of her friends went to backstreet concierges, *faiseuses d'anges*, angel-makers. Some of her friends went to England. Perhaps some of her friends had boyfriends who had the kindness to, as Josée said, "repaint the ceiling." But Josée had the good fortune of dating a young doctor.

Whenever Josée's period was late by two or three weeks, Paul would perform a dilation and curettage.

"But the pain must have been excruciating," I said, crossing my legs as if to ward it off. We'd finished our meal and a bottle of red wine. I got up and opened a second one.

"It hurt a lot," Josée said, perfectly matter-of-fact, as I refilled our glasses. "But when you know what to expect, things hurt much less."

"*Quand même!*" I said, an uncomfortable giggle rising in my throat.

"Yes, well, it's no pleasure cruise," Josée said.

When I researched it later, I would find that contraception was indeed hard to find in France in the postwar years, and abortion was indeed common. Still, the procedure must have been dangerous as well as physically and emotionally painful.

"You didn't think of them . . . as children?" I asked.

"Not at all," Josée said. "Not at all. We called it being delivered . . . delivered of a problem. We did it when we were late by a few weeks—we never waited as long as three months," Josée said.

"It's hard for me to understand," I said. "The way I've heard abortions talked about . . ." I was thinking of my mother, of my friends, of all the women I'd known who were permanently affected by the sense of their lives splintering into possibilities not lived.

"It's stories, all of that. Women who have a crisis of the blues because they lost a fetus." Josée let out a small huff. "It's really all people who have never known war. Those ladies with nothing in their skulls. There are more interesting things to worry about in life. You have to know that a child chooses to come incarnate himself on Earth, and if it doesn't work out, he'll just go back up and re-create himself in the stomach of someone else. It's . . . you haven't *killed* anybody. I think we really feel very sorry for ourselves for so little. People need war or something to shake them up a bit, so that they don't fall into an abyss of doubts."

Josée did worry that the procedures would leave her unable to have children. She did in fact have a miscarriage in her first year of marriage, before Sylvie. The pain, again, had been excruciating, but Paul hadn't intervened. As Josée told it, it was a friend who helped her onto the examining table, another friend who held her hand. The child had been male, the son Josée and Paul had always wanted. But this too was no great tragedy, she said.

After the miscarriage, she went to see a gynecologist for the first time in her life. She discovered that the miscarriage had been due to her retroverted uterus. During her subsequent pregnancies, she would spend the third month lying in bed on her stomach.

"Be careful," she said, "you might have one also. One of my daughters does, I forget which. It's hereditary." I felt a small thrill at her acknowledgment that we were related.

"A doctor told me once that I do," I said. The doctor had also told me that it was common and had no impact on fertility, but I didn't mention that.

"Yes, well, you can know right away," Josée said, "if in coitus you're better on your stomach. If it hurts when he's on top of you, but not when he takes you from behind, then it's retroverted."

I laughed. A February wind blew at the kitchen windows and the clock ticked off the hours of the night. The red wine was very good and it made my arms feel warm and heavy.

"It's all very logical," Josée said. "It either hits up against your cervix or it doesn't. And then, well, the G-spot—but that isn't of my era."

"They didn't really think about female pleasure, in your era?" I asked. Josée took a long unsteady inhale as she considered her answer. She let it out in a whoosh.

"No," she said.

"You hesitate," I teased. Like my mother, Josée was not easy to tease.

"Well, because your grandfather fucked well. He liked it. I don't know if he did it well, but he really enjoyed it. No. It isn't like today, women with their sex toys. *Pfff,* you've all gone and made things so complicated."

"But female pleasure isn't so complicated," I said.

"*Effectivement.* But . . . when they say women now have ten orgasms in a row! It just seems exhausting to me."

"Ten times seems exhausting to me, too," I said. "But that women have orgasms at all seems to me important."

"I don't think in my day men gave themselves a whole lot of trouble trying to find a woman's clitoris. I don't remember your grandfather ever asking me if I'd had a good time."

"But didn't that leave you feeling frustrated?" I asked.

"No, I mean, we knew that we *could.* If it came on its own, that was good. But we weren't going to go out searching for pleasure, saying, 'Me too, I'm going to . . . it's my right!'"

"But the same way men talk about how . . . if you excite them and don't follow through, they wind up in pain? I've had the same thing happen to me—I go a bit crazy, I get angry, I cry."

"Really?" Josée asked. "You?"

I flushed and stumbled. "Yes," I said. "There's just . . . a lot of emotion."

"Something is missing," Josée said slowly, trying to understand. "Something hasn't been released?"

"Maybe," I said, my cheeks burning hot. I strung several words together that did not form a sentence. I was fascinated but nervous. There was electricity in the air, like at a slumber party when someone suggests Truth or Dare.

"I don't know," Josée said. "Maybe I'm a bit of a prude. You know, it's been more than twenty years since I had sex."

She laughed and I joined in.

"I don't know what I'm talking about," Josée said, shaking her head and looking down.

"And did you ever . . . caress yourself?" I asked, trying to slip back into interviewer mode.

"Mélanie used to tell me not to touch my flower," Josée said. "I didn't understand what she meant."

"But it's something that all girls discover at some point, no?" I asked.

"No. For me it was a man who made me notice that I could . . . orgasm. I'd had no idea. It was a boyfriend, when I was seventeen. He told me that, when I was alone, I had to take a warm bath, light a candle, listen to some gentle music, caress myself. And then, supposedly, I would find myself *aux anges*. But I don't have any memory of a life-changing experience in a bathtub. Perhaps I'd put the candle in the wrong place."

"It's something that I've always taken so for granted," I said. "If a friend told me that she had never had an orgasm, or that her boyfriend paid no attention to her pleasure, it would shock me now," I said.

"Here we are in the twenty-first century," Josée said, waving a demonstrative hand across her kitchen table. "It wasn't of our day, all this. And I didn't talk about it with my friends. We had other cats to whip, trips to go on, dinners to plan." It occurred to me that it was unlikely Josée had ever spoken this frankly about sex with anybody.

"I just feel like I would go a little crazy if I couldn't express that part of myself," I said.

"But you, you started at what age to discover your body?" Josée asked.

"My body? When I was very young. Eight or nine," I said.

"You didn't caress yourself when you were eight!" Josée said, her eyes widening.

"I did. A long time before I understood what sex was. No one ever told me not to touch my flower," I said with a self-conscious shrug.

"*Ah bon!* At eight or nine you discovered that all by yourself!"

"It wasn't a sexual act . . . but still I knew that it was something to be done in private. It was part of my . . ."

"Of your well-being," Josée supplied.

"I guess so," I said. "It wasn't . . . goal-oriented."

"Huh," Josée said. "Well, I suppose nobody ever told you it was forbidden."

"No," I said. I had no memory of my mother trying to explain sex to me, nor of ever wondering what it was. When I hit puberty, she had bought me carefully chosen explanatory books, books that celebrated masturbation and discussed homosexuality without judgment, but I had been quietly reading my parents' collection of obscene comics since long before.

"And you didn't have to go to confession!" Josée continued. "When I was ten, the priest put all sorts of ideas in my head about impure thoughts. But I didn't have any. I looked carefully at the boy who went to school across the street and I rolled down my socks into little sockettes so that it would be more sexy. But that was it. Even when Gerard and I were fourteen, I was only afraid I might become pregnant. I had no idea there could be pleasure. A kiss didn't make me boil." Josée began to muse that if her grandmother had told her not to touch her flower, then it must have been because she herself was told that as a girl. Which meant that Mélanie, too, had had a flower, and had discovered it. This had never occurred to Josée before.

"It's quite poetic, when you think about it," she said. "And I, I don't know if my daughters ever touched themselves. I never asked them."

"Well, no," I said.

"You see, I never talked about these things with my daughters. Not like I can with you. These are the kinds of conversations only grandmothers and granddaughters can have," Josée said with a warm smile. I smiled back.

It was past midnight when we stopped talking and I hugged her good night, taking her small body in my arms. As I lay down on the convertible sofa in her living room, I felt a belated stab of discomfort at the turns our conversation had taken. *You've always lacked a clear sense of boundaries*, my mother had said. And yet at the same time I felt the incredible pull of Josée's smile. She beamed at me as if her love were a physical thing she could give me. I wanted this new intimacy we were forging. I did not know the rules.

IT HAD ALWAYS felt natural to keep the women I dated secret from my French family. As my mother said, "Why would you want to give them ammunition?" I kept much of my personal life from them, not that anyone asked me many questions.

But now, as I pressed Josée for intimate details, I felt compelled to share my own. My girlfriend would be coming from New York for a visit and I wanted them to meet. A few weeks before she arrived, I went over to the houseboat. I was more nervous than I had been in a long time. In the rest of my life, I always corrected people who assumed I dated men, even when I had no desire to create discomfort. I considered it a small political act to do so. But, I realized, as I walked the long stretch along the Seine from the subway to the boat, I had never really "come out" to anyone before.

"I wanted to talk to you about something," I said, standing and tugging at my fingers, while Josée set the table on the roof of the boat. She paused and looked up at me.

"You know my boyfriend I've told you about? The graphic designer in New York?" I said. She nodded. I took a gulp of air.

"His name isn't Louis," I said. "Her name is Lindsay."

"What do her parents do?" Josée asked mildly, straightening a napkin and reaching for the silverware.

"Her dad is a doctor," I said. "Her mother manages the family affairs."

"Well!" Josée said, relieved. "She comes from a good family.

That's all that matters." I laughed, and relief weakened my knees. I sat down.

"Did you think it would matter to me?" Josée asked. "As long as she appreciates you and makes you happy. That's all I care about."

WHEN JOSÉE FIRST TOLD Paul she had applied to be an airline stewardess, he laughed and brushed her off. It was an impossibly glamorous job in 1951.

Many gorgeous young women responded to the open call. Josée bit her tongue and waited. In March, the women who had applied were called all at once to the TWA offices on the Champs-Élysées. A man read off the names of the accepted in ranked order. Josée was called first.

"I was called *first*," she told me often, with a very rare flash of pride. Not only was she called first, but because there was still a month to go before her twenty-first birthday (and therefore a month before she could be legally hired), they made an exception for her. They let her fly on test flights. They flew her to New York.

For Josée, Americans were the ones who had covered her city with bombs, saying they were aiming for the Germans and instead spraying all of Paris. The Americans had liberated France, they had died for France in Normandy. And yet for Americans, Europe didn't count. They had come only for the Germans. Americans weren't people "like us." They were big brawny superheroes; they were rotten with cash.

Josée saw New York. It fell on her face in all its excess and grandeur. The South Street Seaport bustled with boats, the Empire State Building towered above her. But it only fit with what she had imagined: a scene straight from the movies. Americans were from another planet. They were beings of constant excess, with their loud voices, their hugs, their too-tall buildings. The whole city lit up at night. *What degeneracy!* Josée thought. Even after the war, she carefully extinguished and saved her candles.

Josée could no longer remember a specific moment of that time in New York. She was there for ten days, she saw what she expected to see, and she left with no wish to return. She would see many things as a hostess: the electricity in Egypt was unreliable, Greece was lovely, all of Italy was in flower. Wherever they traveled, the crew were received like movie stars. Bottles of champagne were sent to their hotel rooms and their pictures appeared in the papers. Josée was paid incredibly well. Her already high salary was in strong American dollars. She gave Mina part of the money, saying that it was for rent on her childhood bedroom. She rarely brought back souvenirs for her mother or her brother, but for Mélanie she stole whole bags of the mints she passed out to passengers.

Paul chased her from city to city, driving hours in his Citroën, Paris to Rome, Rome to Milan, only to discover that she had already taken to the air again by the time he arrived. Fed up, he used the only means he had to force Josée to quit. The stewardesses were contractually obligated to be single. He proposed. "Who would give up a job like this one?" the other flight attendants said. "You're crazy!" But Josée was in love. She wanted nothing more than the stability of a family. A year after she had been hired, she quit.

Paul assured her that he had told his parents her secret. Josée thought them very polite for not mentioning it. Paul came to visit Eugène, entering through the office window, and asked for Josée's hand in marriage. Eugène, delighted, slapped Paul on the back and promised a generous dowry. By the seventeenth of June, they were officially engaged. By the thirteenth of July, the engagement was off.

Paul broke it off by telephone. His parents had hired an investigator to compile information on their future daughter-in-law, he told her, and it seemed he had not told them her secret after all. They had discovered that she was a bastard. Paul couldn't marry so far beneath himself, his mother insisted. No matter that Paul's father was only a veterinarian from a small town. No matter that several farm girls in neighboring villages had children who looked suspiciously related to Paul's father.

As soon as she hung up the phone, Josée took off her engagement ring and mailed it back. No note. She didn't even send it by registered mail. Then she collapsed into sobs.

Paul's parents, Josée discovered later, tried to match him instead with a former president's daughter. But whatever existed between him and Josée was passionate. He soon realized his mistake. He spent the summer ringing Josée's doorbell, extravagant bouquets of flowers in hand. Mina answered the door and told him her daughter was out. Josée entered and exited through the servants' entrance in the back. Paul took up vigil in his car across the street. He slept there for ten days and ten nights. He threatened to kill himself. He swore he wouldn't eat until she spoke to him. Mina watched from the window and brought updates to her daughter. "Let him die then," Josée said.

And then she forgave him. When I asked her why she changed her mind, she shrugged her shoulders and said simply: "I loved him."

In the beginning, they were happy together. But Josée alluded to those happy times only vaguely, always followed by a "but then . . ." The happiness had been so often overwritten with anger that I caught only glimpses of it.

Not even a year into their marriage, Josée began to discover Paul's constant lies. She was pregnant with Sylvie when she cut her hand and rushed to Paul's hospital, believing he was working an overnight shift, only to be told he was not there. Soon after, there were other women's belongings in his car. Soon after, she called home and he, mistaking her for one of his mistresses, answered in an angry hiss, "I told you never to call me here." Although these were not the real problems, she told me. A woman you could fight against. A gambling addiction you could not.

On the morning of their first Christmas together, she and Paul had an argument. Mina rang the doorbell, Josée's young brother in tow, both dressed in their holiday best. Paul screamed, "Your whore of a mother is here!" He opened the door, told Mina that she was never to set foot in their home, and slammed it in her face. Josée was furious. But from then on, she saw her mother very little. There was no room for her past in this new world.

Meanwhile, Mina held three secretarial jobs simultaneously, often working through the weekends. She struggled to make the rent on her apartment, but still refused to give it up. She sent Josée's brother to the best schools and cut corners everywhere else. She worked until she was well into her seventies, but her taste for finery never faded.

In one of our more intimate conversations, Josée told me that one of her few regrets was not helping her mother more in those years. On Josée's brief visits, Mina would occasionally intimate that she needed certain things, that, for example, her washing machine was broken and she couldn't afford to have it fixed. "It would have been very easy for me to help," Josée said. "We had piles of cash stashed all around the house. I helped myself to it when I liked. Paul would never have noticed. But I didn't." Though when I asked why, she said, "It didn't occur to me. I was far too busy being a wife and a mother."

One of those Sundays when Mina babysat while Josée and Paul went to the track, Josée bet on a horse named Mélanie. The horse was not favored, and it was a sentimental whim. But the horse won, the bet was multiplied fourteen times, and the winnings were huge. Josée giddily gave all of it to Mélanie that evening. It was money that Mina, who ran the household, could have put to good use. But it was also enough to emancipate the aging Mélanie from her dependence on her daughter. And yet, upon Mélanie's death in 1961, they found the bills, untouched, tucked away in the back of Mélanie's sock drawer.

"Why do you think she didn't spend it?" I asked.

"Because we found it in her sock drawer," Josée repeated testily.

"No, I mean why, in your opinion, didn't she spend the money?" I said.

"Oh!" Josée said. "You mean, if I were to put myself in Mélanie's place and try to imagine?" She hesitated, the exercise unfamiliar.

"I don't know," she huffed eventually. "You know, people who have known the war . . ."

I tried to reconstruct a scene of one of the Sundays when Josée dropped Françoise off for babysitting. In both Josée's and

Françoise's tellings, those afternoons had gone the way of all things routine, a blur of collapsed time. But now I pictured it as a frozen instant. I saw Josée sitting in the driver's seat of a fancy new car, one hand raised in a distracted salutation. She would have been on her way to the horse track, effortlessly elegant in the latest sixties style. I pictured Mina in the doorway in a dress she had sewn herself, perfectly coiffed in anticipation of this moment when she would step outside. And I imagined Françoise running from car to doorway, all scraped knees and short hair, suspended in motion.

And I saw now what my mother had not, at the time: that Mina must have felt a stab of jealousy to see her daughter awash in the wealth she had only so tenuously known herself. That Josée must have sensed her mother's envy, and felt a certain inevitable pleasure.

And then my frozen moment sprang back into motion. Josée's car pulled off into the road, Françoise fell into Mina's arms. Mina took Françoise, Josée's least favorite daughter, and loved her ferociously. I saw a pattern forming, like a series of skipping stones that sent ripples through the generations: all the granddaughters and grandmothers who loved each other, all the mothers left stranded in between.

chapter eleven

I called Josée from the train.

"*Oui, mon chat!*" she said as she picked up the phone.

"Just letting you know I'm on my way," I said.

"Train six one five five, car six, upstairs, seat one fifteen, arrives at three oh five p.m.," she said, apparently from memory.

"Yes," I said, laughing, "I'll see you very soon."

The TGV bisected the countryside, speeding south. Vineyards whipped past the windows. As the train pulled into the Hyères station, I scanned the platform. I didn't recognize Josée right away. She was wearing a pale yellow headband that held wisps of blond hair away from her eyes, and a soft yellow shirt that came down to the top of her thighs. She looked soft where I was expecting sharp.

She was gazing the other way down the platform. I tapped her on the shoulder. "Ahh!" she said with delight, turning toward me, her face lighting up. Her blue eyes appraised me quickly. I felt the charge of her energy on me. Up close, she became young again. And I became younger, too. My voice went high, my steps turned into a shuffle. Glancing at my reflection in a train window, I half expected to see a little girl in her best red velour dress.

As we got into the car, she outlined all the outings she had planned for us: friends we would visit, beaches we would see. She had told me that we would drive back to Paris together on July 7, but now she told me that she'd decided that we ought to stay down south until the thirteenth. I felt kidnapped, but aloud I agreed happily. I had no good excuse to go back earlier. I went heavy with the deep discomfort of being a guest, of being on somebody else's schedule. As she spoke, laying out a verbal calendar and shuffling it around, I noted the urgency in her planning. When it looked as if there weren't time for something, she didn't say we would do it next year, and that broke my heart. Josée's health had gone through many dips these past few years, but each time she'd recuperated. I refused to believe she wouldn't live at least another decade.

We sped down the highway. In the opposite direction, cars were stalled in traffic that moved at a crawl.

"I hope you didn't have to sit through all that on your way to pick me up," I said.

"No, that wasn't there. And anyway, nothing could have put me in a bad mood this morning. I was so excited you were coming, *je trépignais.*"

"What does that mean?"

"*Trépigner?* It means jumping from foot to foot like a child."

"Oh, that's very sweet," I said. It sounded like what I had felt that morning, trepidation.

"Do you want to go straight to the sea for a swim? Or go home and settle in? If we go home, I'm just warning you, we won't leave again this evening. My friends are coming over for dinner."

I hesitated, trying to guess what the right answer was. I would have preferred to go settle in—I am the kind of person who takes twenty-four hours to travel, no matter how short the trip—but I had a feeling it was the other one.

"Let's go to the beach," I said.

"That's what I thought!" she said. "I always want to jump in the water as soon as I get here."

She went on to tell me a story about driving down here to the South of France with Sylvie, taking turns at the wheel. Josée had the final stretch, and Sylvie fell asleep. She drove the car straight to the beach, parked, and went swimming. When Sylvie woke up, it was getting dark, and she was annoyed. She insisted on having milk for breakfast the next morning, and the store in the village was about to close. "I told her to relax and enjoy the ocean but she refused to get out of the car, she just went on: *the milk, the milk*. So I struck up a conversation with the owners of this little cabana on the beach. I told them, 'My daughter is acting out an operatic tragedy about milk. Do you have any to spare?' The woman went into the back and miraculously produced this little carton of milk, which I, soaking wet and triumphant, brought to Sylvie. '*Voilà! Voilà* your milk,' I said, 'Now will you just relax?' And immediately, she started in about how we needed to get home before the milk spoiled. *Ha!* That girl."

Josée had told me a story about Sylvie, but all I could hear was how much this story was about her. Impulsive, free-spirited—this was the self that appeared in many of her stories, especially those where her daughters played the straight man. We got out of the car, and she helped me change into my bathing suit in the parking lot. "You have fifteen minutes to swim," she told me. She sat on a bench to wait. The sun was setting and the air was cool. The cold water tickled as it climbed my body. My stomach pulled into my spine. I took a deep breath and plunged, happy as soon as the water hit my temples. I swam quickly, straight out into the ocean, my thoughts smoothed out by the rhythmic strokes. I had this tugging feeling, a half-formed thought. It was the feeling that I'd met someone my mother would like. A memory rose without breaking the surface, just suffusing me with the emotion it contained, like a dream. It was of that time in Brazil, when my mother had pulled over so that she and my brother and I could go swimming during the thunderstorm, while my father waited anxiously in the car. *Yes,* I thought to myself dreamily as I swam, *it's a shame. My mother would have really liked Josée if she'd known her.*

JOSÉE HAD ANOTHER BEACH, a secret beach. You could rent a chaise longue and they'd bring you food and drink from the snack bar, which was true of many of the beaches along that small stretch of coastline. But this one had the clearest blue water and was neither too crowded nor too expensive. She wouldn't tell her friends where it was. "Oh no, I can't meet you at the beach tomorrow," she'd say. "We're going to *my* beach. Nadja can tell you, it's the best one around." Then she'd insist that she'd be unable to give them directions, although each time she unerringly found her way there.

She presented me to the women who ran the beach, *les plagistes,* and they kissed us on each cheek. "They lick your peach," my grandmother said of their matronly embrace. The young man who waited on the lounge chairs would probably tend to us with renewed fervor now that she was accompanied by the most beautiful girl on the beach, she continued. I blushed, not feeling beautiful in my too-soft body. I looked around and noticed that I was the youngest woman there. And when he placed two espressos by our feet, Josée said loudly, "Look, Nadja—you have coffee and a handsome French man kneeling in front of you. What more could you want?"

"Nothing," I said with a lascivious laugh and a completely uncharacteristic wink. He stiffened and walked off quickly.

The next day, Josée's friend Julien invited us to lunch at his beach.

I liked Julien. He was seventy-eight and madly in love with my grandmother. He walked with a silver-tipped cane and wore smart tan linen suits and made grand pronouncements about ennui. He read history books about strong women. Josée said he tired her because he didn't enunciate his words. She had very little patience for those who'd grown frail.

"You'll need to dress up," said my grandmother. "His beach is very chic."

I showed her two different outfits, because I thought she would be prouder of my appearance if she'd vetoed one. I wound up in high-waisted printed silk pants, my bikini top, and a see-through silk blouse open to the waist and tied.

She told me that the restaurateur was extremely handsome, and sometimes she brought her friends to this beach just so they could throw themselves at him. "He used to play on the French national rugby team," she said meaningfully, and I made a sound like I was impressed. "He'll surely find you very attractive."

"Oh," I said. I sank into worry. I knew she would be disappointed if he didn't.

As we walked down the boardwalk she said, "There he is! That big broad back, I'd recognize it anywhere."

Facing away from us, at the entrance to the restaurant, a middle-aged man with a physique like an upside-down triangle was talking to a tall tan blonde in her sixties. Josée walked purposefully toward them. Just before she tapped him on the back, she turned and whispered to me, "Be beautiful!"

I didn't even have time to flip my hair back. But I thought to myself, *Okay. Okay. Be beautiful.* My shoulders pushed back and my chin leveled up and I tightened myself deep in my stomach.

"*Ma beauté!*" he exclaimed over Josée, bending to grab her shoulders and kiss her.

"*Je te presente ma petite-fille.*" Josée gestured to me with a sweep of her hand.

Be beautiful, I commanded myself.

He kissed my cheeks, then leaned back and looked me up and down, his eyes lingering on my chest.

"*Elle est ravissante,*" he said, turning his face toward Josée but keeping his eyes on me.

"Of course she is," Josée said briskly. "I wouldn't show her off if she weren't."

He put his hand on her shoulder.

"Your lover is waiting for you over there, at that table," he said, leaning low to speak in her ear.

"At the very center of the restaurant?" Josée said with disdain.

"He insisted on it."

"He's not my lover," Josée said, and we walked over to greet Julien.

Josée and Julien ordered grilled shrimp with risotto. I ordered a salmon tartare, because it sounded healthy but I had seen that it came with French fries. Josée worried about how little I had to eat. "You're going to die of hunger!" she said. I glowed, delighted. My salmon was served in a delicate cup that was much deeper than it looked.

Julien was telling me about one of his three ex-wives. "She had the second most beautiful conversation in Paris," he said. "That's what everyone said about her."

"Who had the first?" I asked.

"The wife of the minister of the interior," he replied without hesitation.

"What does it mean to have beautiful conversation?" I asked.

"Oh, what a wonderful question!" he exclaimed. "It's a dying art, like literature or music, but an art all its own. There's a quality that's hard to describe—it's conversation that's light yet intelligent, with an ability to discuss a wide range of topics and put everyone at their ease. It's very rare these days." He added, "Her son never liked me much. I think he was jealous."

"Of what?" I asked, salting my French fries.

"Oh, how she wounds!" Julien exclaimed. "She's vicious, your granddaughter, with her seemingly innocent questions."

"That's not how I meant it!" I said, laughing.

"Of what!" he repeated, clapping his hand to his heart.

The restaurateur came and asked how we were doing. Josée complained that her shrimp was dry. He clasped Josée's hand between his two huge palms, pulling her arm toward him across the table. "Did you know that bonobos . . . ," he began.

"*Vraiment*," Julien said petulantly. "You promised me you wouldn't talk about the bonobos today."

"Julien and I talked about this this morning," the restaurateur said. "He wants to keep the information for himself. But did you know that bonobos solve every conflict, between males and females, females and females, no matter, they solve every conflict by making love?"

"How interesting," Josée said dryly.

"So my dear Josée," the restaurateur continued smoothly, "I feel we're having some tension, you and I . . ." Josée laughed coquettishly and squeezed his hand once, quickly, before putting hers back in her lap. Julien scowled.

When he was gone, Julien asked me if I had a boyfriend and I blushed and mumbled yes, looking down.

"Is he in New York?"

"Yes," I said, pushing my food around on my plate.

"Does he miss you?"

"I hope so," I said.

"What does he do?"

"He's a graphic designer," I said, willing the conversation to end and unable to raise my eyes from my plate. "Though sometimes he draws comics."

"Really?" Josée asked, surprised.

"You see!" Julien crowed with pride. "It's all about asking the right questions. I bet you didn't plan to tell us that your boyfriend draws comics."

"No," I said truthfully, and Julien, sensing my discomfort, moved on.

After lunch, Julien held Josée a long time by the shoulders as he said good-bye. He tried several times to make another date to see her, but she told him that it was unlikely. He went home to nap and we returned to her beach.

"How do you do it?" I asked as we settled into our lounge chairs. "Will you teach me? How do you make so many men fall in love with you?"

"It's innate," she said. "Don't worry, you have it. Your mother does, too."

But I knew that wasn't true. Men lost interest in me as soon as they began talking to me. So I asked again.

"You can't be afraid to be disagreeable," she answered. I laughed and begged for more specifics.

"It's like having a dog—you have to let men know that they have a master and that the master is you. And, oh, you flatter them, and you mother them a bit, too, but then you flatten them straight out. You keep them in line. Did you see, at lunch, Julien interrupted me and I looked straight at him and said slowly, 'I am speaking'? They need to know who's in charge, just like a dog. But a pretty dog, too, one you're happy to show off."

"What else?" I demanded.

"Well you must always have at least three suitors," she said after a moment of thought. "One and he's bored, two and they get caught up fighting each other, but three and they're all jumping through hoops for your attention."

"But how?" I asked. "How do you get them interested in the first place?"

"*Le regard,*" she said, surprised I did not know something so obvious. "You scan the party for the one that pleases you and you give him *le regard*. Then you look away, and you wait for him to come talk to you." She told me, also, that it was important never to be the best-dressed woman in the room, especially if you were the host but even if you were not. You must look flawless, but not like you were trying, and you must always wear comfortable shoes.

"But in my generation, men courted you. Perhaps it's different with young men these days."

"Hm," I said. "Maybe." I pulled out my book to read.

"You know," Josée said, "I was glad you said 'he' when you were talking to Julien."

"It means a lot to me that I can share that part of myself with you," I said. "I don't need to tell all of your friends. I figure you'll tell them if you want to."

"Of course you can tell my *friends*!" she said. "Just not Julien. He's the village concierge. It would give him gossip for weeks. If you wanted to come back here with a boy one day you'd have to explain yourself all over again."

"*Mmhmm*," I said. "I don't mind. It's still true, in all the ways that matter. I'm in love, the person is in New York, she does draw comics sometimes. The pronouns aren't important."

"I understand," she said. "You're in love with a being." She stared out at the ocean. "Do you think you'll make your life with her?" she asked quietly.

"I don't know," I said. "I'm still too young to be sure with anyone. But I love her. It seems possible."

She nodded. I felt Josée understood this part of me, in all of its constant fluidity, better than anyone else I had ever spoken to—better, even, than I often understood it myself. I wanted to ask her if she had ever had experiences with women. But when I turned toward her, mouth open, trying to phrase the question, she'd already gotten up. She was walking out toward the ocean.

W HEN I DID MANAGE to ask, a few months later, Josée responded without hesitation. She told me about a passionate affair with a woman who was a famous tennis player. I looked up photos of her on the Internet as soon as I got home. She was not beautiful, but her gaze was intelligent and seductive. She was masculine in appearance, just like the women who'd always attracted me. In many of the photos, she was behind the wheel of a race car. In one, she had a baby cheetah on a leash. This tennis player, Josée told me, had seduced all of the most beautiful women in Paris.

She'd seduced Josée as well. In the summer of 1981, they'd spent a torrid night together on the houseboat. The next morning Andrée complained of the noise they'd made. The tennis player put Josée in her convertible car and they drove down south on a whim, all the way to Saint Tropez, the wind whipping at Josée's hair. They'd had a wonderful time, Josée told me, but their affair was brief.

"After that," she told me, "I renounced women. They're even more possessive than men."

On our last night, Josée took me to a restaurant a friend of hers had recommended. It was set back from the road, built right on top of a sleepy beach at an inlet where the ocean dipped into the curving coastline.

We sat outside on the wooden terrace, at one of the tables closest to the ocean. We ordered a pitcher of rosé and a plate of shrimp, mussels, and sardines grilled over a fire of grapevines. The other tables slowly filled with couples on dates and well-dressed families. Their low murmur joined with the sound of the wind and the waves. Over Josée's shoulder I could see a stone staircase that wound down a hill and straight into the ocean.

"I am just . . . ," I said, breathing in deeply and sweeping my hand to take in the table, the water, the stone staircase. "I am just so . . . *happy* right now."

I smiled, but I didn't even need to smile. My veins were filled with light. An uncomplicated, inexplicable joy surged through me, taking me by surprise. I tried to keep it in my peripheral awareness. I knew how happiness slipped into the present only in bright, brief flashes. Most of the time, it belonged to the past or to the future: "I was happy" or "I will be happy" and not, or almost never, "I *am* happy." Even trying to savor the moment tinged it with nostalgia.

Josée beamed at me, her cheekbones lifting her face.

"*La plénitude,*" she said authoritatively. "A feeling of fullness—nothing more you could want."

"Yes," I said, "yes, exactly." But the feeling was already beginning to slip away.

As I savored my last spoonful of dessert, Josée said, "We should give them back the table. They must need it for other customers."

"Okay," I said, casting a final wistful glance at the ocean.

"Do you want to take a swim?" she asked.

"Yes," I said, caught by surprise. I had my bathing suit on under my dress.

"Then go—go! The night is soft and the ocean has been heating all day."

"Are you sure you don't mind waiting?" I asked.

"If I'm suggesting it, it's because I would do it myself if I were younger," she said. She took a book from her bag. I went back to the car to get a towel and a beach chair from the trunk. I set it up on the sand in front of the terrace.

"What's that for?" Josée asked.

"For you, so . . . so you can sit and watch me," I said, stumbling.

"Watch you?" she said, perplexed. "No, I'll be fine inside by the stove. Fold that thing up and go off to the side so that you don't provide entertainment for the whole restaurant."

I shed my dress and walked down the deserted beach, the sound of the restaurant receding behind me. The water was nearly as warm as the air. I swam hard along the shoreline, my body stretching out impossibly long, until I reached one of the cliffs that bordered the bay. I swam back until I was in front of the glittering lights of the restaurant, far from the shore, and floated flat on my back. The Mediterranean rocked me gently, the salt catching my body like a cushion. I tried to count the times I had lain in the ocean on the last day of summer. Each time, I stored away all the physical sensations, the feeling of water tickling around my face, and the memories were so clear and so similar that this moment became all the moments, like a thread pulled tight through gathered fabric, as if I had never done anything but bob in the ocean.

Underwater I could hear thousands of shells clicking together, as if I were eavesdropping on the ocean's private thoughts. Then I listened more carefully. Deep, black water. I was seized by an ancestral terror. I sputtered upright, gasping, adrenaline flooding my veins. I was very far from the shore. My grandmother was indoors by the fire. I was engulfed by darkness and all alone. I made myself breathe deeply. There was no danger here. I swam back to shore, my heart still pounding.

I walked up the sand toward the restaurant with my back self-consciously straight, aware that many of the diners had turned to stare at me.

"*Elle est bonne?*" a round man in his midfifties called to me from his table.

"*Délicieuse,*" I answered softly, my head down, as I toweled off.

"*Alors, ma bichette,*" my grandmother said, and I whipped around in surprise. She was still at our table. She'd put away her book, and her chair was turned toward the ocean.

I walked over to her and she gathered herself to leave. Right outside the door to the restaurant, we paused. We were under a streetlamp and the air was cool on my wet skin.

"As you were swimming this way," she said, "there was someone else swimming the other way—you crossed each other. It was very beautiful to see."

I hadn't seen anyone else in the water. Perhaps she'd just seen me twice. Still, I understood what she was telling me: she'd watched me. I put my hand gently on her arm. Without a word, she took her sweater from her bag and reached up to tie it around my shoulders, draping it over me with a few absentminded pats. It was soft, a beige cashmere, and it smelled like her. I rolled my shoulders against it in joy.

ON OUR WAY BACK UP to Paris, we spent a few nights at Josée's friend Renée's house outside of Frejus. She and Josée had known each other since 1952. I admired the worn, comfortable closeness of their relationship and considered Renée among my favorites of my grandmother's friends. Her elegant reserve gave way to profound kindness when she let down her guard. I had the sense that once she'd decided to love someone, she never changed her mind. I had been to this house with my parents one summer when I was three or four years old. My mother often told the story of how, a day after she'd enrolled me in the local school, I'd come back speaking French with the regional twang. My grandmother told me that my class had been caught near a giant vineyard fire, black smoke obscuring the rolling hills, and I had never mentioned it, even then. I had no memory of either of these things. But Renée remembered my visit vividly, and remarked several times on how delightful it was to see me in this same swimming pool, all grown up.

The days at her house were peaceful. After lunch, the hours

slipped by with nothing more to show for them than a flip from stomach to back on the lounge chair. I worried about the ease with which I fell into this rhythm. My wrist dangled beneath me, the back of it pressed up against a glass of iced tea that my grand-mother had brought me unbidden. I had become so tan I was nearly orange, and the blond streaks by my temples had gone white. We spread out like cats, occupying territory in our sleep. Time passed quick-slow, waterfalls and dams, and I tried to will myself to get up, but the sun held me down like a weight on my chest.

If my mother had been here, she would have been on the phone to New York by now. She'd have set her laptop up on the desk in the hall. She'd have been running final edits through a book or correcting proofs for a cover. She was hard and tight as a metal coil, and I was shapelessness and mush. I had done nothing to deserve this vacation. I had work to do. But I did not open my laptop once.

At six p.m., a murmur rippled across the porch—"Time for the aperitif"—and I pulled myself up to shower and change into a flower-patterned dress. Renée was very traditional, and there were formal rules to obey, even in this summer home among close friends and family. We dressed for dinner and put on shoes. No elbows on the table, no eating until everyone had been served. Cheese after the meal, liquor before it. I was charmed by these rules, as only someone who'd grown up without them could be. We took the aperitif on the table by the pool. We drank pastis, the rich yellow licorice-flavored liquor that clouds as you dilute it with water. I was trying to like it, because a café waiter in Paris had told me that only French people ordered it.

After the aperitif, we set the table for dinner. I could not remember to keep my elbows off the table, and my grandmother kept raising her eyebrows at me and knocking her own elbow on

the table meaningfully. I drank my first glass of rosé quickly, trying to ease the tension that had filled my body.

"Nadja drinks a lot," Josée remarked, "and you notice it when
you count the bottles later." There were polite nods around the
table in response.

"But she holds her liquor very well," she continued, her voice
filling now with pride. "I've never seen her drunk."

"I started early," I said with a wry smile.

"Oh really?" Renée asked with courteous interest.

"In America, we can't drink legally until we're twenty-one, so
we down whole bottles of tequila at sixteen just to prove that we
can," I said, hoping that my use of the royal "we" would preserve
their opinion of me.

I was met with tongue clicks at the sorry state of things in
America.

"My mother once told me," I continued, "that when Josée
came to New York right after I was born, she gave me whiskey to
stop my crying."

"She told you that?" Josée said. "Where did she go find such
an idea! I would never have done that."

"Well, yes," I said, hesitant, "I cried a lot. Perhaps you didn't
give it to me but just suggested it? But it's not so strange. I'm sure
it works well."

"Where would I even have gotten whiskey?" Josée said, QED.

"It could have been some other hard alcohol, I suppose. But it's
not such a terrible thing, just a drop of liquor," I said. "Isn't it just
a cultural difference?"

"I would never have given alcohol of any sort to an infant.
What an idea! What other stories did your mother go and invent?"

Josée gestured toward me. "You need to watch out for this one. She's writing. You have to correct the record."

I let it drop, wondering if I'd somehow invented it all.

And then, as the attention passed from me, Josée laughingly told us a story about how she'd given her daughters cough syrup in childhood to help them fall asleep. One evening, when Andrée was four or five, she'd drunk the whole bottle.

"I wasn't a very good mother," Josée said to the table. "But I've always been a very good grandmother."

THE FOLLOWING SPRING, back in Paris, Josée agreed to host my twenty-seventh-birthday party on the roof of her houseboat. I was grateful, though I had not been prepared for the work this would entail. In the week leading up to the event, she and I cleaned the hinges of her refrigerator with a Q-tip and scrubbed the stairs. Sylvie came in my absence and balanced on a beam over the water in order to plant new flowers. I had imagined a few hours of casual cocktails, but Josée organized a six-course meal for my twenty guests, scrambling to find ways to seat them all. My mother was in Paris that weekend, a stopover on her way to Holland on business. She arrived the morning of the event and, both tired and shy, ate quietly and smiled politely at my friends when they tried to speak to her. Tiki torches and rosebushes in full bloom lined the roof of the boat where we dined. At the end of the meal, the dessert rose from the kitchen on the dumbwaiter, an enormous pyramidal *pièce montée* with small fireworks that shot sparks into the air.

As I plucked a two and a seven out of the caramelized *choux*, I fought a small wave of embarrassment. Some of my friends were turning thirty that year, and even their celebrations weren't as lavish as mine. It was an evening befitting a wedding.

A friend pulled me aside and looked in my eyes with surprising seriousness. "Your grandmother," she said quietly. "She loves you."

MY MOTHER AND I spent the night on the boat. The following day, the three of us would go to a funeral parlor to plan Josée's final arrangements.

We ate lunch on the roof, picking through the leftovers. To Josée's amazement, I called up the music she had chosen for her service on my phone. She suggested we listen to it on the speakers I had brought for the party. Purcell's grand and somber *Funeral for Queen Mary* floated out onto the water as I squinted into the sun, eating the sugary remains of the *pièce montée*.

Josée was in high spirits. My mother was as well. She was pleased to be the daughter chosen to execute Josée's wishes, even though it was in part because her sisters had already refused the honor. I had invited myself along, and now that Josée saw me here, eager, with my notebook already out, she seemed quite glad to have us both. She was not afraid of death, she'd told me often. She knew what to expect. There was a tunnel, bells, and then, finally, all the people you had lost, waiting for you with outstretched arms. There was nothing to fear.

"Did you attend Mina's funeral?" I asked my mother. I remembered the creaking sound of the trapeze in my room, how it had slowed at the sight of my mother's face.

"*Non!*" my mother and Josée said at once, both quite angrily. I started and looked from one face to the other.

"I was quite disappointed in fact, Françoise," Josée said.

"But you were the one who told me not to come," my mother said, instantly small.

"I would never have said a thing like that!" Josée said.

"Mais si Maman," Françoise said. "You called me right away to tell me Mina had . . . You said the date for the funeral hadn't been set. And then you told me—something like, 'It's not worth you flying over. You're so busy in New York.'"

"But where did you go fetch such an idea?" Josée said. "I was very hurt you didn't come."

"I should have just booked a flight anyway," my mother said. "But no one even told me the date."

"Everyone asked where you were!" Josée said.

"It's one of my big regrets," my mother said, staring sadly at the food in front of her.

"It was embarrassing for me," Josée said. "I had to explain that one of my daughters couldn't make it."

My mother sighed and served herself the rest of the salad from the bowl. I saw her take a moment to locate her adult self. Her features rearranged themselves, her voice dropped an octave. She changed the topic, and the lunch ended pleasantly.

It was the weekend of the flower festival in Neuilly and the central square was overrun with bright plants. Parking was unusually difficult to find, even with Josée's special disabled pass.

"I can't wait to be done with all this," she said as she circled the block. "In my coffin, I'll finally get some rest."

The funeral home was the same one where she had made the arrangements after Mina's death. It had the clean and restful anonymity of a doctor's waiting room, with simple furniture and a vase of white lilies. A mild young man, the sole employee on this quiet Saturday afternoon, arranged three chairs opposite his desk and prepared a cup of espresso for each of us.

"But it's scalding hot!" Josée exclaimed as she took a sip. "I'm not here for a cremation."

"I'm sorry, madame," the young man said.

"I can see you're in a hurry to have me dead," she replied, and he reddened. But he walked us through the details calmly. My mother took notes in her notebook, as she always did at every important appointment. I took notes as well, as did the young man. I could tell this pleased Josée, having her wishes recorded in triplicate.

She announced that she did not want the hearse to take the highway when transporting her from the church to the cemetery. "I want a view," she said. "Take the scenic route." The young man made a note of this. We all did.

"Do you still place death announcements in *Le Figaro*?" Josée asked. "Or is it done by text message these days?"

"Yes, madame, we place a notice in the *Figaro*. And we'll mail a death announcement to your contacts as well." He pulled out templates of death announcements. Josée quickly chose the least ostentatious and asked for a copy so that she could edit the language. She would write the death announcement for the paper. She would address the envelopes herself and leave them for us.

"Now, what about flowers?" she asked. The young man replied that the flowers were usually left to the discretion of the family. "It can be healing for them," he said gently, "to make a few decisions themselves."

"I don't want unsightly flowers at my funeral," Josée said. "I'll choose the base and they can add a few wreaths if they want."

Next she inquired about the speech the priest would make

during the service. She did not want him to say the kind of non-sense he'd said at her mother's funeral.

"He'll meet with your daughters to get a sense of you," the young man said. "The family will provide him with a brief welcome text and biography. And then they will also give the speeches they've prepared."

"I'll write the welcome text myself," Josée said. "I've already given Andrée a poem to read." The young man told her that this would not be possible—the church followed its own procedures.

Josée became agitated. "I don't want them to say ridiculous things about me," she repeated.

"My sisters and I will write the texts in advance," my mother promised gently. "We'll let you edit them."

Finally, Josée clapped her hands together and asked to be taken to choose the coffin. The young man led us down to a basement room. "There's the bathroom where I threw up after Mina's death," Josée showed us as we passed it. In the basement, mounted on the walls, in columns sorted by the type of wood, were lengthwise cross-sections of each coffin.

"Oh," Josée said, disappointed. "I wanted to climb inside them." The young man, who by now had warmed to her frank humor, laughed.

"It's not a joke," she said, annoyed. She rolled her shoulders. "I wanted to see how they'd fit."

"I assure you they're all very comfortable," he said.

Josée scanned the room and chose almost instantly. She had a vast store of knowledge, from her many houseboat renovations, and she knew she wanted a coffin made of oak.

"Can this one come with a different lining on the inside?" she asked. "I'd like it to be cream."

"Certainly," the man said.

"Good, ivory has never flattered my complexion," she said. "It makes me look green. Oh look, there's a pillow. I'm going to be quite comfortable in there." She reached out and tested the handles. She declared them painful, the metal cutting into the palm.

"Don't worry," the young man said. "The porters are quite used to it."

"Let's change the handles anyway," Josée said. "No point bothering anyone."

"I imagine my mother would carry the coffin herself if she could," my mother added, amused.

"One last thing," the man said, checking off Josée's choices on a sheet. "Would you like a small cross on the top?"

"Why not?" Josée said. "It might come in handy."

As we climbed the stairs again, not ten minutes later, I remarked that this was probably the fastest anyone had ever made all these decisions.

"Yes, well," Josée said brusquely, "I'm not about to spend the rest of my life picking out my coffin."

As we sat down at the desk to finalize the paperwork, the question of pallbearers arose. The man said that Josée could assign the task to up to three people, and that the fourth would be a professional.

"There are no men in my life," Josée said with a small hint of pride.

"There are your two grandsons," my mother said. "I know my son would be honored."

"You think so?" Josée asked with surprise. My mother assured her he would.

"I would be honored as well," I said. Josée laughed. "No, really,"

I said. "You need three, and you have three grandchildren. I'm pretty strong."

"Can she do that?" Josée asked.

"It's not traditional," the man said with a smile. "But I don't see why not."

"Okay," Josée said. "You'll have to hide your hair under a baseball cap."

I kissed her cheek.

"You won't drop me?" she said.

"I promise," I said, laughing. "I won't drop you." But then I imagined myself actually carrying her coffin. It wouldn't be like my grandfather's funeral, I realized for the first time. I would be devastated.

"You'll stay close?" I asked her quietly, when my mother could not hear. "I mean after. You'll stay close to me?"

"Oh," Josée said. "I don't know. I'll have such a great many things to do."

chapter twelve

On the island of Ischia, off the coast of Naples, there was a resort of natural thermal baths run by friends of friends. The spring of Josée's eighty-fourth birthday, my mother called to suggest the three of us go there to celebrate. It was to be her gift to her mother, and to all of us.

"But that'll be great for my book!" I blurted. My mother's trips to Paris, though frequent, were brief and frenzied. I longed to have the three of us together in one place.

"Yes, I know," my mother said, her tone indulgent. "Finally, something that might make everyone happy."

Josée was thrilled. Emails bounced between us as we planned the trip. My mother would fly from New York to Paris, where we would all meet in the airport and board the same plane for Naples.

The day of our departure, Josée wore an impeccable traveling outfit: a tan linen pantsuit, a cream-colored shirt, light scarf, and pink sunglasses. As we passed through security, her boarding pass disappeared. She'd put it in the bin with her purse, she insisted.

"It must have blown away inside the X-ray machine," she said, showing the security agent the empty bin.

"Perhaps you have put it back in your purse, *madame,* or in your pockets," the woman said, her voice somehow unimpeachably neutral and at the same time dripping with contempt.

"I've already checked there," Josée said curtly. "It's stuck in the machine."

The security agent locked eyes with me over Josée's head.

"Would *you* look in her purse?" she asked me, and her eyes said, *We both know what happened.* I stared back for a beat too long, surprised. Then I dropped my gaze and gently took Josée's purse from her. I dug around inside.

"It isn't here," I said quickly, with relief, though it might have been.

The agent sighed and told us to go get a new one printed at the gate.

"*Alors!*" Josée said as we walked away. "That idiot must deal with this often if she knows exactly how to replace them. What a bad system." We repeated this to each other several times, trying to erase the memory of my hands in her purse.

The screens showed that my mother's plane from New York was delayed. Josée declared that if Françoise missed our flight to Italy, we would go straight on to the island without her. She did not want to waste half her day sitting in the hot gritty sun of Naples. I made a noncommittal sound that meant *We'll see.* I knew I would refuse to leave my mother behind.

The seats on the plane were arranged by threes. Josée had the window seat and I had the middle. I sat in the aisle and put my bag on the seat between us.

"What are you doing?" Josée asked.

"I'll move if someone comes to sit here," I said.

"Of course someone will come sit there," she said. "Don't play games." I sighed and moved over. Seconds later, a woman installed herself in the aisle seat. Josée raised her eyebrows at me meaning-fully. I laughed, conceding the point. Then I turned and anxiously watched the front of the plane. The flow of people had slowed considerably. Josée rested her head against the seat back and shut her eyes.

My mother was the very last person to board the plane. I shouted when I spotted her; her face was so wonderfully familiar that I barely saw it as a face at all. I scrambled over the woman beside me and fell into my mother's arms.

"That cry!" Josée said, a hand on her chest. "That *cri de coeur*! '*Ç'est ma maman!*'" She imitated me in a strangled high pitch. "I'll remember that cry all my life," she said. "You shocked me out of my sleep."

In Naples, my mother and I left Josée by the taxi stand with our luggage—my mother begging her to sit down in the shade, Josée insisting on standing in the sun—while we weaseled answers about the Naples bus system out of the reluctant woman staffing the airport information desk. As we walked away, I ran back to ask for a map of the city. I presented it to my mother with a flourish.

"What a good idea!" she said. And then we took a taxi to the port, as I'd always known we would. My mother was a woman who liked to know her options.

In Italy, my grandmother appeared suddenly old. In her own home, every object was an extension of her. She never seemed frail there, even when she'd broken her wrist and was unable to cut her own food. Her entire being diffused and she became more than her body; she became the whole room. But here, far from Paris, the unfamiliar atmosphere compacted her back into herself. The lines in her face deepened, and I saw her fragile bones and thickly veined hands. I felt the tones and movements other people used to cushion the air around her. Even my mother treated her delicately, taking Josée's weight on her arm as they walked and worrying over every movement she made.

"If she keeps treating me like this," Josée murmured to me as we boarded the boat, "I'll become an old woman."

The sun was on its way back down when we finally made it to the island of Ischia. My mother, who had left New York more than twenty-four hours before, gave no signs of exhaustion. She checked us into the hotel by the spa. Two rooms side by side, one for Josée and one for us to share. When the door to our room closed behind us, my mother and I fell into each other's arms like lovers. I hadn't realized until that moment just how much we had been holding back.

The spa was nestled in a bay. Rich foliage on small cliffs gave way to the beach below. Twenty-three thermal pools were embedded in a labyrinth of stone paths. There were pools with jets and undulating pools with water the exact temperature of the human body. The water came from deep within the island, heated by a dormant volcano and infused with minerals from the earth. Marco, who ran the spa along with other members of his family, explained that the water here held a small degree of natural radioactivity. The body fought against it, he said, then gave way to fatigue. It promoted a deep relaxation.

He ended his tour at the restaurant on the terrace, where we sat and looked out at the sea. A waiter brought us fresh green olives and huge hunks of Parmesan cheese. Marco talked mostly to my mother. He was a fan of the children's books she published and knew them each by name, even those that had come out years ago. I had often sat quietly by while people had similar conversations with my father, but it was rare to meet someone who knew my mother's work so well.

She gently turned the discussion away from herself and toward him. He told us that many men who grew up on the island became sailors. He had tried but had not been suited to the work.

"*Ohhh!*" said my mother with a grin, and she leaned back, sweeping her arm toward my grandmother. "My mother," she said grandly, "lives on a houseboat!"

At night, when the boisterous Italian families with day passes to the spa had departed, only the hotel guests populated the glowing terrace. The pools were still and dark and empty. Waves lapped against folded beach chairs, smoothing away footprints.

"It's far too cold now to swim in the ocean," Josée said. "If only we'd come a month later, the island would have been in bloom."

Over dinner, looking out at the sea, we tried to find a path into the past. I asked my mother and grandmother about the early vacations they had shared. My mother recalled learning to swim on the Côte d'Azur and fishing alongside her father.

"We never ate the fish your father caught," my grandmother insisted, though my mother's memory of eating them was vivid.

"Oh!" I said then, the bright *Oh!* of one who has suddenly remembered something. I turned, placing my hand on Josée's arm. "Did you ever tell my mother the story about the lottery?" I felt her stiffen under my touch.

Haltingly, Josée tried to tell the story. The facts became jumbled. The details changed. There was another girl involved. Josée forgot to say, until I prompted her, that the lottery had never been drawn. The story lost its punch line.

"Yes, then there was the Munich Agreement," Josée concluded. "And so the lottery was never drawn."

"The Munich Agreement?" my mother said, perplexed. The story hung heavily in the air.

"You're not cold?" Josée asked me sharply. She had asked me several times to put on my jacket.

"No," I said. "I'm not cold."

"Just looking at her makes me turn to ice," she said.

"I must have warm blood," I said. "I'm not often cold."

"You're enrobed," Josée said enunciating the syllables— *en-rob-ée*—as if I might miss her meaning.

"Yes, that's true," I said, with a nervous trill at the back of my throat.

"To be enrobed, it's common knowledge . . . the best swimmers carry a small layer of fat like this, like a dolphin or a fish. You would be a good swimmer."

I shrugged, smile in place.

"I didn't know all this," my mother said then, and it was clear that she wasn't referring to my body but to Josée's past. But when she tried to ask about Mina and Mélanie, Josée parried her questions with a fencer's grace. "Would you like some pineapple?" she asked. I felt a tiny prick of pride. My mother did not yet know her way through Josée's rhythms.

THE NEXT EVENING, Josée asked a local man to recommend a nice restaurant. My mother corrected her—we wanted a good restaurant, not a nice one. We wound up in a place with white linen tablecloths and many forks. The waitstaff displayed the fish to us whole before cooking and serving it. I winced at the prices, but I knew my mother was proud to treat her mother lavishly. In that hushed candlelit interior it felt as if time had stopped.

My mother asked Josée a question about her childhood, the answer to which was a story I already knew. Josée glanced up at me across the large round table. I nodded almost imperceptibly. Her childhood unspooled through the courses. She told my mother about the war, the years she'd spent shuttled between hiding places. She had told me scattered anecdotes, ricocheting back and forth through the years, but now a clearer and more linear narrative emerged.

When Josée came to her early years in Nanterre, living with Mélanie on Aunt Lucy's property, and when she mentioned the older cousin with whom she had biked to Mina's apartment in Paris, my mother caught an inconsistency I had not thought to press.

"But Mina's brother died when he was nine," my mother said. "And Mina had no other siblings. Who was Aunt Lucy? Who was this cousin?" Josée's answers were vague—these were not questions she had thought to ask as a child. But under my mother's questioning, a genealogy slowly emerged.

Josée's grandfather, Alfred, had had a wife before Mélanie, and children. Aunt Lucy, Josée conceded, might have been Mina's half sister from her father's first marriage. And, she told us then, though Alfred had separated from his wife when he met Mélanie, he had not divorced her and married Mélanie until several years after Mina was born.

My mother drew her conclusions from this with awe: Mélanie was *fille-mère*. This was the term for a woman who'd had a child out of wedlock: a girl-mother. And Mina, my mother said, had also been a bastard! Josée tried to backtrack—Aunt Lucy might only have been a family friend—but my mother simply *mmhmm*ed and shifted the conversation forward, asking Josée about later years. My mother had told me often how much it pained her, the shame Josée continued to feel over a stigma so long outdated. I could see how much it meant to Françoise, this missing clue in the mystery of her mother.

When dessert was long over and the rest of the restaurant had emptied, I excused myself to go to the bathroom. I stood in front of the mirror longer than necessary, splashing cool water on my face, savoring the moment to myself. When I returned, my mother and Josée were still talking. The staff began setting the tables for the next day. It was only when our waiter apologetically presented the check that Josée and my mother blinked and reentered the world.

Later, my brief absence expanded in my mother's mind to cover nearly the whole meal.

"While you were gone . . . ," she said several times, eager to fill me in. I had been there. I had asked some of the questions myself. But eventually I stopped reminding her of this.

IN THE POOL exactly the temperature of the human body, jets sent up bubbles strong enough to make a person float. My mother and I took turns holding each other under the arms so that the rest of our bodies stretched out on the water's surface. When I twisted to leave my mother's grasp, she gathered my legs against her instead, cradling me like an infant. I rested my head on her shoulder, the water bubbling around us. Josée stood at the pool's edge, a heavy sweater on. The wind had picked up. She was cold and she wanted to go eat lunch.

"I'm doing a rebirth," I told her.

"You should get out and put some clothes on," she said. "You're going to come down with the flu."

My mother asked Josée to take a photo of us and she did, fumbling with the phone's camera for a moment. "Let's go," she said.

"Just a minute longer," my mother said, nuzzling my neck.

"You're both going to die of bronchitis," said Josée, "and I'm going to be left with this stupid photograph, saying, 'Those idiots, I told them to put on clothes!'"

At lunch, my mother mentioned therapy, and how useful she had found it to speak to someone over the years.

Josée was skeptical. "Why would you pay for advice from a, what do they call it in New York again? A shrimp?"

"A shrink," my mother said. "And they don't really give you advice. Mine almost never talks at all. It's hearing yourself talk that's useful. It's talking without fear of being judged."

Josée said that she was perfectly capable of talking to herself for free. My mother, searching for backup, asked me if my experiences in therapy had been similar.

"Not really," I said. "Maybe because I was sixteen. I really wanted my therapist to like me."

"And your parents were paying for it," my mother said. "That makes a big difference. You wanted to go, but your parents were paying."

"I didn't want to go!" I said. "You sent me because you thought I was crazy."

"Josée also sent me to therapy because she thought I was crazy," my mother said.

"Yes, well," Josée said, "everyone gets told they're crazy when they're sixteen years old."

"I wasn't sixteen," my mother said with little-girl hurt. "I was thirteen."

"You always were precocious," Josée said.

Somehow, the conversation wound around to the summers they had spent in Ussel, the summers when my mother, forbidden from playing with Andrée, had grown desperate with boredom and loneliness.

"How old were you?" I asked my mother, although I already knew the answer.

"Twelve," she said with leaden heaviness.

"You were perturbing her," Josée said. And then, seeing my mother's face, "You were perturbing her, but it wasn't kind of me anyway, I'm sorry."

My mother brushed the apology aside uncomfortably. She talked about the solitary walks she'd taken in the woods.

"But I didn't know you were so lonely!" Josée exclaimed. "Why didn't you play tennis?" Doubles matches with visiting friends had occupied Josée's summer months, but her three daughters remembered only being made to chase the balls and rake the court flat after the games.

"I had no partner," my mother said.

"You could have played against the wall," Josée said.

"There was no wall," my mother said.

"Why didn't you tell me!" Josée said. "I would have built you a wall."

After lunch, the three of us sat in beach chairs in the sun, reading quietly. I got up to go fetch sunscreen, and my mother offered to accompany me. When I turned around to see if she had followed, she was still standing behind Josée's chair. She had bent over to cover her mother's neck with kisses. Josée reached up, put her hands in her daughter's hair, kissed her cheek in return. A happy warmth spread through me. My mother looked up at me, her chin in the crook of Josée's neck, and I clasped both hands together over my heart. But my mother pulled her mouth down sharply to one side and arched her brows, an expression I knew meant *Something's wrong*.

"So?" I said as she joined my side and we turned to walk together. "That looked so sweet from afar."

"You know what she said to me?" my mother asked. "She said, 'But I had no idea you'd been so miserable, my poor Cosette.'"

"And that upset you?" I said.

"Cosette like in *Les Misérables*," my mother said angrily. "I don't need apologies from her."

Back in the hotel room, my mother ran her fingers through her hair before the bathroom mirror, styling the curls that fell in her eyes. I had cut her hair that morning on our terrace. It was a tradition I had with her, my father, and my brother whenever we were on vacation—they would sit and I would touch their necks and ears, talking softly as I worked the scissors around their heads.

My mother told me she felt uncomfortable with the turns our conversations with Josée were taking.

"I love discovering who my mother was as a little girl," she said. "But I don't want to talk to her about my own adolescence. I don't want to get into recriminations."

"But," I said.

"Several years ago, I decided to save her number in my phone as 'Maman,'" she said. "It's my present to myself. To let myself have a mother I love. That's all I want." I was silent, and she spoke again.

"You don't understand. It wasn't neutral. It's so painful, to bring all this to the surface. I don't want to settle scores. I don't need her to apologize."

"I understand," I said. "But . . . for me this tension of your shared pasts is interesting. I don't want to make you uncomfortable. And yet I get the sense that Josée is searching for this as well. No one asked her to apologize just now—she offered that on her own."

My mother sighed. She turned to contemplate me for a moment. "Okay. I trust you," she said. "And Josée trusts you. I suppose it's comforting to both of us that you have an agenda." She readied herself to leave the room. I trailed behind her, rubbing worriedly at the back of my neck.

THE NEXT MORNING, we woke up to rain. We ate breakfast together under an overhang on the hotel's roof terrace. We were quiet as we watched the ripples on the thermal pools below.

"This is an island of lemons," Josée said. She ordered herself a fresh-squeezed lemon juice from a passing waiter. She poured water and a packet of sugar into the cloudy liquid.

"I'm going to do a lemon cure," she said. "I want to nourish myself from all these lemons." I took a sip of her drink, knowing that she did not like to share her food but would allow me to do so. The acidity was bracing. It felt cleansing. I ordered one as well.

After breakfast, the three of us went downstairs to Josée's room. We lay on her bed, my mother in the middle with her feet by our heads. She grabbed a pillow to prop herself up, "so I can *see* you," she said. We talked idly, half listening to the soft patter of rain on the parking lot outside. Under my questioning, Josée began to tell us about her boarding school days. But then she interrupted herself to say that none of this was very interesting at all. This was something my mother said to me often when I asked her about her life, and she reacted now just as I always had.

"But for me it's fascinating," my mother said.

"It's interesting *now,* maybe, to talk about it, because it's raining and we have nothing else to do," Josée said. "But otherwise no. You might as well read a good book."

"Discovering that you spent your whole childhood . . . it blows me away," my mother said.

"That I was a child?" Josée said archly.

"No," my mother said, unsmiling. "That you so rarely lived with your mother. I didn't know."

"We never really talked, did we, you and I?" Josée said. "I was a wife more than a mother. And then you left for America . . . It's only thanks to this troublemaker here and her endless interrogations . . ." She swatted me gently, leaning over my mother's feet.

"Did you talk about it with my sisters?" my mother asked.

"No, I never talked about it with anyone," Josée said. "I still don't see why anyone would be interested."

"But weren't you interested in your own mother's story?" I asked.

"She never told me her story," Josée said.

She told us how, after Mina had had a hip operation late in life, they'd gone for a walk outside the hospital and sat on a bench together. "I asked her if she'd ever had the desire to run around on my father—or no, I said, 'My father, did he have other women? He offered you lovely vacations, to have you forgive him.' I told her about a photo I had of her as a young woman on a cruise ship, where she looked radiantly beautiful. And she clapped her hands together and said, '*Si! Si! Le capitaine!*' She smiled this smile I'd never seen before, the one she must have had at twenty years old. She told me she'd had an affair with the Greek ship captain. Apparently, she cheated on my father once. In 1935."

"So you were asking a question, about the relationship between your parents," my mother said thoughtfully, more to herself than to us. "Did I ever tell you what Mina told *me* about her life?"

"You must have, but I've forgotten," Josée said.

And so my mother began to tell the story as Mina had told it to her, in 1978. My mother and father were in France on a visit, and my father had just made one of the first outlines for *Maus*. My mother had translated it into French and typed it up for a small French magazine. When she went to see her grandmother, her head was filled with the stories of Vladek and Anja and she shared them with her.

"You're looking for stories?" Mina said. "I have a story to tell." Over the course of two days, she told my mother her life.

I had heard the story from my mother several times over the years. At first she had told me that I had been there, too, a baby cradled in her arms. But later she'd corrected herself and said that I had not been there that day after all. She had been alone with Mina, she was sure of it. I felt something deep inside me being taken away. The traces I had conjured—Had a teakettle whistled? Had I grasped a cool white porcelain statue in my fist?—began to fade.

This was Mina's story, as she told it to my mother.

MINA HAD BEEN christened Fernande, but she'd never liked her name. She went by the nickname Nanda until late in her life, when Beppo gave her the pet name Mina, which she loved.

Her parents, Mélanie and Alfred, ran an auto shop with a small *buvette*, a canteen counter, attached. I do not know where they lived in 1904, when Mina was born, but in later years they lived together as a family in rooms over the *buvette*. This was in Boulogne-Billancourt, home to the Renault factories, where the

Seine exited the southwestern confines of Paris before making its sharp U-turn back up toward Neuilly. It was a proletarian neighborhood, a typical French lower-class setting, and Mina dreamed of a grand escape. She threw herself into her studies. She was first in her class. But when she was fourteen, her parents declared that her schooling was over. She had received her *certificat d'études*, completing her legally mandated education, and now she was an adult. She was to take a job and help support the family. Mina's teacher came to their home—an extraordinary occurrence—to plead Mina's case. The girl showed such promise. Who knew what a few more years of schooling might bring? But her father refused, and Mélanie didn't take Mina's side. Mina never forgave her mother for that, Françoise often said.

In 1918, Mina took a course in stenography. "She did her formation," one would say in French, so that learning is another act of being shaped, and through being shaped, becoming. World War I had pulled women into the workforce in the vacuum left behind by all the dead young men. Young female workers were organized into vast well-trained secretarial pools.

To capture speech back then was as elusive as capturing emotion, and stenography was as much an art as a technique. One method used a series of strokes to capture consonants, another captured phonemes; one used five hundred characters annotated with dots, another used semicircles that moved like phases of the moon. Secretaries could not decipher one another's notes. Only the woman who had made the markings could expand them back into language. In that way, shorthand was like memory, condensing the gone-by-too-fast into symbols intelligible only to the one who held the key. Secretary, ghostwriter, editor—I called upon the three generations like muses. But I was none of these things.

I was the narrator, giving shape to memories that weren't my own. And that, I was learning, was a much more violent act.

In the 1920s, the image of the young secretary, with her short hair and hemline, represented a popular sexualized fantasy. It was taken for granted that her only dream was to marry her boss. But though Mina knew other secretaries who had tried to go that route, she kept her eyes squarely on her work.

She found her pleasure in the open-air *guinguettes* on the banks of the Seine, where she went dancing every Saturday. The wine flowed freely and the artists mixed with the factory workers. With her wide eyes, heart-shaped face, and Cupid's-bow mouth, Mina was a beauty made for the era.

A young man took her for a spin. He was a *beau parleur*, a smooth talker, and he told her stories about all the things he could show her. He asked for her hand in marriage. By then, Mina was eighteen or nineteen years old. She saw in him her freedom, and she agreed. As soon as the wedding plans were in place, the man announced that they would temporarily move into the rooms upstairs from her parents. His salary was not quite what he'd told her, he said, though it would be soon, of course.

Mina's mother had not told her what to expect on her wedding night. In one gesture, her new husband revealed himself to her. His genitals were diseased. He told her that he had been ravaged by syphilis. They would never sleep together, never have children.

"I married you to be my nurse," Mina remembered him saying.

The following day at work, Mina could not contain her tears. Her boss, Eugène, demanded to know what was wrong, but Mina refused to speak. Another secretary, her best friend, filled him in on the details. Eugène called Mina into his office. He was many years her senior and round as a Buddha. He was married. He wore a pince-nez over his wet eyes.

"I heard about what happened to you," he said. "I can take care of it."

"What do you mean?" Mina asked. Eugène told her what he would ask of her in exchange. Mina could not turn to her parents, her authoritarian father or her unsupportive mother, who would surely only scold her for getting into such a mess. And so she agreed.

Eugène sent Mina to the countryside for a few days. He went to see her husband in the rooms above the *buvette*. He told him that either he could accept a large sum of money and have the marriage annulled or Eugène would arrange to break his legs. The man took the money. Mina returned to Paris, and Eugène installed her in a nice apartment. He visited a few times a week.

Mina was neither happy nor unhappy. It was certainly better than living at home. For several years, her life found a rhythm. Eugène did not ask much of her. She continued to work as a secretary. He provided her with clothes and paid for her vacations. She loved to travel and often traveled alone. I had seen photos of her punching a boxing bag on a ship, on a boardwalk where her hair blew in the wind. I did not know who had taken them.

Then Mina fell in love with a young man her own age. He was the scion of an aristocratic family, poised to inherit a castle and a title. He loved her just as much as she loved him, but his family was violently opposed to their union. They threatened to disinherit him. He vowed to elope with her anyway.

When Mina announced her departure to Eugène, he raped her. She became pregnant with Josée. I'd questioned my mother about the logistics of this. How could Eugène have made her pregnant only this one time and not all the others? My mother replied only that this was what Mina had told her.

Mina was twenty-six years old. She would not leave for another twelve years, when she threw the suitcases out the window, broke down the door, and rushed into Beppo's arms.

THAT WAS THE whole story, as Mina had told it to my mother and my mother had told it to me. But that rainy afternoon in Ischia, my mother did not tell it all to Josée. She stopped with the syphilitic husband, and Eugène's offer Mina couldn't refuse.

"Ah so!" Josée said, getting up and out of the bed. "My father saved my mother."

"I'm not sure Mina—" my mother said.

"That was very brave of him," Josée said, "to go threaten that man. I didn't know he had it in him. My mother must have loved him for that." And with that she took off her dressing gown and began to pull on her bathing suit. The rain had stopped, she pointed out, and it would be a waste to stay inside talking all day.

THAT EVENING, we had drinks by the sea as the sun was setting. Josée was complaining, as she often did that vacation, of the injustices that Paul had visited upon her. She was retelling the story of how her custody of Andrée had been revoked.

My mother interjected to say that during the divorce proceedings she had been asked to testify before a judge about which of her parents would be a better guardian for her younger sister.

"What did you say?" I asked.

"I found it shameful that anyone would ask such a question of a child. And I asked who would be taking custody of me. I was told no one had ever asked for it."

"That's normal," Josée said. "You were *majeure*."

"*Mais non, Maman!*" my mother said, incredulous.

"You were eighteen," Josée said.

"I wasn't!" Françoise said.

"But by then you lived with Jean-Michel!" Josée said.

"*Non!*" my mother said, elongating the word into one long wail.

"When I left with Andrée, all my other children had left home," Josée said with certitude. "She was the last one left."

"Where did you want me to go?" my mother said. "I had no other home."

"In the summer of 1972, you and Jean-Michel went to Afghanistan."

"It was a trip! I wasn't going to spend the rest of my life there! When I came back in the fall, you were gone."

"Yes," Josée said. "I left the first of July. Just as I had told him I would on the first of February. He was raping me one last time in my room. I was looking at an aquarelle we had above the safe—a sunset, black on a gold background. I said to him, very calmly, 'It's the last time.' He was hammering away, in full swing, and I said to him, 'Never again will you touch me. I'm leaving on the first of July.' And I did. On the first of July, I took Andrée, the turtledoves, and the cat—"

"Are those the turtledoves that you told me about?" I interrupted. My mother had told me that her turtledoves often flew free in her bedroom. They'd hatched eggs together. One day, the male escaped through the open window. The female took up a relationship with her only surviving fledgling, another male. After that, my mother did not like the turtledoves anymore. She always made a face of exaggerated comical disgust when she told this story.

"Yes," my mother said, "my turtledoves."

"You had left them behind," Josée said.

"I went on a *trip* to *Afghanistan*," my mother repeated.

"And when you got home, were the turtledoves still there?" Josée lifted a finger in the air, as if she had finally backed the witness into a corner. My mother was silent a moment.

"No!" Josée answered for her, triumphant. "Because I see myself very clearly, leaving with their cage." I stifled a smile and both women looked at me sharply.

"I couldn't carry the cat," Josée continued. "And so your father, who had gone crazy with rage, grabbed it by the scruff of its neck and threw it in my face. Can you imagine? Claws out, straight in my face. It was your cat in fact, Françoise."

"I didn't have a cat," my mother said. "We didn't have a cat."

"Fine," Josée said easily, conciliatory. "Not your cat, but a cat."

"Anyway," Josée continued, "that's how Andrée and I found ourselves living on a houseboat with two turtledoves, a cat, a hamster, a dog, and a turtle." Her voice warmed, became full and lyrical. My mother sat back in her chair, mouth drawn tight, and stared at her hands. But soon she leaned forward again, soon she laughed. Josée was a wonderful storyteller, and my mother could not help but be pulled back in.

THE SUMMER AFTER OUR TRIP to Ischia, my mother discovered a secret recording. It was among the digitized files of home movies she'd had converted from reel-to-reel and VHS, but this one was only audio. It was labeled "*Printemps 72.*" My mother had no memory of ever hearing it before.

Through the static, she made out Josée's voice, though not as it was now, low and gravelly with age. This was Josée's voice shrill with anger, the one my mother had forgotten she remembered, and then remembered, on hearing it, so clearly.

Several times on the tape, Josée asked Paul to speak louder, claiming she was going deaf. She screamed to Andrée to turn down the television in the other room. This, my mother realized, must be one of several secret recordings Josée had made around the time of her divorce. Intentionally or not, she'd given it to Françoise one year in Paris, and Françoise had put it in her suitcase and brought it back to New York. There it had sat, unplayed, for decades.

My mother did not wish to listen to it all the way through on her own. But that summer, she played the tape for me. We paused often so that she could help me decipher what was being said.

"Ah, Paul," Josée says, moments after the recording begins, "I was just telling Françoise that you're refusing a legal separation and want a divorce as quickly as possible. I'm leaving in June with Andrée, and so logically you will claim custody of Françoise."

"I claim nothing at all," Paul says with the careful locution of an educated man, each syllable perfectly rounded. "We were going to talk about this tonight, with Sylvie present."

"Yes, well, she's not here and we still have to talk about it," Josée says.

"*D'accord*, I decide that I'm keeping Sylvie," Paul says.

"So you're taking custody of Françoise and Sylvie," Josée says.

"If Françoise would like to stay with me, yes," Paul says in a hushed voice, pronouncing her name with tenderness.

"Françoise, I told you, her life is Jean-Michel," Josée says, and in her mouth her daughter's name is like the nasal quacking of a duck. After some further back and forth, Josée addresses Françoise. It becomes clear then that my mother has been in the room all along.

"Okay, so that's all settled," Josée says. "I'm taking Andrée and you'll be in your father's custody. Which won't mean you never come to see me."

"Yes," Françoise says softly, in a voice I don't recognize at all. There is a faint don't-hit-me tremor. She sounds *meek,* a word I would never use to describe her now.

"Because even if you had come under my responsibility," Josée goes on, "I'm sure you would not come live with me. It's not important for you. Your life is practically made already. You're portioned off to Jean-Michel."

It soon becomes clear that Josée is pushing for Françoise to marry Jean-Michel in the fall, after their return from Afghanistan. She presents this arrangement as an inevitability. Françoise appears worried that Jean-Michel may not agree to this, but of her own desires she says nothing. She is only a small voice, buffeted by her parents.

"I cannot say that I'll oppose their union," Paul says, "but neither can I say that this corresponds to what I envision for my daughter." He speaks with the finesse of a character in an old play. It is not a quality I remember about him.

"I think it's premature," he continues. "And, as Françoise knows, this is very egotistical, but her union with Jean-Michel turns her away from our shared medical vocation, a mutual passion that gave me infinite pleasure. It was one of the great joys of my life. Everyone who worked with me shared the same sentiments and thought I was a blessed man to have a daughter who was young, pretty, and intelligent . . . No, but it's the truth, Françoise. You're very very very pretty. A very very beautiful girl."

My mother paused the tape. She gave a short sharp laugh of pain. "But it is premature! There's no reason for us to get married at seventeen, no reason except to leave my father completely alone, with his daughter married off to the son of his wife's lover." She shook her head, pressed play again.

And then, Jean-Michel arrives. The invisible room fills with ghostly voices, taking on the surreal quality of an ensemble piece in a theatrical production. There are the sounds of glasses clinking, a chair being pulled across the floor to accommodate the guest. I knew I was supposed to feel that this was the objective past, truer than all the rest, yet it felt like a radio play.

"Ah, Jean-Michel," Josée says. "We were just discussing Françoise's custody. I asked for custody of all three children, but Paul said I couldn't take Françoise and Sylvie even if they agreed. Because Françoise no longer exists as our daughter, Françoise is your wife. It's certain that she's no longer at the stage where someone needs to take custody of her."

The tape ended abruptly, in the middle of one of Paul's monologues. My mother rested her arms on her knees.

"Oh," she said, hand on her forehead. "Her *voice*."

I said, "I'm so impressed you survived all that." But I was surprised by how empty-handed the recording had left me. I had expected it to contain a miraculous and impartial Truth. Yet while it corrected certain facts—Josée had said she'd leave in June, and not in July—the narrative that strung these facts together remained as complex as ever.

My mother had been correct in saying she'd still lived at home that fall. Josée's relationship with Louis Guérin was uncovered before the date for the wedding could be set, and the plan was derailed. But Josée had also been truthful when she'd said she believed Françoise was already gone. She was not reinventing the past. She had willfully tried to make Françoise leave home, creating that reality, even then. In a sense, Françoise had been both out of the house and not. She was in that liminal space, where so much of our shared history lay.

I kept stroking my mother's back ("Her *voice*," she repeated), and somewhere deep in my stomach, unfair yet uncontrollable, I was jealous of her. I was jealous that on the rest of the hard drive there was only video after video of my brother and me tearing open mountains of presents, playing dress-up, blowing kisses to the camera. Inside myself, I had retained the vivid emotions of my adolescence. But there was no external record of those dark difficult moments with my mother, the ones that I was now becoming less and less certain I remembered.

IN ISCHIA, the evening after Josée and Françoise had argued about the events of that summer, the three of us dined at one of the island's many oceanfront restaurants. A waiter brought us a plate piled high with small fish fried whole, my favorite dish. Grease stained my notebook. A question arose: When, exactly, had Josée begun seeing Jean-Michel's father? Was it the summer just before the two girls were sent to boarding school—when Josée appeared eager that Sylvie pursue her *petite aventure*? Or was it the summer after, the one during which my mother became pregnant? Josée refused to be pinned down on a date. The tone of the conversation became more and more strained. My mother asked point-blank if Josée and Louis Guérin were already sleeping together when he accompanied Jean-Michel to their home to arrange for her marriage.

"I don't even know what we're talking about anymore," Josée snapped. "You're ruining my birthday with all of these questions."

My mother let the topic drop. She knocked my hand and signaled for me to put my pen away. A false calm covered the rest of our meal.

But when we returned to the hotel room, my mother leaned against the closed door. She looked dazed. She asked for my notebook and began making a timeline, using the clues Josée had given us. "It's just as I thought," she said, putting the pen down with a gesture that had all the drama of a scene from a movie. "Her relationship with Louis started before I began dating Jean-Michel. If only she could have acknowledged the role she played. I don't want an apology, but just, oh just an *acknowledgment.*"

She went on, stepping further and further into the past, seeming younger and younger as she spoke. It was as if with each sentence a veil dropped, shortening the distance between my mother and the girl she'd once been.

She thought back to those summer nights when she and Jean-Michel showed up late to dinner and ate quickly, hair tousled and cheeks flushed—*she knew, of course she knew.* She thought back to when her parents had asked her, in that grand echoing living room, if she was having sex—*she already knew it was too late.* She thought back to the marriage arrangements—*she had discussed it with Louis Guérin, two lovers planning to wed their children to each other.*

"She *knew,*" she said, "she *knew* I was going to get pregnant. Before it even happened, she *knew.* She *let* me get pregnant. She *wanted* me to get pregnant. She used me as a cover for her affair.

And then . . . and then . . . and all this just to punish Paul, all this just to say: Look, your daughter, the prude, *sainte nitouche,* went and got knocked up."

She stood, she turned toward me, she staggered and fell into my arms. She sat down again on the bed. She reached out one arm toward me, grabbing my shirt as if to steady herself. I sat next to her. She hugged me, burying her face in my neck, and began to sob. "Oh but what good I did to leave all this, what good I did. What a viper." Only later would I realize that my mother had never cried on my shoulder that way before. In that moment, I felt she was not my mother but the young girl I had never known.

She took a deep breath to calm herself, then let it out, whispering *ow ow ow ow ow.* She rocked back on the bed and lay on her side. I curled myself around her.

"I'm sorry," I murmured to her. We fell asleep like that, her body shaking softly until she slept.

WHEN I AWOKE, I was alone in the room. I was getting dressed when my mother returned. She and Josée had had breakfast together and laid out plans for the day. My mother did not mention the night before, but it was there in the fatigue that tugged at her swollen face. I asked her gently if she was okay. She sighed heavily and looked at me hard, narrowing her eyes, though I could see that her gaze was actually turned inward.

"The last thing I wanted to do this morning," she said, "was to go see my dear little mother and figure out what I could do to make her happy. But I did it. It's done."

This day passed as easily as the one before, more easily even.

The explosion of the previous evening left almost no trace. It was our last day and we had our routines by now, our favorite pools. Josée appeared happier, relieved—perhaps because neither my mother nor I asked her any more questions about the past. Instead, we each took one of her arms and pulled her on her back through the water, as we had done once on a vacation long ago.

"My dolphins," she called us. "My mermaids."

WE GOT TO THE AIRPORT EARLY, which was rare when traveling with my mother. We sat on high stools in a fluorescent-lit café, drinking espresso from paper cups. My mother glanced at her watch and asked me to go check if our flight had begun boarding. I craned my head to look down the long airport hall and told her that it had not.

"Just go over there and check," she said.

"I can see from here," I said.

"Don't be difficult, Nadja," she said. "Just go over there!" I sighed dramatically and got up, walked across the vast white expanse and back again.

Later, laughing bitterly, my mother recounted the exchange that had followed.

"Did Nadja just offer to go check the gate?" Josée said. "How sweet of her!"

My mother mumbled that it had been at her request.

"She is so considerate," Josée said, ignoring this. "All my friends ask me what I did to get such a sweet, considerate granddaughter. And do you know what I tell them?"

"What?" my mother said.

"It's innate!" Josée said. "It's just innate."

On the plane, my mother and I sat next to each other, Josée several rows ahead. We placed a bag on the seat between us. No one came to claim it, and the seat remained empty, the only empty seat on the whole plane. In the hum of the recycled air, we had the first truly private conversation we'd had all week. I apologized for pulling her back into the past. She had followed me, and it had been dangerous.

"It was useful," my mother said firmly. But she had always been able to see difficulties as challenges, and my conscience was not eased.

"Maybe it wasn't," I said. "Maybe it was just hard."

"It was useful because we survived it," she said. "It's all still there—she's the sweet aging mother whom I can take on vacation and try to please. I'm the adult daughter who built her life an ocean away. And she's also still that person who can destroy me. I'm also still that little girl with no resources. And now we know that we can go there and return, the fire isn't going to burn us alive. We can touch those things, and we can survive."

I thought of the naturally radioactive waters of the spa, how they broke your body down until it relaxed. I hoped that there was some benefit to all of this, and was not sure.

STANDING IN LINE at customs in Paris, I leaned my forehead against my hand, tired. I felt a long, hard scratch down the side of my spine. I jumped and turned around, glaring. Josée grinned at me mischievously. She raised a crooked finger.

"*Ow!*" I said. A look of distress flashed across her face.

"Oh, come on," she said, composing herself. "That didn't hurt."

I realized then that she had meant only to caress me but hadn't known how.

"No," I agreed, and meant it. I pulled her, stunned, into a hug. "No. It didn't hurt."

epilogue

My mother stopped dyeing her hair. She told me this over
the phone. At a party the night before, she said, a woman
had told her she admired the "bold" choice. Other women had
joined in, piling on the compliments so heavily they stung.

"I look old now," my mother said sadly.

"So why don't you just dye it again?" I asked. My mother had
dyed her hair for as long as I could remember. Her sadness seemed
strange to me when the solution was so simple.

"Oh, *chaton*," she said, and I heard the distance she put between
us when she knew I could not understand. "I'm turning sixty. I
am old."

Her birthday was only a month away, and this was the real reason for her call. She wanted to mark its passage by organizing a
trip that would resemble our time in Ischia two years before. She
decided on a weekend in Deauville, that city on the northern
coast where Paul and Josée had laughed as they struggled to carry
huge buckets of lobsters, water splashing their sandy legs. It was
an easy drive from Paris, what the Hamptons are to New York. At
my mother's request, I booked us rooms in the grandest hotel, a
day at the spa. "It's a folly to come to France just for a weekend,"
she said. "But I'll only turn sixty once."

When she arrived at my Paris apartment, she looked no different to me than she always had. What I noticed was the short purple silk scarf knotted around her neck, girlish and colorful. It was the sort of French foulard that my father had drawn her wearing in *Maus* but that I'd never seen her wear. She saw me looking and, with a bashful smile, put her hand to it. She told me she had worn it on her first flight to New York, all those years ago. I wondered if this weekend felt to her like an ending as well.

She took off her heavy backpack and headed straight for the table of plants by the window.

"They're thriving!" she said, impressed, turning their leaves in her fingers. I did not tell her that I had just replaced many of them with new ones from the store.

"I'm so proud of you," she told me over and over as we sat down to the breakfast I had prepared.

"For what?" I said each time, my intonation fluctuating between curious and dismissive. For everything. For keeping a plant alive, for living in Paris, for making reservations in Deauville, for knowing how to buy cheese. I waved aside her praise. I was embarrassed by how easy my life was, and how little I had done with it. And yet, of course, I also wanted her to continue, and she did. I was filled with the buoying sensation that often came from being with her, that feeling of invincibility.

When people tell you things you don't want to hear, it is easy to focus your resentment on the moment they choose to speak. It was evening. We'd just left my building and had ducked into a side street. We were walking quickly—we were running late to meet her sisters. I was checking the map on my phone often.

She inhaled sharply.

"I read the beginning of your book," she said.

"Oh," I said, stunned. I had not given it to her to read. I had shown it to almost no one. It was still a draft. She had said she would never read it. I had wanted to believe that.

"You left it on the computer in the living room last time you were in New York," she said.

The memory came back to me: a rush to print, a file forgotten on the desktop.

"I knew I'd have to read it sooner or later," she said.

"Okay," I said. There was a sharp pain in the side of my chest. Anger welled as well, a heat at the base of my throat. But I locked my jaw. She had given me her most intimate stories to tell. I did not also get to control when she read them.

"So," I said.

"It was hard to read," she said.

"Oh," I said.

"It was just strange," she said. "I didn't recognize myself."

"It's already so difficult to see oneself in a photo, or on film," I said. "To be written about must be worse."

"It's more than that," she said. "I recognized myself in the parts about my childhood. But as soon as you were in the scene, as soon as I was seen through your eyes, I didn't recognize the woman you described at all."

"Oh," I said.

"For example," she continued, "you say my lipstick was perfectly applied. But I never wear lipstick! *You're* the one whose lipstick is perfectly applied." This was true, I realized. When my mother put on makeup, she emphasized her eyes, not her lips. She did not own a single tube of lipstick, though I owned half a dozen. I had one specific memory of watching in a bathroom in Paris as my mother put on lip liner, then blended it with lip balm. She had done the same on my face then, her hands cool and soft on my cheeks. But even that was rare. I'd allowed that moment to permeate the years and become a trait she did not have.

"I am a very private person, as you say," my mother continued. "And these stories about me, I wouldn't tell them to anyone. But I told them to you. And you wrote them, as I knew you would. It's a reality I'll have to adjust to. I'm still not sure how I'll do it. But I will."

Having a writer in the family is like having a murderer in the family, I thought. I touched my chest, oddly grateful for the tangible pain there.

"I love you," I said.

"I know," she said. "There were so many moments where I wanted to say, *That's not true, that's not true.* But it's your book. I have to think of it as being about your fictional mother. And there were a few things that did ring true, of course."

"Like what?" I asked.

"That dinner party where I say my children are in all of my memories. I don't remember saying that, but I agree with myself. And that story Siri tells, 'The bear was seen.' That's a great line."

The heron was seen, I thought, but saw the irony in this and did not correct her.

"But then when you say that your weight was always a problem between us," she continued, "that's not true. I never cared how much you weighed. It was your father who had a problem with it."

A slipping vertiginous feeling took hold, one I had felt many times. It still felt as if my mother could talk me out of my memories.

"Maman," I said, "I cannot have this fight again. I just can't do it anymore."

"Okay, it's just, I always thought you were perfectly—" she said.

And then we were back in it. I could not stop myself. We were each insisting on the same points we'd insisted upon so often, as if somehow this time, this time, this time the other would hear them.

"We can each have our own versions!" I repeated after each accusation I leveled, but I was only trying to end the conversation on my own. If I allowed her to speak without contradiction, even once, I felt the enchantment would be cast and unbreakable. I would never find my way back into myself, the bread crumbs I had so carefully laid out blown away.

"I'm just letting you know what it is that *I* remember," she said. And then we had arrived where we were going. I pushed the door open and we smiled for her sisters. There was no time for another word.

The next morning, we went north. Josée rode shotgun. The buildings of Deauville looked sprung from Germanic fairy tales, with their peaked roofs and decorative dark wood beams. It was a city built for tourists: the grand casino, the high-end designer shops, the steaming platters of mussels and fries. The northern seaside was an odd choice for a late October weekend, but my mother liked the romance of chilly abandoned beaches with their folded umbrellas.

We had come mostly for the thalassotherapy. The spa was all blue lights and white floors, more clinic than haven. We bathed in Jacuzzis filled with salt water, wrapped ourselves in seaweed, applied lotions that contained the mineral richness of the sea. Outside, the waves slammed against the sand. It seemed to me a particularly French invention, this signifier of the ocean without the ocean.

The first evening, after Josée had gone to bed, we went to the casino. I tried to imagine the space as it had been in the past, women in sequined gowns, smoke floating from cigarette holders to the high gilded ceiling. Now it had all the aspects of a carnival. Semiclothed girls handed out candy canes, people drank neon-colored cocktails in the flash of neon lights. We did not gamble, just wandered and watched. Time passed strangely, as it was meant to, and soon we had been there for hours. When we left, the streets were oddly calm. It was nearly two in the morning.

"You go on back," my mother waved. "I want to go down to the beach."

"Now?" I asked.

"I haven't touched the water yet," she said.

"Can I come with you?" I asked. She nodded. The night air held the sharp reminder of approaching winter. I shivered under my light sweater.

"You know," my mother said, noting my shivers, "some of my happiest moments have been on the beach alone."

"Do you want to be alone?" I asked.

"No, it's okay," she said.

We walked in silence. As we reached the sand, we slipped off our shoes. My mother was barefoot but I was wearing tights. I placed my foot tentatively, braced for the damp, but the water was still a long way off. It was the widest beach I had ever seen, the ratio of sand to water reversed. They say that the town of Deauville is closer to Paris than it is to the ocean. Where we stood, the water was still so far away from us as to be nearly invisible, a thin black strip below the black sky.

Halfway there, we stopped. Deep puddles from high tide caught and fractured the light. I did not want to step through them in my stocking feet.

"Go ahead," I said. "I'll wait here for you."

"It's okay," my mother said. She linked her arm through mine, and we looked up at the sky.

"We're in the stolen hour," I said. It was the evening that the clocks got set back, creating earlier winter dawns, earlier winter sunsets. At three a.m., the hands would turn back to two. This hour would disappear.

My mother turned to hug me, her breath in my hair. Then she pulled away and walked off toward the water.

"You're going in?" I said to her receding form. She did not answer.

She was several feet away before she turned around. She walked back toward me. Without a word, she handed me her shoes and her bag. Then she took off toward the water at a run. Her scarf whipped in the wind. Her bare heels caught the moonlight. She became smaller and smaller across the endless sand. She became a white dot. She disappeared.

I felt the night air on the back of my neck. I felt the cool sand underfoot and the weight of my mother's purse. I listened carefully and heard, beyond the waves, the distant rumble of a solitary car. I looked straight ahead. Through the layers of darkness, I could almost make out my mother's shimmering form.

acknowledgments

Thank you to my editor, Becky Saletan, whose talent and extraordinary efforts made this book possible. She illuminated my Paris apartment through late-night Skype sessions and, on top of it all, became a mentor and a friend. Thank you to Anne Fadiman, who knew what it meant to be a daughter and saw me as myself. The project began under her wing. Thank you to Rebecca Nagel for finding the perfect home for my work. Thank you to Jynne Dilling and Katie Freeman for their extraordinary promotional powers. Thank you to Karen Mayer, who took this book to heart. Thank you to Megan Lynch, who first pulled me into the Riverhead fold. And thank you to the rest of the Riverhead team—in particular Grace Han, Gretchen Achilles, Amy Ryan, Janice Kurzius, and Geoff Kloske—for all the work they have done behind the scenes.

Thank you to CJ Hauser, Snowden Wright, and Ruth Curry who, in New York, convinced me I could start writing a book. And thank you to Jacqueline Feldman, Kate Kornberg, Ian Dull, and Isidore Bethel who, in Paris, convinced me I could finish one. Thank you to Lynda Barry for the flash cards that summer. Thank you to Andrew Wylie.

Thank you to my friends, without whom I'd be lost, too many to name without forgetting one. Thank you in particular to those who sat by me while I worked: Jasmine Roudenko, who always knew when I was on the Internet, and Rosa Rankin-Gee, who made me laugh loudly in libraries. Thank you to Yelena Moskovitch for her inspirational text messages, and to Daniel Fromson for being my writing partner when this all began. Thank you to Lindsay Nordell, who taught me how to love. Merci à Sarra Kherrat, qui m'a aimée mieux que je n'aurais su le lui demander. Thank you to all those whose lives were folded into this book and who will be impacted by its publication. Thank you in particular to my aunts, who have always extended a loving hand. I know you each have your own different versions to tell.

Thank you to my brother, who asked to appear little here but looms large in my heart. I am so grateful for you. Thank you to my father, who never meant to be the tree that cast the shade, yet in whose shade I grew. His work informs this book. His love informs everything else.

Thank you to Josée, who took a chance and loved me, and allowed me to fall in love with her in return. She is much more than a character in a story. I am so grateful for the sharp, witty, caring woman I came to know, and more grateful still that she happened to be my grandmother. I will carry the moments we shared forever. I hope there are many still to come.

And thank you, more than thank you, more than words, to my mother, who gave of herself without reserve. I know that there is still so much of you I do not know, and that you will never be fully captured by my writing. But the more I learn about you, the more I love you. You never asked to be admired by me but, at the risk of sounding like a second-grader, you are my role model and my hero. And *regardes*, Maman. I can fly.